Michael Tippett O.M.

A CELEBRATION

Michael Tippett O.M.

A CELEBRATION

Edited by Geraint Lewis

THE BATON PRESS

Frontispiece Sir Michael Tippett, O.M., by Mike Evans

Compilation © Geraint Lewis, 1985

First published in UK in 1985 by
THE BATON PRESS LTD.
44 Holden Park Road,
Southborough,
Tunbridge Wells, Kent, TN4 0ER

ISBN 0 85936 140 3

Printed in Great Britain

CONTENTS

PETER MAXWELL DAVIES

Foreword

MICHAEL TIPPETT is the most ruggedly individual composer among today's composers — an elemental force, a prime mover. Even upon first hearings of Tippett's work in the late Forties, it was the ecstatic quality which caught the musical imagination, and was the impetus to always attempt to be true to the ecstatic and innocent qualities of one's inspirations in the process of composition. This element has intensified and deepened throughout Tippett's output, to inform his recent work with a transcendent and visionary quality which is a continuing example not only to composers, but to all who care about the possibility of music today expressing man's highest aspirations.

Peter Maxwell Davies

Acknowledgements

IT IS MY pleasure to thank many people. My publishers – Raymond Green and John Chambers – and all connected with them have been wonderfully supportive and encouraging from beginning to end. I must especially thank Kathy Morley-Clarke for her painstaking editorial work, Elizabeth Thomson for instigation and liaison, and Frances Rae for her enterprise and flair. Schott and Co Ltd have been most graciously co-operative and I thank Sally Groves and Alan Woolgar in particular. All Sir Michael's music is published by Schott and Co Ltd, and the musical examples here are reproduced with their kind permission.

I also owe an enormous amount to the expertise and patience of Nicholas Wright and the insight and unfailing helpfulness of Meirion Bowen, while Professor Ian Kemp has been characteristically generous in offering his advice and authoritative comment. I am indebted to both Richard Armstrong and Andrew Davis for illuminating and entertaining conversations and to my Director of Studies at St John's College, Dr George Guest, I am particularly grateful for a special favour. I also wish to express my great appreciation of Professor William Mathias's constant enthusiasm and musical perception. My family, friends and colleagues too have provided much invaluable support, practical assistance and inspiring tolerance.

I thank all contributors for their response and accept all responsibility for any final faults in my presentation of their work. Editorial royalties are donated to the Michael Tippett Musical Foundation and it will not surprise anybody that the prevailing spirit of all involved in this venture has been a dedication to and love of the man and music being celebrated. It is my privilege to wish on our behalf – Happy birthday, Sir Michael!

Geraint Lewis

Cardiff
January 2nd
1985

GERAINT LEWIS
Introduction

IAN KEMP's *Symposium on Michael Tippett's 60th Birthday* was a pioneering volume in every sense. Its first section is a fascinating collection of biographical tributes organized to reflect the 'mosaic' tendencies of Tippett's music at the time, while the second half is a series of analytical chapters very sensibly grouped genre by genre. These cover everything up to and including the Concerto for Orchestra (1963) and one writer looks forward eagerly to the work in progress provisionally called *Fenestra* which in 1966 was first performed as *The Vision of Saint Augustine*.

Over the last twenty years Tippett's output has continued to evolve and not surprisingly a considerable bibliography has developed. David Matthews and Meirion Bowen have both contributed lucid volumes: the one introductory and the other more involved, while Eric Walter White neatly summarised the four operas in a book which also contains a fascinating series of letters relating to *The Midsummer Marriage*. In a related field Meirion Bowen has edited the composer's notebooks on *A Child of Our Time* and these appeared in *Music of the Angels* – a successor to the earlier collection of Tippett's writings called *Moving into Aquarius*. More recently, Arnold Whittall explored Tippett's music in relation to that of Britten in his volume subtitled 'Studies in themes and techniques' and in the autumn of 1984 – in anticipation of the 80th birthday celebrations – Professor Kemp's magisterial study appeared in which we have the most intimate and detailed treatment of Tippett's life and works so far.

What then of this book? It is not a biography and neither is it a guide to the entire output. As outlined above these areas have already been covered on a variety of levels. It was partly designed as a successor to Ian Kemp's *Symposium* in being a varied collection of tributes, and one important priority was to cover all the major works heard *since* 1965 in some way. This therefore provides a loose chronological thread to the second half of the book in particular, and the chapters preceding that on *The Vision of Saint Augustine* are either concerned with some major early work, or deal with broad areas and particular themes – so ranging over a number of works and periods in a way not perhaps possible in more exhaustive or comprehensive studies. Interspersed amongst these larger chapters are shorter tributes and essays and a special feature of the book is its sequence of musical tributes from fellow composers of all generations.

As to the nature of the analytical writing, it is deliberately as varied in style as possible – there has been no attempt to impose any uniformity of approach. Some chapters are generally descriptive while one or two others are much more complex in nature! This range is designed not only to appeal to a wide cross-section of readers who might wish to dip into the mode they find most congenial, but also to demonstrate that Tippett's music can be viably discussed in many ways. It provides too an indication of the scope of present day writing on Tippett and will hopefully show that there are many paths still to explore.

It emerged during the gathering of material that two works in particular – *The Knot Garden* and Symphony No. 3 – were proving to be central in Tippett's post-1965 output, since a number of writers referred to them in the course of their essays. If there are apparent moments of duplication (which I have mostly tried to avoid) I hope they may be forgiven and taken in the context of each writer's particular approach. Beyond this I have aimed to present a diverse celebration which, while tentatively modelled on the wide-ranging synthetic style of Tippett's current music, can only hope to add a little to our insight, knowledge and appreciation of the rich life-work of one of the greatest living composers.

BIRTHDAY GREETINGS

Dame Janet Baker

It is a privilege and joy to have the opportunity of wishing you a Happy Birthday, Michael, and to express the gratitude and love we feel for the light, the hope and the beauty your music brings to the world.

Janet Baker

Sir Isaiah Berlin

I am happy to salute Michael Tippett on his 80th birthday. The first work of his I heard was *A Child of Our Time*, to which I was introduced by our mutual friend, the late Miss Anna Kallin, of the BBC, and have ever since been an ardent admirer of this noble and profound composer.

   I consider it a great honour to be allowed to pay him tribute.

Isaiah Berlin

Printed by kind permission of The London Sinfonietta and Michael Vyner.

From Elizabeth Maconchy

ROBERT TEAR

'. . . a Child of Earth and of Starry Heaven . . .'

A CERTAIN philosophy, a specially perceived aura, renders me a begging prey. In my early times, even before any desired form could be invented by my short intellect, my feelings were mysteriously inclined. Questions without answers were preferred – intuitions invariably warmed while certainties froze the cockles. When a kind of maturity arrived and questionings could at least lead a hesitant way, I discovered that other people's writings and supposed feelings could be aligned with mine. Those people who feel a necessity to define the unutterable called these others 'mystics', or again to make dully plain, those who feel they have a one-to-one relationship with God, or however the observer would wish to define the feeling. The Saints Augustine and Francis played leading roles, Meister Eckhart and St John of the Cross no less. Thomas Traherne and Lao Tsu were the impresarios, Nietzsche the Feste of the piece, Blake the producer, Redon the designer, Vaughan Williams . . . but his Wordsworthian pantheism fell a little short of obsession. There could only be one composer to write my 'Magic Life' – he is Michael Tippett. Messiaen might have done, but in some way he flies too near authority. John Taverner the elder would have done, but I felt a certain commitment to living links in my blessed chain. Michael has provided my link to Blake, Palmer, Herbert, Quarles, Chesterton, Watts and many more, and I thank him and am grateful.

At frequent times during my singing life (which is quickly claiming its silver jubilee) I have been faced with Tippett's notes. Sometimes those notes have been quite new, waiting to be breathed into life; other times, older works have waited for the new interpretations that must arrive with new voices and thoughts. Michael has been a constant in my life. But with old and new I receive a remarkably faithful impression. This is of breathlessness (I am not now talking of technique) and a feeling of drunkenness and blessedness. I can be transported so that I no longer occupy my usual area – the earth recedes, the self falls away and security becomes an idiocy. I remember that my first awareness of this state was clearly noticed when I performed *The Heart's Assurance*. The showers of notes in 'O journeyman' and 'The Dancer' quite overwhelmed me. When the whirlings became too much, suddenly there was a sunlit plain with Martinesque vistas – quiet, beautifully sad music, but never sentimental. When I look back and remember the wonderful soul-uprising figures in *Boyhood's End* alongside the oft-voiced criticisms that there are 'too many notes', I simply know that this whirlwind of sound followed by areas of stillness is essential to the mesmeric effect that Tippett achieves. I remember sitting in a London church, listening to the 'Western Wynde' mass of John Taverner (when I say listening, I mean the battering of my head and soul by whirls of eddying notes) and thinking that this is the technique that frees the mind from its logical chains. Michael Tippett well understands this phenomenon.

Michael tries for the impossible and at most times he succeeds. The Nothing is clearly a difficult concept to elucidate in any form. Words cannot do so for their nature renders them concrete and misunderstandable. Plastic art sometimes, almost by accident, achieves its end. Where nothing must be said, music finds itself in the best position for saying it! It is abstract and ill-suited for political or even programmatic purposes. Programme music is a corruption of the medium, turning it into second-rate poetry. Mozart achieves the non-didactic truth without effort. He stands free, knowing nothing, telling all. Michael, in my terms, stands in a similar position. He cares deeply for the stupidities of pride and all that affect most men. He cares, writes, and yet remains, as he must, a watcher with a clearer eye. He views from above, benevolent, hawk-like – tries to better our sense and love – and will always fail.

Michael has always remained optimistic, confident that things are shareable and in swift evolution must change. Therefore he has followed movements with avidity. Having taken on the transcendental in the Double Concerto, *Corelli Fantasia*, *The Midsummer Marriage,* and *Boyhood's End*, he moves on to more political issues in *The Heart's Assurance*, a mixture of the pseudo-political with historical timeless myth in *King Priam* (what a masterpiece) and then to the burning questions of the Sixties – sexual identity and acceptable morality – in *The Knot Garden* then further again to the so-called ideas of 'political freedom' in *The Ice Break,* to return unbroken and incorrupt to the innocence of the Triple Concerto and *The Mask of Time*. My reaction to this homecoming is a sigh of great relief. To my spiritually biased view I found the exercises that Michael took into the politico-care arena very disturbing. I considered him a man, more than any other, to be able to communicate the 'eternal now' to us, quenching our mystic thirst and refilling our bowls. To see this paragon dealing with the 'instant now' in such sincere terms worried me greatly and warned of misunderstandings. However he has returned to me, and being unusually adamant about my spiritual loneliness, I am glad.

There has always been that difficult time, when my chosen heroes become political, or rather take a political stance from their exalted unified position. Blake, Tippett and Nietzsche never could have been 'political animals', because they were not, as most politicians seem to be, in spiritual exile, but were always in touch with their selfless ground. Their dealings with the arid soil of politics must be taken as a concern for the good – selflessly, eagle-eyed,

14

always seeing what is, yet separate in their loneliness. This is how I can accept *The Knot Garden*. Although it is inspired by *The Tempest*, it seems not to be bound in to the effect of the inexorable elements on man and his desire to be with them, but rather to deal in the instant relationships of people with little understanding of themselves or indeed of the unity of their fragmented selves with time. This is my difficulty – Michael has no such difficulty. He sees and occupies. Yet at the base of his occupation there exists no self-love, no self-seeking, no wanting, but an understanding of, or rather an acceptance of, the inexplicable.

As to us performers, we occupy the most odd position. It is at once most careless and responsible. Michael has never written for anyone in particular, never for any quirk of technique, never for any thank you. He has always written his truth, irrespective of those who might perform it. Not for him the close tailorship of Mozart or Britten but, instead, the straight donation of Beethoven. He has always enjoyed his music, sitting back content, immoderately happy. He has no fears. He has abandoned self and consequently self-doubt. I am sorry to take such a Buddhistic position but cannot explain things otherwise. The best that Michael can say is 'Take it, do it,' – we know he will rarely intervene. We are left with golden problems in our tarnished minds and throats.

The frequently-aired criticism concerning the quality of the libretti with their often sudden 'modernisms', which are always a little passé compared with the inspirational sounds, is easily answered. Do not divide, do not separate. Tippett is at all times a unity. Any autopsy will declare imperfections. What of the libretti of *Die Zauberflöte* or *Fidelio*? Tippett's words are way above the level of these. What of Wagner with his endless alliterations in such a bourgeois concept? Michael, in spite of occasional prolixity, is trying to describe the unnamable – is concerned with the ultimate. Far too much is made of these so-called weaknesses.

Michael Tippett's music gives me the feeling of endless possible joy. Joy, however, only to be grasped under certain conditions. The freeing of the mind from time and planning, the ability not to look before and after, is the most important of these. The gift to be able to see that thought is meant to conceal the truth is another. The best of Michael's music allows me to become more aware of my physical relationship to the universe and this is what I think the true mystical experience is. 'Life cannot be frozen or compartmentalised or conceptualised or even grasped. Life is something that simply keeps happening,' said Alan Watts. I thank Michael for the music which helps me to see it.

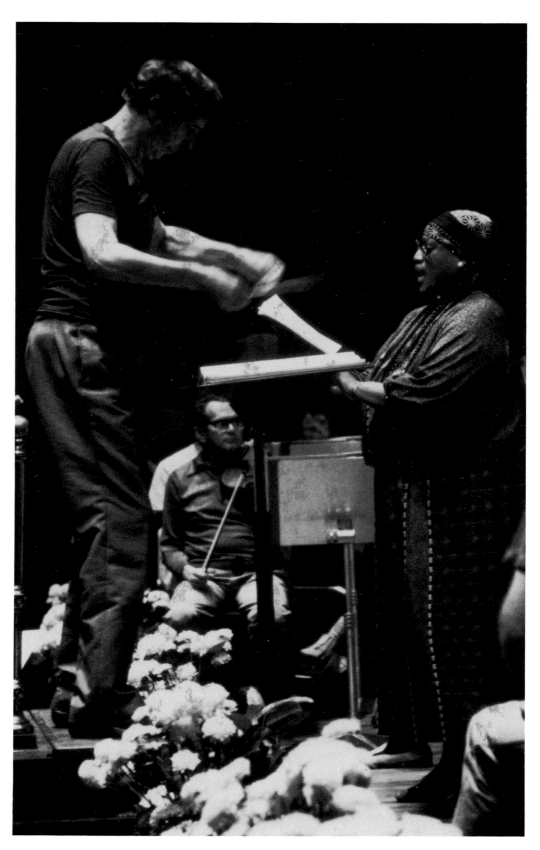

Jessye Norman rehearsing
A Child of Our Time
with Sir Michael Tippett,
Summer, 1979.
(Photo: John Rogers)

16

JESSYE NORMAN
Tribute

IT WAS my great pleasure to have participated in a recording of *A Child of Our Time* by Sir Michael Tippett, with Sir Colin Davis conducting the BBC Symphony Orchestra, and I also had the special honour of singing this work under Sir Michael's direction at one of the BBC Promenade Concerts. In this great choral work, his use of the Spiritual – in his own words 'as Bach uses the Chorale' – is an inspired and successful idea. Since I have been acquainted with the Spiritual as long as I can remember, I was fascinated to find how very easily these songs combine and intertwine in *A Child of Our Time*. To have experienced in so personal a way this vital spirit, in my mind the very essence of Sir Michael's artistic genius, is a source of great joy to me.

18

MICHAEL BERKELEY

A Man of Our Time

THERE ARE those who feel that the purity of music lies in its abstraction, in its freedom from external influence. They find embarrassing the concept of music with a message. Certainly there is much to be said for an art form in which the artist's initial motivation remains absolutely private and in which the onlooker is guided by his own interpretation. But it is impossible to imagine the music of a composer like Michael Tippett failing to reflect the world he inhabits, because he is so vibrantly involved with his perception of that world. It's just a passion that makes for compulsive and spontaneous statements. These frequently manifest themselves in tangled musical relationships that lead to explosive outbursts, yet somehow belong to the everyday, even if they are approached from a highly individual stance.

In fact, several of the most telling moments in Tippett's work come when he manages to marry his own language to a universal idiom. This can be a dangerous road; the line between the banal and the inspired being tremulously thin. How masterly therefore are the arrival of the spirituals in *A Child of Our Time*, driving home the impact of each section with irresistible poignancy. Tippett was obviously aware of the perils here – he directs the chorus to swing the music but *not* to sentimentalise it. In *A Child of Our Time* there are many pointers to Tippett's make-up: the tearing suspensions in the chorus both echo the early English vocal style at its greatest and at the same time anticipate the cataclysmic choruses in *The Midsummer Marriage*. As for the spirituals; well Tippett's music has always been full of the blues. Sometimes subconsciously, as in the *Corelli Fantasia* or the First String Quartet, but frequently with overt fullness, as in the Double Concerto for strings or the later orchestral writing and, of course *The Mask of Time*.

It was suggested that, having myself written *Or Shall We Die?*, I might specifically mention works like *A Child of Our Time*. At first this struck me as rather presumptuous until I recalled a conversation with Tippett in which he ridiculed mousiness. Indeed, part of his own youthful vigour (both in person and music) comes from his intense concern for the exchange of ideas with the younger generation. It matters to him that he communicates with them. And young people do feel a burning need for music that articulates their feelings and fears. They want to be moved and they want (like Tippett) to stand up and be counted, and they want works like the *War Requiem*, *A Child of Our Time*, and even *Or Shall We Die?* But they would not want them if those works had been composed merely as vehicles for the needs of others. They all had to be written primarily out of a burning *private need* to speak out; to risk blasphemy at the altar of purity and show their balls. And if they achieve varying degrees of success as works of art they nevertheless all contain that one vital element – the power to move. This essential could never materialise had not the composer justified the music to *himself* first and foremost. In this context Tippett's career has been remarkable. Through thick and thin he has believed in his own vision and refused to compromise, despite years of obscurity and critical indifference. This experience has, I think, left him more his own man than ever before though he has always been guided by fierce, sometimes confusing, ideals and convictions. I think of his pacifist stand almost half a century ago. It's somehow typical that Tippett's darting mind should have landed him in the Scrubs where many a more *clinically* organised mind proved persuasive. One wishes that, rather than listen to Tippett's philosophy, the Tribunal had simply listened to his music – for that is where the philosophy basks with radiant conviction.

In *A Child of Our Time*, Tippett takes care to avoid specifics. Let us not, he seems to be saying, get over-involved with the individual at the cost of the greater implications. But inevitably it *is* the tragedy of the individual that most touches the heart, and few of us can remain unmoved by the plight of a fellow creature suffering from greed or cruelty, especially when his or her story is told simply and dispassionately. This simplicity speaks volumes where rhetoric tends to splash around in the shallows.

While I did not consciously model *Or Shall We Die?* on *A Child of Our Time* or the *War Requiem*, I have been fascinated by a common need for a Greek chorus: the Bach Chorale. It seems to me that Britten used the movements of the mass for this purpose even if they are also the foundations of his *Requiem*. In essence, Tippett's spirituals come even closer to Bach's Chorales both in construction and effect. They are pivotal points at which we all join in a form of musical communion. In the case of *Or Shall We Die?* Ian McEwan provided me with lines from William Blake at crucial points in the narrative and the four-line stanzas immediately suggested a chorale-like treatment.

The quality that sets Tippett apart from his distinguished colleagues is that of *vision*. Through his steadfastness his unworried use and amalgamation of the past, he has created a world which, while not technically innovative, is totally personal and magical. Vision is not a tangible property – we simply know that it's there, adding that extra dimension that separates the gifted from the sublime. In voicing his fears for, and his love of, a caring humanity, Tippett has succeeded in creating works of great beauty. It's hard to think of a finer way to state your beliefs – to recognise that sometimes it is important to extend yourself beyond the abstract and, despite the risks, embrace the more dangerous world of the man on the street. And in that sense *A Child of Our Time* is just such a work – it belongs to us all.

SIR LENNOX BERKELEY

Tribute

WHEN TIPPETT'S music first became known in this country many of us felt that he was bringing something new that was destined to make itself heard and to provide something that was wanted – perhaps a kind of freshness. This did not involve any discarding of the existing musical language that, on the contrary, Tippett has enriched. Listeners who heard *A Child of Our Time* were unanimous about it. I have a great admiration for Michael both as a person and as a musician.

Lennox Berkeley

To Michael – with affectionate greetings –

From "Journeys and Places" (Edwin Muir) 1971 – R.O.

22

WILFRID MELLERS

Song and Dance Man

MICHAEL TIPPETT, on reaching eighty, can look back on a life's work adventurous in variety, as well as creatively rewarding to him and us. In this he resembles two composers he greatly admires, Beethoven and Stravinsky; and between these two disparate artists stands Charles Ives, whose music has increasingly fascinated Tippett over the last fifteen years. Ives is a Beethovenian composer with a difference, in that he belonged to a democratic New World. One aspect of his demotic nature lies in his use of sundry popular music and of jazz which, during and after the years of its genesis, also made an impact on composers in Europe. We may learn something about Tippett's unique contribution to twentieth-century music by way of *his* interest in jazz, considered comparatively in relation to European Stravinsky and to American Ives.

Jazz was itself a product of the confrontation of two worlds, one new, the other very old. The African Negro, transported in slavery, took with him to his white new land his native musical traditions which were corporeally rhythmic and vocally modal. These came into contact, and before long into conflict, with the harmonic conventions of the Western world, specifically with the white march and hymn. Out of this tension was generated the classic form of the blues, the heart of the jazz experience. Yet although this 'form' was adapted from the white world, jazz was never formal, being a manner of performance rather than an artistic convention. Variety of timbre and malleability of rhythm are as important to it as melodic contour and more important than harmonic progression since jazz, springing from the movements of black bodies and the cries of overburdened hearts, is a manner of doing and acting rather than, in our Western sense, an art. Through it black men and women in the first two decades of our century created a music that gave aural flesh not only to their protest against dispossession and oppression, but also to a nostalgia for – in Allen Ginsberg's words – 'the beauty of his wild forebears – a mythology he cannot inherit'. This is understandable enough. What is more remarkable is that this black melodic-rhythmic, non-harmonic music began to exert a potent influence on white people, too, at first in the United States, then over most of the so-called civilized world. Modern Western man was himself, as D.H. Lawrence put it, 'like a great uprooted tree'; if not persecuted and oppressed, he was to a degree alienated and dispossessed. From that state he recognised in the black man's largely improvised music a spontaneous vitality which he, in his modern self-consciousness, had lost.

While jazz was germinating in America Stravinsky, a cosmopolitan European, was turning away from the moribund traditions of nineteenth-century romanticism, seeking renewal through a rediscovered primitivism, as did men like Picasso and Modigliani in their visual arts. The improvising Negro found his creative energy in tension between his melodic-rhythmic music and the harmonic and tonal prison of white America: which prison had its origins in those very European conventions Stravinsky was discarding. He may have found this relinquishment feasible because, as a Russian, he was partially outside 'Europe'. Even so, he could rediscover the primitive only by being self-consciously unself-conscious: as is indicated in the fact that *The Rite of Spring* is scored – however 'savagely' Stravinsky employed conventional instruments in defiance of what was accepted as their 'true' natures – for a mammoth orchestra, that triumphant apotheosis of nineteenth-century industrialism. And although in *The Wedding* he emulated the sound of a peasant band, he does not claim that the mimed ritual is for real. Both works are ballets, stylised games of let's pretend. They remind us of lifesprings we had forgotten, to our cost; but their negative, therapeutic value, expiating the violence of the war years, may be stronger than their positive revocation of vanished power.

When, during and just after those war years, Stravinsky wrote music that overtly betrays the influence of 'barbaric' jazz, he does so in a negative, deflatory sense. At that time Stravinsky had heard no jazz but had merely seen a few printed copies of piano rag – the Negro's attempt to create a 'respectable' notated music which, being based on white marches and quadrilles, could compete with his white masters. The inane eupepticism of piano rag was a wish-fulfilment, a pretence that the new Negro might be on top of the New World. Rag could jauntily but precariously disturb by syncopation the self-confident rhythms of dance or march, but could not manifest jazz's essential characteristic: the creative tension between, on the one hand, the freely pitched and rhythmed solo lines and, on the other hand, the disciplined regularity of a military beat and of formalised Western harmony. This is why rag tended to sound like, and to be played as though it were, a music of automatons; the 'nigger minstrel' grin is a mask, and the glinting texture and chirpy metre disguise the palpitations of the heart. The appeal of this music to Stravinsky, at this anti-romantic stage in his career, is obvious. Rag sounded like pianola rolls and was frequently recorded on them. Stravinsky devised works for pianola more or less contemporaneously with his ragtime pieces.

His pianola studies were written in 1917; *The Soldier's Tale* appeared in 1918. The scoring of this theatre piece is similar to that of the New Orleans or Dixieland bands, though Stravinsky may well have picked it up from street bands of Europe, and Satie had employed a comparable ensemble for his *Le*

24

Piège de Méduse as early as 1913. It is however significant that Stravinsky gives to the fatuously cheerful sound of the Dixieland band a satirical astringency; and that he associates jazz with the principle of negation, indeed with the devil himself, who corrupts the soldier hero, destroying his soul by hypnotic boogie rhythms and disruptive syncopation. This might be described as anti-jazz, since the obsessive boogie rhythm freezes the marrow instead of liberating the body. The fiddle's open-stringed double stops sound like rattling bones; the contractions and elisions of metre stab one in the solar plexus: so that jazz techniques turn out to deny the vivacity of the sharp sonorities. The lyrical and rhythmic verve of New Orleans jazz are remote from this music, though of course this is not a criticism of Stravinsky's marvellous score, which sounds as new-minted today as when it was first performed.

Stravinsky's 'anti-jazz' coincides in date with the 'death of Europe' in the First World War, immediately after which he produced direct imitations of jazz in the *Ragtime for Eleven Instruments* and the *Piano Rag Music*. The latter, notated without bar-lines to encourage rhythmic freedom, makes some approach to the raucous improvisatory style of the old barrelhouse pianists, whether or not Stravinsky had any experience of this unlettered and scarcely notatable music. Nonetheless it remains deliberately dry, skeletonic if exciting music, far removed from the red-blooded exuberance of Negro jazz; and Stravinsky's references to jazz in later years continue to exploit its 'negative capability': as is evident, for instance, in the jazzy dislocations of 'European' metre and harmony in the *Symphony in Three Movements*. In 1945, having settled in the United States after his second deracination, Stravinsky composed another work overtly in jazz idiom – the *Ebony Concerto* dedicated to Woody Herman's big band. Although by this date Stravinsky had heard Negro jazz in Harlem and Chicago as well as on records, it says much for his self-knowledge and acute intelligence that, having heard the music, he made no attempt to emulate it. The *Ebony Concerto* is the most convincing of Stravinsky's jazz pieces, but is so because it is good minor Stravinsky, not because it is jazz. Significantly, Woody Herman's band disliked playing this neo-baroque concerto, which is devoid of what jazzmen call 'flight' and which, in its undulating pentatonic minor thirds, recalls the archaic ululations of Stravinsky's primitively Russian phase rather than the corybantic fervour of jazz. The lyricism that, in tension with the beat, makes 'swing' possible is absent. Stravinsky is still using jazz negatively, for his own legitimate ends.

A decade or two before Stravinsky produced his first crop of jazz pieces Charles Ives had embraced jazz in both pianistic and orchestral terms. The distinction between the composers is basic, though both ended up in the same land. Stravinsky was a European cosmopolitan with three homes, first on his Russian estates, then in Paris, then in Los Angeles and New York. As *the* representative modern composer he was shoring such fragments as he could against Europe's ruin: whereas Ives, never leaving his New World, accepted it in its emergent chaos as well as in its burgeoning promise. He was the first composer of democratic principle in that he found his materials in the world around him, making no arbitrary distinctions between the artistic and the demotic. Music was sounds made by people, in a multiplicity of social contexts. These sounds included art music, especially that of the 'manly' classical composers, notably Beethoven, alongside hymns and marches, parlour ballads, and the rag and jazz of bars and shanty-town 'caffs'. Clearly such an approach must override barriers between formal artistic processes (in which Ives, trained at Yale, was well versed) and ad hoc creation. It was basic to Ives's position and to his radical Americanism that, despite his technical skills, his acute ear and exceptional intelligence he should have deliberately remained an amateur. He was a most uncommon Common Man who, making a substantial living in the insurance business, used his music to define a faith that – again in accord with American pragmatism – was at once real and transcendental. This profoundly American combination of naiveté with sophistication is pertinent to our future also, should we have one.

Given Ives's empirical approach to his art it is not surprising that his jazz explorations should be, unlike Stravinsky's, positive rather than negative, authentic in spirit and technique. As early as the 1890s he was making barrelhouse piano music which he sometimes inaccurately termed 'rag'. Two such pieces, originally improvised at student hops during his years at Yale, are incorporated into the magnificent First Piano Sonata. The Hawthorne movement of the Second (Concord) Sonata embraces still wilder jazz elements, alongside the circus-band music to which rag was initially related. More recently unearthed are the astonishing *Three page Sonata* and the *Piano Study* and *Take-off*. Many of the 'theatre sets' composed between the 1890s and around 1916 contain 'sketches' for jazz or theatre bands that suggest the white heat of improvisation, eschewing finalised notation. Indeed there is no 'definitive' version even of Ives's most famous work the *Concord Sonata,* let alone of the Fourth Symphony, his most adventurous piece. All Ives's jazz pieces contain jazz's quintessence in that they involve tension between the corporeal energy of the beat, the often levitatory 'flight' of the melodic lines,and the empiricism of the fortuitously consonant or dissonant harmonies precipitated, from traditionally hymnic and martial elements in the heat of the moment. Ives's unformalised notation – at the opposite extreme to Stravinsky's meticulous precision – attempts to capture the moment's frenzy, insofar as this is possible. His 'democratic' techniques include not only normal sound-creation but also imitation of acoustic phenomena (bands passing one another on the march, and so on), parody, game-playing, problem-solving, partial and total recall of past experience, and, most significantly, the mechanics and semantics of improvisation both within and outside notated composition. Many years later such notions are to be explored by the European and American avant-garde; all of them Ives had observed and practised in his local environment, seventy or eighty years back. We can get a remote idea of how apocalyptic was Ives's approach to performance by listening to the few extant tapes of his playing of his own piano music. These demonstrate, among other things, that Ives was, in the years of the First World War, the only 'art' composer animated by the spirit as well as the letter of jazz. With one exception, I think it is still true that Ives is the only composer to have used jazz positively and 'authentically'. That exception is Michael Tippett.

Stravinsky was a cosmopolitan European; Ives was an indigenous American; Tippett is an Englishman, with Celtic ancestry. He resembles Stravinsky in that throughout his long career he has been a seeker, passing through a succession of apparently disparate phases which add up cohesively. He resembles Ives in that his music stems from a specific environment. Like Ives, he is at once naïve and sophisticated, but from the twilight of an old world rather than from the dawn of a new. It is hardly oversimple to say that Tippett's music is about growing up. This relates him to his younger contemporary Benjamin Britten, all of whose work centres around the theme of Eden's Forgotten Garden, revealing the innocent heart's ultimate invulnerability, even in a corrupt world. Britten's technical lucidity and spiritual grace are beyond Tippett, but that is because the older man has chosen, like Beethoven, to grow up the hard way. A technical consequence of this is that whereas Britten was never deeply preoccupied with the sonata principle and had no more than tepid interest in Beethoven, Tippett, with sonata in his blood-stream, in youth revered Beethoven fanatically, and still admires him above all composers. If Beethovenian sonata is one pole of Tippett's art associated, in Blake's sense, with Experience, the complementary pole – that of Blakean Innocence – is often represented by folk song and by jazz, to which he was early addicted at a time when, in conservative British academicism, such musics were taboo. Ives was unique in the early years of the century in being an 'art' composer who was also part of the jazz world. He was also a Beethovenian composer in his concern with sonata as a compositional principle auralising the process known to philosophers as Becoming. Since his exploration could not accept Beethoven's European, eighteenth-century-rooted positives of form and tonality, Ives's Becoming was both more radical and less rewarding than Beethoven's. Nonetheless, they are composers of the same ethos. Tippett, as an Englishman, is poised between their two worlds, old and new.

Tippett was a late starter and his First Piano Sonata, the work that initially brought him to our attention in 1938, was written in his thirtieth year. It is distinguished more by Innocence than by Experience; and though it is called Sonata it has no movement in sonata form.[1] The variation-set with which it opens develops out of its glinting linear textures and its metrical contrarieties a measure of sonata-like tension. Even so, this inauguratory Tippett work affects us mainly with its boyish exuberance, and it is no accident that its youthfulness should entail an intuitive response to jazz and folk song. The metrical intricacies of the first movement and of the scherzo are jazzily buoyant; the rondo finale has an explicitly negroid, pentatonically dancing tune that in its guileless rhythmic elisions may make us laugh out loud; the slow movement, based on a real Celtic folk tune, harmonises it with the plangency of the black blues.

That this relationship to jazz was intuitive, not the self-conscious imitation practised by other European composers such as Stravinsky, Ravel, Hindemith, Lambert, even Weill, is testified in Tippett's first indubitable masterpiece, the Concerto for Double String Orchestra of 1939, a wondrously life-asserting piece written on the eve of Europe's most cataclysmic war. Here the lyrical, quasi-vocal character of the themes, the buoyancy of the rhythms, the multiplicity-in-unity of the counterpoint, still derive from techniques that dominated European music before the schism of sonata, so that the music creates a spontaneous affirmation of life rather than an introverted struggle between the will and the world. Yet even in this early work Tippett's preoccupation – one might call it an obsession – with false relations not only points back to the string music of England's seventeenth century; it also relates to Vaughan Williams's creation of an English symphony distinct from German tonal tradition, springing from vocal modality yet capable, through techniques evolved from false relation, of the inner tension and incipient drama of sonata. Originally false relation had emerged, in European music, from a dichotomy between two views of the world: from a collision between the monophonic modal melody, usually with flat seventh, characteristic of folk song and of plainchant; and the harmonic tonality fostered by the Renaissance, which needed the sharpened seventh to formulate cadence marking, through 'leading' notes and 'dominants' – the imposition of will on Time.

Tippett's false relations likewise testify to his precarious equilibrium between worlds old and new; and this bears on the fact that false relations have, in the twentieth century, recurred in the so-called blue notes of the black Afro-American in his white world. The Negro's pentatonic and modal roulades, inherited from his African ancestry, clash with the harmonic, tonal and metrical symmetries of the white American march and hymn. An Englishman, Tippett could make this black-white alienation vicariously his, as could Ives, a native American, and as Stravinsky, a cosmopolitan European, could not. On reflection, we may realise that the blue notes – false relations indeed – of Afro-American music may represent as crucial a moment in man's history as did the false relations occurring at the transition from the Middle Ages to the modern world.

In the Double Concerto Tippett's liaison with black American music is manifest in melodic, rhythmic and harmonic terms; and these black techniques parallel elements having roots in 'old' English traditions. Thus in the first movement all the themes sing, and at the same time liltingly dance. The metronome mark gives minim equals 110; but the notation is in $\frac{8}{8}$, owing to the prevalence of 'numerical' rhythms (especially rumba-like patterns of 3 plus 3 plus 2) within the duple beat, and because the melodic stresses ride over the bar-lines. As in seventeenth-century polyphony, bar-lines exist to keep the parts together, but have little accentual significance. The melodies float, 'swinging' over and through the beat, the ebullient effect being emphasised by antiphony between the two orchestras which doesn't imply a dualism of harmonic and tonal conflict, as in a classical sonata. There's a continuous polyphonic interplay of themes, producing modulation through inner permutation rather than as part of a tonal argument. In its singing-dancing flow this allegro is a canticle of praise at once physical in rhythm and metaphysical in melodic proliferation. The coda reveals an identity between the two originally distinct themes, leading to joyous release. We are 'sent' by the music, as we are by a jazz break of Louis Armstrong, who also heals breaches between flesh and spirit. He created power and joy from the squalor of the New Orleans slum he was born into, assimilating its terrors into memories of a racial past. English Tippett, with centuries of European culture behind him, also made his music swing in rediscovering our seventeenth century, when flesh and spirit still sang and danced together before, from their separation, the modern world was born.

The slow movement makes a more direct return to England's past, for its beautiful melody is very like a folk song. Yet the English false relations with which the tune is harmonised also sound profoundly 'blue' and Afro-American; the present discovers the past and the past is *presented*. This is why the middle section's slightly frantic attempt at fugal unity doesn't prevent the music from becoming chromatically insecure, and from acquiring some of the rhythmic ambiguity of the first movement. When the da capo of the 'folk' tune begins on solo cello, syncopated figures continue to recall the first movement's initial theme: so that the apparent repose of the movement can lead to a finale which has the first movement's singing-dancing vivacity, with more positive, forward-thrusting energy. Although the movement is in rondo, not sonata form, it is a developing rondo with sonata-like characteristics. The intricate polyrhythms, the lyrical flights, the side-stepping modulations exist, with both spiritual and physical grace, in an eternal present. Yet the movement does progress, having beginning, middle and an end in which the song-like tune proves to be a derivative of the folk-like melody of the slow movement, purged of any hint of blue nostalgia, and accompanied on the other orchestra by a medley of $\frac{6}{8}$ metres against the tune's $\frac{2}{4}$ lilt. The work has remade England's past in the light of her present, jubilantly growing from the knowledge, in nerves and blood, that what we were we may still, even in those storm-clouded years, potentially be.

Technically and experimentally this knowledge involves a synthesis of the Old world with the New. This is demonstrated — more overtly because in literary and theatrical as well as musical terms — in the oratorio which was Tippett's next sizeable work. In *A Child of Our Time*, for which the composer wrote his own text, Tippett confronts the Second World War head on, telling a (true) tale of modern anguish and persecution. The story of a young boy victim of Nazi terror becomes a twentieth-century myth. By relating the lay-out to Handel's *Messiah* Tippett suggests a kinship with the oratorio-going British public; by substituting Negro spirituals for the Lutheran chorales in Bach's Passions he uses an oppressed people as symbol for the stifling of the human spirit in a ravaged world. In so doing he makes direct use of the jazz idiom implicit in his own sensibility: so it is not surprising that his choral 'arrangements' of the spirituals are by far the most convincing made by an art composer. The soaring melodic roulades and polyrhythms generate something approaching the exaltation of black Gospel singing; in a committed performance the spirituals can sound as though they are being improvised here and now. Jazz elements appear intermittently throughout the solo music, which includes a haunting tango. But more significant than the occasional jazz 'number' is the basic conception whereby vocal and verbal rhythms are in tension with a corporeal beat. The composer was on the mark in comparing his methods with the 'sprung rhythm' of Gerard Manley Hopkins, a poet who more extravagantly emulated Shakespeare's balance between latent metre and the natural inflexions of speech, and who complementarily commented, in a memorable sonnet, on Purcell's musical exploitation of the 'thew and sinew' of the English language. Apart from the spirituals, the jazz elements in *A Child of Our Time* are not totally integrated into the music, which is sometimes strained and unfulfilled. Of its nature jazz should be a spontaneous liberation of spirit and flesh, as it is, beneath the surface, in the Double Concerto. Brought *to* the surface in the oratorio, it does not fully convince, though the validity of feeling finally conquers. Without offering any solution to our social evils, without castigating us for our wickedness, the oratorio culminates in a thrilling chorus wherein the polyphony swells, and the solo vocal lines burgeon, in ecstatic arabesque. What keeps us alive, the music tells us, is the human impulse to dance and sing, whatever man's bestiality to man. That is what Louis Armstrong also affirmed, as his trumpet bounded from the exuberant body to the spirit's delight.

The end of the oratorio affects *The Heart's Assurance,* to quote the title of the marvellous song-cycle that Tippett wrote to a series of poems about death, by two young poets killed in the war *A Child of Our Time* had heralded. He's reached that point by an apprehension of the interdependence of light and dark forces: a duality inherent in the phenomenon of false relation itself. Certainly *The Heart's Assurance,* though not patently in jazz idiom, is pregnant with blue notes: as is his first (and still greatest) opera, the central work in his career, on which he worked from 1946 to 1952. *The Midsummer Marriage* is that of the body's and senses' joy with the spirit's mystery. The compulsive rhythms of this superbly luxuriant score are a wilder version of the Purcellian tension between vocal reflexion and bodily dance movement; the polyphonically derived harmony owes much to seventeenth-century modal variety; while the flowering of the lines into ever smaller note-values parallels the seventeenth-century technique of divisions on a ground. There's a baroque, sensuous excitement in the curling tendrils of Tippett's vocal lines; yet the airborne rhythms give the music spiritual buouyancy also. The relation to jazz, though latent, is profound; and bears on the fact that in this score Tippett has achieved something very rare in our time: an act of celebration.

In some chamber works composed during these fecund middle years, we may trace the manner in which Tippett's jazz-orientated 'celebration' comes to terms with his Beethovenian exploration. In the string quartet he found a medium which has affinities both with the polyphonic string consort of the seventeenth century and with the classical sonata as supremely practised by Beethoven. The second (and most frequently played) of his string quartets is described as being in F sharp major-minor, the bitonal ambiguity referring explicitly to the blue false relations that pervade it. The first movement displays the madrigalian flexibility of rhythm and the melodic compromise between modality and diatonicism such as characterises the Double Concerto. The slow movement, though austerely linear, is closer to the baroque notion of fugue; while the finale reconciles Tippett's 'evolutionary' song-dance with the dualistic conflict of Beethoven. As in *The Midsummer Marriage*, strife between positive and negative forces generates jubilation. Tippett resembles Ives in that his jazzy 'innocence' proves inseparable from his Beethovenian 'experience', this life-assertion being here more potent than it is in the next phase of Tippett's work, centred around the opera *King Priam*. In the mosaic and collage techniques which Tippett explores in this period, rhythmic animation is enhanced rather than dampened but it is less jazz-like, being more separable from forward-thrusting line and harmonic progression. When jazz recognizably reappears in Tippett's music, in what we're coming to think of as his third period, it is in connection with words and, at least implicitly, with theatre. The keywork is the Third Symphony, which refers directly to both the blues and Beethoven. Significantly, it is also a work in which Tippett's fascination with Ives is strikingly operative. Through Ives the new world and the old world – the demotically extrovert and the spiritually introspective – meet.

The symphony is in two parts, each conceived on a large scale. Structurally the first part has something in common with the progressive evolution typical of post-Renaissance music, but more in common with the static, and to a degree non-Western, principles of composition that Tippett had explored in his second period. The composer says that the music is polarised between Arrest and Movement, using the terms metaphorically to imply a positive compression and explosion of energy, on the analogy of a jet engine. 'At the halfway point of Part I the polarity changes to that between a pattern of discontinuous music "in the heights" (the music of a windless night sky) and a flow of continuous music "in the depths" (the song of the ocean currents).' Opposite poles of experience are again juxtaposed, but they are not 'worked through', as in *The Midsummer Marriage*, let alone resolved. After uncompromisingly stating the divisiveness of modern man, Tippett goes on to ask whether we still have any right to sing an Ode to Joy such as Beethoven assayed when, as finale to his Ninth Symphony, he set Schiller. Tippett's conception is closer to that of Schiller's contemporary Blake: whose humanely religious preoccupations are in turn mirrored in Beethoven's third period music. Indeed, Beethoven's last three piano sonatas might almost be said to be 'about' the reconciliation of Blake's Tyger and Lamb: a parallel which Tippett, describing his symphony, invokes. Even from the depths of our late twentieth-century hell it is still possible, Tippett believes, to celebrate: so what he is attempting in the Third Symphony is a latterday, more inward, more agonised reappraisal of the 'human predicament' he'd faced in *A Child of Our Time*.

After this bold statement of divisiveness, Part II at first relinquishes duality in being kaleidoscopic. For it opens with a scherzo which, telescoping a multiplicity of wild and whirling, very fast, very different musics is the closest Tippett has come to Ives's 'democratic' acceptances of the flux of appearances. Often, in his orchestral incarnations of life-as-it-is in the volatile present, Ives quotes a medley of disparate sources, artistic and popular. Tippett does the same, or at least gives that impression, and concludes the scherzo with an unambiguous and cataclysmic quotation: the famous-notorious dissonance that forms the ultimate climax to Beethoven's Ninth. This dissonance, embracing every note of the chromatic scale, occurs in the retrospect of fragments from the previous movements that is to lead into the finale's Joy theme. At that point Beethoven calls on vocal (and verbal) as well as instrumental resources. Tippett again follows suit, except that he asks for a single soprano. What the soprano sings is explicitly called Blues, slow and fast; and Tippett's own words give a more inwardly Jungian twist to the dialogue of positive and negative forces he'd initiated, more than thirty years earlier, in *A Child of Our Time*.

The philosophical and psychological, perhaps even the physiological, point would seem to be that our divisiveness can be healed only by a return to the corporeal-spiritual identity which the blues may represent. The opening of Tippett's first blues promises this, for blueness is potently realised in harmony and scoring, as the obbligato parts on flugelhorn and other jazzy instruments interlace in painful ecstasy with the soprano's soaring flights; although notated, the music gives an impression of immediate invention. The trouble is that this invention cannot be sustained into consummation. Of its nature, improvisation cannot be simulated. As the soloist's ululations and the orchestral dialogue grow increasingly frantic, words and music acquire a portentousness that denies the heart of the matter. 'We sense a huge compassionate power,/To heal,/To love'. Only perhaps we don't: not as we did in the early Double Concerto, at the end of *A Child of Our Time*, throughout *The Midsummer Marriage*, in *The Heart's Assurance*, in the string quartets, the Second Symphony and the Concerto for Orchestra.[2] The two late operas, *The Knot Garden* (1966-9) and *The Ice Break* (1973-76), come up against similar problems. Both start from the ratiocinative process; the 'head' – Tippett has a very able one – reflects on man's plight, and intelligently exploits the findings of psychology, anthropology and sociology in so doing. He modifies his musical resources to suit, calling not only on jazz, an organic part of his sensibility and technique, but also on electrophonic rock and pop as counterpart to the dramatic themes. This is valid enough, since what the operas are 'about' is precisely the motivating force that has moulded those demotic musics. Yet of its nature, semi-improvised ritual music cannot be replanted in Establishment theatre. The blues-songs for Dov are as intrinsically beautiful as they are original; yet although each opera fascinates and stimulates, neither is entirely satisfying in the theatre, as is the magic ritual enactment of *The Midsummer Marriage,* or the intuitive absorption of jazz into the Concerto for Double String Orchestra.

In this context the distinction, as well as the similarity, between Tippett and Ives is worthy of comment. Ives drew on jazz and many other pop musics because as an amateur he belonged, despite his professional accomplishments, to the worlds those musics stood for. He heard his father directing the Danbury town band; he improvised barbershop harmony with bi- and tritonal embellishments in the family parlour; as pianist he beefed out music hall numbers and rags for his college glee-club and at local junketings; he played (often wildly improvised) hymns and voluntaries in New England chapel or New York church. Such embracements of pop musics were grist to the mill of his unpop art, and were feasible because there was no musical Establishment within which he had to work. This gave his music its full-blooded if raw authenticity; but the penalty of his amateur status was that his 'serious' music was little performed and was even considered unperformable. The disadvantages of this are obvious; the advantage was that he was free to experiment. That Ives gave up composition in the early twenties, though he lived until 1954, was a consequence of his lonesomeness: the illness from which he suffered was almost certainly in part psychosomatic. Yet the essence of his achievement is that it was incomplete and never to be completed except by death, and perhaps not even then. The Americanism of Ives's music depends on the fact that it is life in the making: which is why it is still relevant to the future, as it was at the far-off time it was created.

Tippett, on the other hand, has been for half a century a respected composer and has now become an international celebrity. One can't, it seems, have it every way; that kind of success can find no place for the blues and for electric rock as 'performance art'. Stravinsky, probably the greatest and certainly the most representative composer of the twentieth century, owes his documentary significance to the fact that he evaded the implications of both jazz and Beethoven. Ives and Tippett accepted both, revealing the necessity of the one to the other in any future mankind might rationally and irrationally hope for. Whereas Ives didn't intellectualise what he was about, Tippett has attempted to do so. To intellectualise the inadequacy of intellect is a paradox of which Tippett does not always escape the consequences. Even so, one cannot but admire his courage, and one has to admit that, important though the unearthing of 'primitive' levels of experience has been, there never was a time when we've been more, not less, in need of 'consciousness' and all that incorrigibly Western phenomenon entails. After the collage techniques of the Second Piano Sonata, of *King Priam* and of the Concerto for Orchestra, Tippett seems, in 'third period' works like the Third Piano Sonata and the Triple Concerto, to be paying direct homage to late Beethoven. These works may indicate the direction in which the music of this inexhaustibly fecund creator will evolve. If so, it may well be that future works will make less overt reference to jazz: which is not to deny that, but for jazz, his uniquely significant contribution to twentieth-century music would have been impossible. Like Beethoven, Tippett has always awakened 'beginnings' which he must explore for himself, and which will in turn be launching-pads for those who come after. Remembering Eliot's dictum that 'old men ought to be explorers', we may add that in his eightieth year this Child of our Time is just *beginning* to be old.

NOTES
1. Tippett sees its scherzo as a disguised sonata-form movement! Ed.
2. For a different view of this aspect of the work see 'The Third Symphony' by John McCabe – Ed.

DAVID MATTHEWS

'Mirror upon Mirror mirrored'

Some notes on Tippett's allusions

MOST COMPOSERS today are eclectics who, since they no longer inherit a tradition automatically from their immediate predecessors, must forge their own links with the past as best they can. With the enormous increase in our knowledge of the past, 'tradition' is now the whole history of music. Composers will choose their ancestry from whatever means most to them; consequently there is not just one contemporary language but a plurality. Those who find tradition a burden may decide to ignore it altogether, just as others are tempted to seek refuge in the simpler, safer world of the past. But knowledge of the past need not be inhibiting; it can and should be a rich stimulus to the creative imagination. Michael Tippett has always found this to be so; his music is a continuous and fertile dialogue with the past. When Tippett alludes to the music of his predecessors – and his allusions are almost always conscious – it is both a gesture of the kinship he feels with them and at the same time a desire and a need to give his music greater resonance, to enlarge its range of meaning.

In 1952, Tippett wrote: 'I hold for myself that the composition of oratorio and opera is a collective as well as a personal experience . . . If the traditional forms of oratorio and opera can contain the collective experiences of any time then composers will generally use them.'[1] It was in order to realise this idea that Tippett, in *A Child of Our Time*, first wove into a major work a complex pattern of allusion. Whereas Elgar in *Gerontius* was concerned with his own private response to Newman's poem (and the occasional musical similarities to *Parsifal* are not deliberate attempts to identify Gerontius with Amfortas), Tippett tried to make his oratorio a public statement, as if it were the collective response to the tragic events narrated in it. Bach had done this in the Passions; but then Bach was working within the tight framework of Christianity. In order to draw some of this Christian heritage into his own work, Tippett made allusions to the Passions, and in particular to Handel's *Messiah*. He found a substitute for Bach's congregational hymns in Negro spirituals and further broadened his musical language with references to popular song: for instance, the solo tenor's 'I have no money for my bread'. His text mixes biblical references with allusions to Blake and Jung. *A Child of Our Time* remains, however, a problematical work, partly from the intrinsic

35

difficulties of the form, partly because by constantly subjugating the personal response to the universal, Tippett cannot avoid a certain anonymity of style and of tone. In *The Midsummer Marriage*, distilled personal experience is as equally important as the collective aspect, which is brought in by means of a still more complex musical and literary background. This is one reason for that work's exceptional power.

In the case of the non-dramatic works, the allusive background is generally more straightforward. One starting point for Tippett has been the experience of hearing the work of another composer. The Piano Concerto, as is well known, was conceived when Tippett heard Walter Gieseking rehearse the first movement of Beethoven's Fourth Piano Concerto and was so affected by Gieseking's interpretation that he felt impelled to write a concerto himself 'in which the piano is used once again for its poetic capabilities'. In fact, the Beethoven is a fairly remote archetype for the finished work; Tippett's direct musical allusions are rather to Brahms (deliberately? – see the first movement, figure 19ff) and to his own *Midsummer Marriage*. But it is important to know the role of the Beethoven concerto as a background presence in order to understand the kind of piece Tippett was aiming at. The Piano Concerto has, indeed, just those qualities of poetic lyricism and classical purity that had initially inspired it; it is markedly different from the typically percussive concerto of the time by Bartók or Prokofiev.

Beethoven, of course, looms behind much of Tippett's music. In the 1930s Tippett held the view[2] that tonality had been misused by composers since Beethoven, a decline he coupled with the loss of psychic wholeness: 'The tonal system related to sonata form is a highly polarised system. Modern people are not polarised, they are split.' The uncompromising implication to be drawn from this theory was that if a modern composer wished to write tonal music, he should return to Beethoven's principles and start again. This is precisely what Tippett himself attempted to do. The results may be seen at their most puritanical in the finale of the Second String Quartet of 1941-2, which is closely modelled on the last movement of Beethoven's C sharp minor quartet, Op.131. Like Beethoven's finale, this is a sonata movement, the only one in the quartet and one of the strictest Tippett was to write. It is worth looking at the similarities in some detail. Though the quartet's overall key is F sharp, Tippett begins his finale in Beethoven's key of C sharp minor, the dominant of his home key. There is a further parallel here, since Beethoven's finale could be said to begin with the short slow movement (No. 6) which is really a slow introduction in Beethoven's dominant key of G sharp minor. The second movement of Tippett's quartet is a slow, chromatic fugue, inevitably recalling the slow fugue that begins Op.131. The opening of Beethoven's finale (Ex.1b) is a refashioning of the opening notes of his fugue (Ex.1a). Tippett similarly transforms his fugue theme (Ex.2a) into an allegro theme at the opening of his finale (Ex.2b). A still closer link with Op.131 is established when at bar 11, in the bridge passage to his second subject (see Ex.3a), Tippett quotes the actual notes of Ex.1a in the order they appear in Beethoven's finale as the second idea of his first subject group (Ex.3b).

36

Both Tippett and Beethoven have soaring, cantabile second subjects: Beethoven's is in the relative major, E; Tippett's a semitone lower in the relaxed key of E flat. The return to the first theme in both quartets is the beginning of the development section: Tippett begins in B minor, Beethoven in F sharp minor, and though they don't progress through the same keys, Tippett follows Beethoven in his modulation by fifths. Tippett's development section is a little longer than Beethoven's and more extensively worked, but his recapitulation is more orthodox; he simply repeats his first theme, still in C sharp minor, verbatim, whereas Beethoven hugely expands his. Tippett's second subject this time is a fourth higher in A flat; Beethoven's – again expanded – begins in D major and moves smoothly to the tonic C sharp major. The two codas are quite different. Beethoven characteristically has what amounts to a second development; he keeps up a furious energy until the very end and the change to the major mode for the last few bars does little to soften the tragic mood. Tippett continues his fourth-higher transposition by restating the B minor music which began the development in E minor; but the music soon slows down into its peaceful conclusion, the disruptive B sharp of the C sharp minor sections (see Ex.2b) becoming a calm C from which Tippett twice modulates into F sharp major. In these last few bars the Beethoven sound-world recedes as the seventeenth-century allusions that had pervaded the first two movements – to the English madrigalists and to the Purcell string fantasias – briefly come again to the fore, to end the quartet as gently and gracefully as it had begun.

It is the return of this 'fantasia' music at the end that may summon up doubts as to the total success of this movement. Although Tippett skilfully avoids pastiche, we may feel that the music has been unnaturally forced into too restrictive a frame. The fact is that the tautness of Beethovenian sonata form does not marry perfectly with Tippett's instinctive lyricism. The more spontaneous flow of the fantasy-like first movement, and especially the dancing, additive-rhythm scherzo, underline the truth of this, while the fugue points towards the different solution Tippett was to propose in his next quartet.

In the major works of the next years, the First Symphony and the Third Quartet, Tippett continued to explore the possibilities of using late Beethoven as a model, but concentrating on Beethoven's amalgam of sonata with fugue. The last movement of the symphony and the first movement of the quartet are both fugues with long, athletic themes similar to that of the finale of the 'Hammerklavier' sonata. In the quartet, with its three fugal movements interleaved with two rapt slow movements, all prefaced by a slow introduction whose sonorous opening chords immediately bring to mind Beethoven's Op.127 quartet, Tippett, for the first time since the Concerto for Double String Orchestra, finds a wholly successful solution to the problem of integrating his language into a classical mould. He also comes closest both to the sound and to the spiritual world of late Beethoven. The achievement of the Third Quartet, the climax of Tippett's obsession with Beethoven's musical language, is not yet fully appreciated. Throughout this piece Tippett almost miraculously recreates a classical (not a neo-classical[3]) style, so intensely does he identify with its spirit. Tonality has rarely sounded so fresh this century.

It was not until some twenty-five years later that Tippett renewed his obsession with late Beethoven, in the Third Symphony of 1970-2. Here he confronted – this seems the right word – no less a work than the Ninth Symphony. The Beethoven-inspired works of the 1940s were composed against the background of classical form and tonality; the Third Symphony's background, on the other hand, is Beethoven's philosophy, his optimistic humanism, as supremely expressed in his setting of Schiller's *Ode to Joy*. We now know that Beethoven's confidence in the brotherhood of man was, to say the least, premature. As Tippett has written: 'What is "out-of-date" in Schiller's concept of joy is any romantic notion of its universality and inevitability. All that has happened since, in aid of various political utopias, has but deepened the disillusion. Yet if now is our Season in Hell, then when we do occasionally celebrate, as we must and if we can, we do so from a deeper need and with a sharper pang.'[4] In his recent music, Tippett himself has been unable to make the kind of unequivocal affirmation that he made in the works of the 1940s, culminating in *The Midsummer Marriage*. The tonal confidence of those works is no longer valid for him – or rather, the works remain valid, but he cannot now, in a darker and more dangerous world, confirm their particular certainties. Tippett's recent music is much more questioning and ambiguous, though it has not ceased to celebrate.

Tippett begins the finale of this Third Symphony (it follows on without a break from the scherzo) by directly quoting the opening of Beethoven's finale. It is important to distinguish what Tippett is doing here from the practice of some other composers who have introduced quotations into their music. When Bernd Alois Zimmermann, in his orchestral work *Photoptosis* of 1968, quotes the same passage from the Ninth Symphony together with the plainsong 'Veni Creator Spiritus', Skryabin's *Poem of Ecstasy*, *Parsifal*, the

'Dance of the Sugar Plum Fairy' and the First Brandenburg Concerto, he would appear simply to be saying, with Eliot, 'These fragments I have shored against my ruin' (there is sad irony in the fact that Zimmermann took his own life two years later). But for Tippett the quotation signals the start of a deeply involved dialogue with the meaning of Beethoven's great work. As Arnold Whittall puts it: 'The quoted Beethoven seems to represent the intensely pure vision which must disintegrate, the broken dream which begins to be remade through the extraordinary transmogrification of the blues: no longer bitter, but expressing a profound sense of the sorrows which modern generations inherit.'[5] It was a superb idea, analogous to the introduction of the spirituals into A Child of Our Time, for Tippett to follow the Ninth Symphony quotation with three blues for soprano solo, the first of which alludes specifically to the classic recording of 'St Louis Blues' by Bessie Smith with Louis Armstrong. (When Tippett appeared on the radio programme 'Desert Island Discs' he chose this as his favourite record.) In Tippett's 'transmogrification', the harmonium of the original becomes a low wind and brass choir and Armstrong's solo is metamorphosed into a flugelhorn which comments rhapsodically on each line of the verse, just as in the recording.[6] That the jazz and blues of the early part of this century may serve as a vernacular for the serious music of our time (as it does for contemporary popular music) is a brave hope of Tippett's – we certainly need a new vernacular to replace the exhausted vein of folk music. To use the collective language of the blues was both the nearest Tippett could get to an equivalent to Beethoven's famous tune (which has fittingly now become almost a World National Anthem) and the most poignant contrast with it: Tippett's music of personal sorrow complementing Beethoven's music of universal joy.

Tippett's fourth and final song (in fact a dramatic scena) is introduced by a second quotation of the Beethoven, corresponding to Beethoven's own restatement of his opening immediately before the first vocal entry. This time Tippett follows the quotation with an energetic reworking of Beethoven's cello and bass recitative: compare Ex.4a (from the opening of Beethoven's finale) with Ex.4b (Tippett). The solo soprano sets off exultantly, accompanied by a fragment of Beethoven's D major tune. Tippett's words allude to Schiller's: 'They sang that when she waved her wings the Goddess Joy would make us one.' But mention of the Gulag and the concentration camps (sung over music from the slow movement) freezes her in her tracks. This sets the pattern for the rest of the scena: the music's progress, urged on by more injections of Beethoven, is several times halted by reminders of human suffering. Although Tippett eventually builds up a sustained, rapturous climax to the words 'We sense a huge compassionate power/To heal/To love', (the hushed melismas on the words 'heal' and 'love' parallel Beethoven's ecstatic meditation on 'wo dein sanfter Flügel weilt' just before his final Prestissimo), he cannot sustain a Beethovenian momentum right up to the end. But as we listen to his ending, with aggressive brass chords, like those at the very start of the symphony, alternating with quiet, compassionate chords for six solo strings, recalling the blues-inflected solo string passage that had

immediately followed the first Beethoven quotation, we cannot also be unaware of Beethoven's own exultant conclusion. The ambiguity in our present-day response to it is mirrored in Tippett's ambiguous – though not negative – ending. The final section of the Third Symphony is one of the richest in allusive power in all Tippett's music.

The Third Symphony is the climax of Tippett's musical development during the 1960s and is, I think, his best work since *King Priam*. After ten years of searching for new directions the symphony begins a new period of consolidation. The allusion-by-quotation technique works more happily here than in the works in which he first tried it out, *The Knot Garden* and *Songs for Dov*. This is, I would suggest, because of the weight of obsession behind it : Tippett's lifelong empathy with Beethoven as composer and man which has, as it were, granted him the right to use Beethoven's notes here as if they were

40

his own. Similarly, his forty-year obsession with the 'St Louis Blues' gives his own transformation of it exceptional resonance. Dov's blues, in *Songs for Dov*, urban blues of alienation relating more to Chicago than to New Orleans, are less successful because less assimilated. In *The Knot Garden*, I find the introduction of Schubert's song 'Die liebe Farbe' into the second act somewhat forced, despite its appropriateness to Flora's character and its tonal links with the beginning and end of the opera (which Arnold Whittall has noted).[7] This may simply be because of the slight superficiality of the music that leads up to it: *The Knot Garden* as a whole has never seemed to me one of Tippett's most deeply-felt works; it is, above all, a reflection of his confusion at that time about the way his musical langage should progress. The opera's sibling *Songs for Dov*, a treasure trove of quotations from *The Knot Garden* itself and from Beethoven, Wagner and Mussorgsky,[8] is also a curiously unsatisfactory work. The collage technique seems awkwardly handled; the allusions and quotations in the text and in the music distract rather than enrich. (Quotation can be a dangerous game; after you have exhausted the fun of work-spotting – which in a piece like Berio's Sinfonia may keep you going quite a long time – you begin to worry if that wasn't the chief interest of the piece.) Dov is a typically confused young man of the 1960s, a Bob Dylan or John Lennon figure; but Tippett can no longer offer a simple solution to his dilemma, as he could to Mark's, or as Dylan or Lennon themselves might have offered, musically at least. *Songs for Dov* is work in progress. The Third Symphony is based on more solid ground – Beethoven! – and is altogether a more achieved work. If it is, as Whittall suggests, 'Dov's Symphony', we can be grateful that Dov has learned so much from his *Wanderjahre* in the song cycle.

A conclusion that may be suggested from the works I have looked at here is that conscious allusion, if it is to enrich the work that contains it, must arise, in the first place, out of strong feeling, and will then seem appropriate and natural. Perhaps this is only to echo distantly Tolstoy's theory of art. I have said enough about Tippett and Beethoven to indicate the peculiar strength of their relationship. Tippett is not Beethoven reborn, but he is the most Beethovenian composer of our time, both in the character of his music and in the attitude he takes towards artistic creation. For him to allude to Beethoven is indeed to acknowledge kinship. Since the Third Symphony he has produced three more 'late Beethoven' works: a 'late piano sonata' – the Third; a 'late quartet' – the Fourth; and a 'Missa Solemnis' – that is, a large-scale summing up of fundamental beliefs – *The Mask of Time*. We may tentatively hope for more 'late quartets' in the future (though in the meantime he has surprised us with a 'late Schubert' piano sonata in the Fourth).

In pursuing the Beethoven relationship I have been unable to say anything here of the equally strong affinity Tippett feels for Stravinsky, whose example inspired the renewal of his language in the late 1950s, which also was made along Stravinskean lines. The first product of that renewal – the Second Symphony – has claim to be considered Tippett's masterpiece, and the fact that Stravinsky and Beethoven stand behind it, for the first and only time, as equal presiding deities, has much to do with its special quality. I have only hinted, too, at the literary allusions that haunt Tippett's texts and closely parallel the musical ones. But many other echoes inhabit Tippett's garden. The title of this essay is a Yeats quotation sung by Hermes in the last act of *King Priam*; it is no surprise to open the vocal score of *The Mask of Time* and find on page seven a quotation from Yeats's late poem 'High Talk'. Those whom Tippett loves best go on resounding through his work.

NOTES

1. M. Tippett: *Moving into Aquarius*, (London: Paladin Books, 1974) p50
2. See his 1938 article 'Music and Life', reprinted in Tippett: *Music of the Angels*, (London: Eulenberg Books, 1980)
3. The distinction is a fine one; but I would claim that a neo-classical composer like Stravinsky stands much more apart from his models. Tippett himself adopted a more neo-classical stance in such Stravinsky-influenced works as the Second Symphony.
4. M. Tippett: *Moving into Aquarius*, (London: Paladin Books, 1974) p159
5. A. Whittall: *The Music of Britten and Tippett* (Cambridge University Press, 1982) pp266–7
6. Meirion Bowen (*Michael Tippett*; London: Robson Books, 1982 p121) calls the flugelhorn solo 'Miles Davis-inspired' and admittedly it *sounds* more like Miles Davis; but I am sure that the Armstrong original was at the back of Tippett's mind. The allusion just becomes more complex!
7. A. Whittall: *The Music of Britten and Tippett* (Cambridge University Press, 1982) p242
8. Meirion Bowen identifies them in a careful examination of the work in his *Michael Tippett*, pp147–52

*Michael Tippett in
Cornwall.*

43

[Copyist: see P. 2]   "Rebecca" Prelude   (new prelude
                                                re-begun on)
                                                2/IV/82
                                                Wilfred Josephs

Allegro con fuoco (♩=c120)

Wilfred Josephs ©1983
Vocal Score   Novellos   Page 3
              1983

"Rebecca" Act — Scene —
d.126
PRELUDE

WILFRED JOSEPHS
Tribute

T HERE CANNOT be many English composers of my generation who were not, at some time in their early careers, influenced by the music of Michael Tippett.

His great early masterpiece, the Concerto for Double String Orchestra, was such an inspiration to the English composer seeking something thrilling, innovative, brilliant and also intensely moving, that I suppose many others were, like me, entrapped by its delights.

Certainly my own early Essay for Strings, performed at an SPNM Public Orchestral Rehearsal in the Royal Festival Hall, had a first movement which was so Tippettian that even I realised it – and withdrew it after one performance! The middle movement still survives as my opus 13; it was not at all Tippettian – more Bartokian in fact, but it *had* a little of me in it.

During the break in the rehearsal, Ben Frankel, the Presenter, told me that I was too good a composer to let the Finale stand and, after the performance, I agreed with his suggestion of scrapping the two outer movements and keeping only the Elegy for Strings, as the central movement is now called.

The only other contribution I could have made in Tippett's honour would have been to allow part of the Essay to be printed here, but I am loth to include something which I am not happy to own up to. Equally I find it very difficult to write a short piece 'just like that' in Michael's honour, nor do I wish to parody his music in any way whatever.

For these reasons I have chosen to include a copy of the first page of the vocal score of my recent opera *Rebecca* – a tribute from a composer 'young' in opera to one 'old' in opera, but very young in everything else.

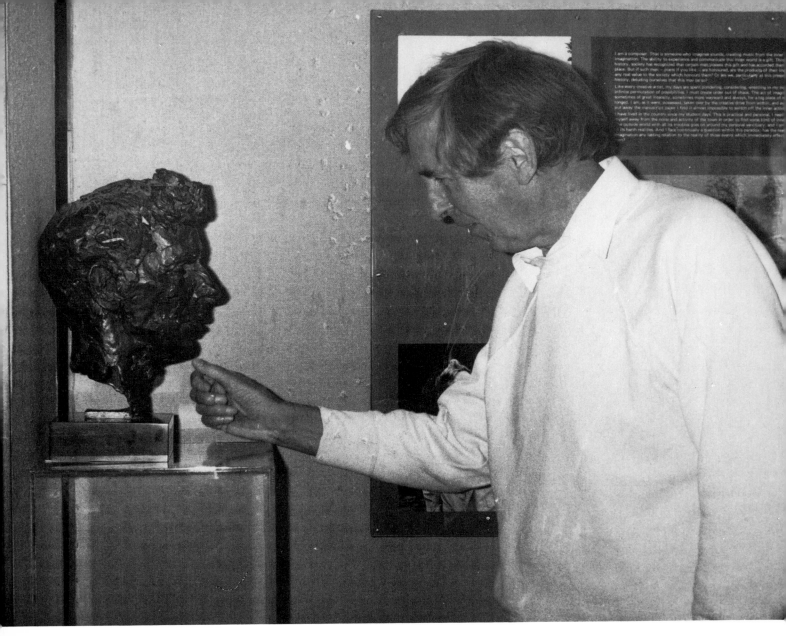

Tippett at the Royal Festival Hall showing of the exhibition A Man of Our Time, *with sculpture modelled by Gertrude Hermes: on permanent loan to R. F. H. from Schott and Co.*

SYMON CLARKE
Birth and Renewal

I N WRITING about the use of metaphor in the works of Tippett I will confine the discussion to only a few works. The nature of this kind of subject is elaborate and difficult to confine with precision; I will, therefore, consider two interrelated areas within the same subject.

The first concerns a brief analysis, based on the views of Tippett himself, of the problems encountered when attempting to apprehend a particular work of art and thus to comprehend the construction and intention of the metaphorical language it might contain. Secondly, I wish to look specifically at Tippett's metaphorical inventions by examining two kinds of metaphorical conceptions; the use of separate individual metaphors and then how they might combine into conglomerations and thus constitute more general conceptions in conjunction with the large scale architecture of his compositions.

An example of the single metaphor might be 'We shall give milk and kisses', a line from the text of the Third Symphony. An example of a generalised conception would be the problems concerning man's understanding of Time, expressed throughout the text and related musical superstructure of *The Vision of Saint Augustine*.

It is clear already, I think, that it is easier to quote words and discuss their implications as examples of metaphorical constructions rather than abstract music – an issue that Tippett is strongly aware of, and I would submit that his perceptions concerning this are reflected in most of his actual compositions, using words or not. His attitude towards the communicative power of words and music, albeit idiosyncratic, is nonetheless a profound contribution to artistic creativity.

Tippett makes a distinction between knowledge about art and knowledge about a particular work of art. He maintains that a work of art itself can only be apprehended (and comprehended) as an 'image', the impression given – deriving its impact from the inner feelings and experiences of its individual creative artist. However apparently representational the mode of expression might be, the idiosyncrasy is that the composition is always about the individual's inner world and can only really be comprehended by another inner world. To use our language of words to explain the substance of this 'image' further externalises its essential nature, leading us adrift from the points of communication and contact within it. Art, Tippett surmises, is able to fulfil a fundamental need to communicate with the inner world of us all[1].

The artist also needs to create a mechanism whereby it is possible to translate his inner world into an outer one and for this he uses his technique and craft of compositional processes, developing and refining his tools until they become symbiotic with his inner ideas and images. This translation is necessary as the listener would otherwise not be allowed to recognise the inner world through the outer. The resulting work of art is thus always representational to some degree.

But to reverse this process of translation in an attempt to return to the ideas of the original inner-self means that the 'image' of the individual work becomes obscured; a well-known problem for musicologists! Stravinsky put the case in one kind of context by saying that the only real criticism or analysis of one work of art is the creation of another. The artist is thus faced with the continual questioning: Why do I create and what do I create?

The 'why' for Tippett, is inextricably connected with the 'what' and he is able, in some of his compositions, to draw attention to the links between them. Tippett's subject matter in the representational mode, the 'what', contains a profound amalgam of topical yet perennial issues and visionary elements. The 'why' is intrinsic to the visionary qualities.

In *The Midsummer Marriage* Tippett uses the figure of Sosostris as a direct intervention of the visionary from outside but the metaphorical implication is that her powers are contained within each of us. Sosostris sings to King Fisher:

> Who hopes to conjure with the world of dreams,
> Waking to life my visionary powers?
> He draws inexorably out from the vast
> Lottery a dream to dream himself[2].

During the second act of the opera the visionary element appears again, as from outside. But this time the metaphor allows us to look within by virtue of purely musical structures but with the integrated dimension of dancing.

The 'Ritual Dances' occur in *The Midsummer Marriage* as climatic sections to the working out of the dramatic conflicts and questionings of the characters and the music at the ends of Acts II and III. The music of the dances serves, metaphorically, to illuminate the inner worlds of the characters and their situations but also to place their dilemmas in a universal perspective. The balletic element, carefully associated with symbolic ideas taken from various vegetation myths of birth, death and renewal, articulate a kind of universal imagery of redemption, through explanation of the universality of the natural world – the thematic construction of the dancing being allied to the central idea of the opera, that of 'our ignorance or illusion about ourselves'. The first three dances depict a female pursuing a male, in the natural, for in this opera the universal world also contains the innerself, so the Hound chases the Hare; the Otter hunts the Fish and the Hawk hunts the Bird. The final dance 'Fire

Summer' is music rich with the imagery of transfiguration. King Fisher dies, allowing the union, through inner knowledge dispelling illusions, of Mark and Jenifer.

Tippett uses Ground Bass techniques in this music with almost vocal counterpoint in the upper parts, comprising elaborate yet finely wrought textures. The movement of the music is episodic but harmonically continuously coherent with diatonic chords decorated and expanded by the constant use of layers of fourths. In the final dance the chorus sing:

> Fire! Fire! St Johns' Fire!
> In the desert of the night[3].

Here, to music that emerges from the previous contrapuntal textures the diverse elements finally unite into a kind of chorale – the verbal imagery indicating the notion of final cleansing by fire.

The discovery, through depiction, of the internal world is also explored by Tippett in *A Child of Our Time*. The context is very different however, the natural environment being replaced by specifically human activities of oppression, war and politics. Here the composer eventually wrote his own large scale text for the first time: the notion of a Poet (deriving from the Greek 'to make'), is interchangeable with that of a composer[4]. A full assessment of the gestation of this composition may be deduced from Chapter 4 of Tippett's book *Music of the Angels*. I wish only to concentrate on the metaphorical language of the Negro Spiritual settings but seen within the metaphorical implications of the whole work.

With regard to the Spirituals, Tippett writes: 'I had to elevate this musical vernacular to take charge of feelings of a rather higher order without at all losing its immediacy of impact or appeal[5].' The use of the words 'impact' and 'appeal' are significant. Here Tippett denotes generic qualities that he sees impregnated into the metaphor of the Spiritual – a topicality already implying a universal perspective; a metaphorical construction that can contain the impact of a particular event but outside a particular time. The oppression of the Negro is at once an individual and a collective experience; the spontaneity of the individual inventing freely the words and music for himself as a slave on the plantation is preserved metaphorically by Tippett. This potent imagery of lamentation is also a therapeutic activity by the very act of singing from deep within. A process that external, pragmatic oppression cannot extinguish.

The tripartite scheme of this oratorio, imitating Handel's *Messiah*, expounds collective images of oppression in the first part, individual imagery linked to a specific story during the second, but in the third part includes the Spiritual again, now alluding to the power of the inner world, with its potential capacity to unite and renew. The context for rebirth however, is imbued with irony. 'I would know my shadow and my light[6],' from the penultimate section indicates a polarity, the resolution of which can only be a perpetual balance. This may be possible for the individual singing from deep

49

within but is impossible for the collective, because the same process of inner reconciliation would, at present, be disseminated among self-righteous groups and societies. These groups are the perspective established by Parts I and II of the work – the questioning is only made clear in Part III, when Tippett searches for the moral and ethical implications directly. He concludes, again with nature imagery, 'the moving waters renew the Earth. It is Spring[7]'.

The music of the Spirituals was absorbed by Tippett into his own creative vocabulary of techniques from an original recording heard on the radio. Their original construction influenced the whole harmonic ground plan of the composition of his own spirituals and the work as a whole. The use of the minor third, arising naturally from the flattened seventh and the fifth of the tonic below, became a structural device in the oratorio. The linear texture of the original spirituals was clarified and also dramatised by placing the soloists in opposition to the chorus.

The Blues songs in the Third Symphony also occupy the same kind of metaphorical world as the spirituals in *A Child of Our Time* and similarly their closeness to the vernacular creates an equally daunting and compelling impression.

The context for the Blues songs and the final dramatic scene in the Third Symphony is yet again different. The representational mode consists of a fifty-minute structure, the solo soprano entering only towards the end after three complex and argumentative orchestral movements. Any symphony attempting to combine abstract instrumental music with a specific verbal text is bound to relate to what Tippett calls that 'famous hybrid work' – Beethoven's Ninth Symphony. This relationship becomes fundamental to the metaphors of Tippett's own symphony. To introduce the voice he actually quotes directly the raucous presto opening of the Ninth Symphony's last movement. The metaphors for Tippett and Beethoven are here the same – a vehement interruption and implied rejection of the previous musical argument, but whereas Beethoven reviews music from the previous movements and finally overthrows them to embark upon his 'Ode to Joy', Tippett recalls music from the previous movements during his finale. Notably – the percussion music of the first movement to the words: 'What though the dream crack', and the solo viola phrase from the second movement but now on the cello[8]. This structural procedure aids the metaphorical commenting of the text, itself a comment on the 'Ode to Joy'. Tippett inevitably asks, 'what price brotherhood today?' What here becomes specific in the text is implied in purely instrumental terms in the earlier parts of the symphony and regenerated by including music from the previous three movements. This gives further weight to the musical gestures at the beginning of the symphony but now with ironical hindsight.

Only at the end of the work do the ironies coexist with any comfort. The closing page of the score reveals the germinal idea transmuted into 'tough' versus 'tender' in some metaphor of acceptance.

The Blues songs add further connotations; the text highlights the individual, occupying the hostile world of the conflicting materials of the instrumental movements. The problem, as Tippett sees it, with Schiller's 'Ode to Joy', is that in our century it 'lacks any romantic notion ... of universality and inevitability[9]'. Tippett focuses directly upon Schiller, so that:

> Alle Menschen werden Brüder
> Wo dein sanfter Flügel Weilt.

becomes

> They sang that when she waved her wings
> The Goddess Joy would make us one.

Beethoven's 'Ode to Joy' theme is quoted and then distorted at this point by Tippett; a gesture clear from the score but often difficult to hear in the concert hall. The past tense of Tippett's comment on Schiller's original alludes to the improbability of the sentiment sufficing for us today; for Tippett also fashions the metaphors of 'My sibling was the torturer' and 'Did my brother die of frostbite in the camp', adding powerful vernacular intimations. The family connections at this point are for the individual looking out towards the collective but also for the proposed brotherhood of mankind. The individual is, however, so strongly aware of the ironies that only 'milk and kisses', simple yet basic compassion, mixed with renewal, will be able to help from within and by extension, effect a change outside. Finally Tippett is explicit about his ethics. He says, in the last lines, that we can 'sense a huge compassionate power/To heal/To love'. The collective is implied by the 'we' but only a 'we' that an individual, with the possibility of other individuals following, can form a collective experience. The collective may only be comprised of these singular elements, each asking similar questions in the face of the ironic polarities and the confused territory between them. This is Tippett's way of supplying a replacement in our time of the missing 'romantic inevitability'.

The treatment of the Blues songs is, like the Spirituals in *A Child of Our Time,* a product of Tippett's absorption of their vernacular significance. Between the composition of these two works – some thirty years – the literal metaphorical import remains largely a musical gesture. In the Third Symphony the text is entirely Tippett's own. He undertakes a kind of re-composition with reference to the 'blues style', something that is peculiar to himself and particular to this work. Ambiguous harmonies, deriving from the use of the flattened seventh are a hallmark of the original style but unlike the techniques of *A Child of Our Time* where Tippett merely extends and expands the original music, he creates in the Third Symphony his own ambiguous harmonic language. It is sophisticated and of the European West but still retaining the character of the original, if only through gesture. This empirical approach still uses the slow-moving, Blues-orientated, bass line but with almost modal Messiaen-like brass chords on top. (See page 131 of the score – the slow blues song.)

The second Blues song is fast and uses more directly an original technique, the 'riff'; this is a relatively short phrase repeated over a changing chordal pattern. Again, this is music of the European but the link with the original is stronger – a quotation of characterised intention rather than verisimilitude.

The Fourth Symphony, composed during 1976-7, is a work that Tippett

51

has referred to as a 'birth to death' piece; a composition that does not include overtly the notion of renewal through any transcendent activity as in the previous works mentioned. This work has no vocal dimensions and Tippett has created a cyclic structure of gradually expanding individually characterised blocks of material. The symphony falls into seven sections, interlocking to form a continuous single movement, lasting some thirty minutes. The structure incorporates elements of sonata allegro, scherzo and fantasia. The fundamental structural material is stated during the first third of the work and is subsequently expanded and reworked in blocks of increasingly elaborate development, each longer than the last – the dénouement of the work being the juxtaposition of a similar 'tough' and 'tender' motive as in the Third Symphony, with low pitched breathing sounds produced either by actual breathing through a microphone or by using a synthesiser. The final dying breath does not hint at a rebirth but instead relates to the breathing sounds with which the work commences. First breath to last – a process encountered in Mahler's Ninth Symphony and Liszt's *Von der Wiege bis zum Grabe*. Unlike the Liszt however, Tippett retreats from programmatic allusions, allowing the music its own ontology to convey the process in purely argumentative musical language. The renewal processes in this work occur during the actual 'life' of the musical journey of birth to death. The rejuvenation of an inner spirit.

There is, in fact, a particular metaphorical gesture in this piece, heard several times, where the woodwind, strings, tubas, piano and percussion repeat notes very fast in a jittering fashion: to this motive Tippett ascribes the analogy of the fracturing and rebirth of cellular molecules, thus creating a new life[10]. He saw this happen in a film, shown during the 1920s where the foetus of a rabbit was seen subdividing and shaking. Of course, without Tippett's verbal explanations it would not be possible for us to make the same analogy from the music alone but nevertheless Tippett still considers the metaphor significant, if only as a mechanism of translation within himself to create the right musical gesture that could be absorbed into the otherwise 'abstract' musical arguments. I remember coming out of the Albert Hall with him after the first British performance of the work, at the Proms, where he was pounced upon by a small boy, who, having obviously studied the programme note, asked: 'Did the rabbit die at the end?'

A good example, I think, of the danger inherent in attributing verbal explanations to musically-orientated metaphors without including words with the music to make the associations explicit.

I have concentrated on a mere handful of Tippett's compositions and a study of his imagery and conceptions concerning the processes of and between birth and renewal would need an entire book. The point is really that the book is unnecessary – Tippett has already written it and is, incredibly at the age of 80, still writing it. His art needs only the experience gained through listening to his compositions. Works like *The Vision of Saint Augustine* and recently *The Mask of Time* deal with perennial questions of considerable complexity, but the nature of Tippett's own inner questioning and his ability to translate it into a representational mode that actually communicates, means that these works and their subjects become not only accessible but also enriching. His metaphorical language is idiosyncratic – it could never, for a great artist, be anything else, but his capacity for asking the questions provides the elements, through eventual translation and transformation into sound, of the visionary. The final metaphor of *The Vision of Saint Augustine* is apposite. Sung in the language of the country of performance, unaccompanied, by the chorus: 'I count not myself to have apprehended.' Tippett considers the visions of the saint a possibility, a mystical experience, but for us, we cannot rely upon visions of a future eternity. As Dr Zhivago says, in the book of the same name: 'Man was born to live, not to prepare for life.' Despite the visions Tippett's music belongs to a land of the living.

NOTES
1 Ideas here taken from *Music of the Angels*, (Eulenburg Books, London, 1980) p17, etc.
2 *The Midsummer Marriage*, Act III, scene 5, (Libretto p44)
3 Ritual dances Schott score Ed 10207, p124
4 M. Tippett: *Music of the Angels*, (Eullenburg Books, London, 1980) p28
5 *Ibid*, p121
6 *A Child of Our Time* Schott score Ed. 10899, p136
7 *Ibid*, p139
8 Symphony No 3, Schott score Ed. 11148, pp209-10
9 M. Tippett: *Moving into Aquarius* (Paladin Books, London, 1974) p159
10 Symphony No 4, Schott score Ed. 11395, pp18-19

© Part of *Little Christmas Cantata* by Anthony Payne, by courtesy of Chester Music.

54

ANTHONY PAYNE
Tribute

MICHAEL TIPPETT was one of the first modern composers I came to terms with in my adolescence, and I am deeply grateful that such an affirmative, life-enhancing vision helped to form my introduction to contemporary music. I imagine that many who, like me, grew up in the early 1950s must have shared my experience, for the basic conservatism of musical education at that time meant that the continental avant-garde, not to speak of their forbears Webern, Messiaen, Varèse and others, was a closed book to most of us. This was a lamentable state of affairs, as all contemporary styles ought to be available for the emerging young composer to sample; and yet, I can not find it in my heart to regret that I came across Tippett before, say, the Second Viennese School. I now feel that what I wanted then was to feed my growing consciousness of belonging to the English soil. English roots had to be strongly developed before I felt in a secure enough position to take what was wanted from outside sources, and Tippett's firm links with Elizabethan music and Purcell, as well as with such as Stravinsky and even Hindemith, made him a wonderfully nourishing agent.

It has been said that what one loves one makes one's own; so I feel that a small part of Tippett's spirit has always been burning somewhere inside me. He encourages us to be ourselves, open ourselves to other music without abandoning a native shrewdness, in fact to admire without slavish submission, and more important still, never to lose sight of the fact that music is rooted in song and dance, and is the body's as well as the spirit's expression. Finally there is the significant fact that Tippett has always remained true to his time without becoming a prey to 'isms' and factions: is contemporary but never modish.

Such was for many years my apprehension of Tippett and my conscious debt to him, until a friend revealed more tangible points of contact which had probably been too close to me previously to be noticed. There were, for instance, proliferating lines in my music which in unguarded moments I might have attributed to the influence of Boulez or perhaps Ligeti, but which I suddenly realised were as much akin to Tippett – the *Corelli Fantasia*, perhaps, or parts of the Second Symphony; while more recently I found myself responding to a carol text in my *Little Christmas Cantata* with dancing syncopations that certainly sprang from a long standing love of the Concerto for Double String Orchestra and the Second String Quartet.

In sum, along with many of my contemporaries, I am deeply indebted to this golden-hearted music, visionary yet uninhibitedly physical. It has provided an inspiring antidote to parochialism and anonymous cosmopolitanism alike, while encouraging a sense of the English tradition and an openness to outside influences. Self-pity, despair and narrow introversion, pitfalls for the modern artist, are all combatted by the constructive optimism of Tippett, and we have been lucky to have had him working amongst us.

*Tippett conducting in St.
Louis, 1968.*

warmest greetings to Michael Tippett on his birthday

(from Fioriture)

Alun Hoddinott

RICHARD ELFYN JONES

Ritual, Myth and Drama
The Midsummer Marriage

THE OPENING of Act II of Michael Tippett's *The Midsummer Marriage* evokes presences and powers that hover mysteriously around and above reality. The composer has pointed out that he 'could not have written the opening of the second act, when you have the afternoon sun of midsummer, without Wagner . . . who showed that it was possible to fill an empty stage with nature'.[1] There is also in Tippett's work a Wagnerian approach to myth (through the symbolic projection of the soul states of the protagonists) which is strongly rooted in the Romantic tradition, and which has been criticised by a number of commentators as being too idiosyncratic. For Tippett is in lineal descent (via Eliot) from the Symbolists, as Mallarmé might have confirmed by his assertion that 'to name an object is to suppress three-quarters of the enjoyment of the poem'. That the symbolic method should be first instigated in music, and by Wagner (as originator of the structural analysis of myths) is a significant fact. For is it not natural that the search for a middle way between aesthetic perception and logical thought should find inspiration in an art form which Claude Levi-Strauss describes as the 'only language with the contradictory attributes of being at once intelligible and untranslatable?'[2] Even if Tippett's debt to Jung and other modern interpreters of myth was very great, he must surely have sensed in Wagner a most remarkable feeling, some time before the heyday of psychology or anthropology, of the psychic import of ancient phenomena. Richard Wagner and Michael Tippett, both in their respective ways, express the psychic fundamentals in a manner impossible in words. Also, Tippett's final resolution of this midsummer drama provides a significant parallel to Wagner's 'redemption through love' by means of the forging of human relationships through sacrifice as a consummation of inner reconciliation.

Robert Donington, himself a writer who has provided an approach to Wagner along the lines of analytical psychology, admits to being perplexed by Tippett's idiosyncratic symbolism, which incorporates private versions of images 'which are themselves archetypal, so that we recognise them as they do grow familiar – but with more difficulty'.[3] The range of most mythological references is so wide that there is no real end to mythological analysis, no hidden unity to be grasped once the breaking-down process has been

Sheila Nadler as Sostrosis in the American première of The Midsummer Marriage *at the San Francisco Opera, 1983. (Photo: David Powers)*

60

completed. Themes can be split up, disentangled and separated, but when knit together again can imply other far-reaching implications. The same is true of myth within the context of modern analytical psychology (Jungian for instance); the confusing range of symbolic meaning enriches myth almost beyond the range of an intelligible usefulness. One has only to consider the different interpretations of simple phenomena to see how confusing is the significance of 'dog', 'lion', 'forest', and so on. One of the major obstacles in applying a Jungian interpretation here, or in any work of art, or indeed in understanding Jung's analytical theories at all, is his multiplicity of ill-formulated definitions for the same thing. But despite the ambiguities which result from Jung's predilection for dividing the mind into separate 'personalities' and his adoption of a terminology in which mental functions are treated as people, there is little doubt of its appeal to the poet, dramatist and librettist. Obviously, by reversing this process and treating people as mental functions (as well as dramatic characters in their own right), Tippett stands in a hallowed tradition which stretches back to antiquity. In the opera it is Jung's world of symbols which predominates – not his theory of types and, as in many other comparable works, symbols interrelate at different levels so that images taken from many different sources are intermingled and coexist. The complete work is itself symbolic of a single idea, which may be described

The Hawk (Anne Elizabeth Egan) poised to attack the Bird in the third Ritual Dance *at San Francisco. (Photo: David Powers)*

61

as representing the inner reconciliation in the hearts and minds of certain individuals – what Jung called the process of individuation. This is the main thread running through the opera and it is derived from Jung. The other symbols clarify and ornament this central idea.

The means by which the tale is told rests on a much older tradition which is Greek in conception. The very fact that this is a comedy immediately implies the comparison with the greatest figure in Greek comedy. Any play by Aristophanes shows a number of procedures which can be seen as prototypes for the dramatic events of *The Midsummer Marriage* and the following quotation indicates how closely Tippett has followed his model. In his introduction to *The Complete Plays of Aristophanes* Moses Hadas describes their regularity of procedure as follows:

> The prologue, frequently a master-slave conversation, sets forth some fantastic scheme – a descent to hell, a sex strike or the like – and the rest of the play is worked out on the assumption that the premises are the most commonplace in the world. In the *agon* the 'good' side naturally wins and the bad is discomfited. The bad side goes off, often literally bruised, and the good goes to a riotous celebration, often accompanied by gay females. This is surely some relic of some sort of 'marriage' which was the culmination of a fertility celebration; psychologically it is the only acceptable solution of a comedy. The endings of tragedy, however grim they may be, are psychologically satisfying but how else is a comedy to end?[4]

Aristophanes' plays fall into a regular pattern, and perhaps because of their religious origins their structural regularity makes for a ritualistic effect which is to some degree recaptured in Tippett's opera. But the basic form of an Aristophanic play as outlined above was not rigid. There might be a prologue (so-called) in which the argument or opening situation was expounded. Then the *parados* or entry of the chorus was often marked by a long and varied song-and-dance movement. The *agon*, or formal debate, was usually the central scene, and in it speech was balanced against speech and song against song. The *parabasis* was quite strict in structure with a carefully pre-ordained pattern of three songs and three speeches, and often characterised by a remarkable passage which was to be rattled off very rapidly (in one breath) – the *pignos*. It is evident that at least some of the characteristics of Aristophanes' art are imitated in *The Midsummer Marriage*, notably the *parabasis* in Act III, Scene 8, where the She-Ancient comes forward to speak directly to the audience. The very technical nature of Greek comedy (Old Comedy) was one of the subjects explored by Jane Harrison in her comprehensive and scholarly study of the social origins of Greek religion, *Themis*, a work which seems to have had a strong influence on Tippett. In *Themis* Miss Harrison explores the elements of the Eniautos myth and describes certain factors which we recognise as Aristophanic – a contest, a *pathos*, a death or defeat. In the Theseus myth this appears in the death of the old king, 'A triumphant Epiphany, an appearance or crowning of the victor or the new king, with an abrupt change from lamentation to rejoicing.'[5] The nature of Michael Tippett's involvement with the Greek experience was such that it was conditioned by his close interest in this and

other modern interpretations of the classical attitude. Gertrude Levy's *The Gate of Horn* is another work whose influence rests heavily on the symbolic apparatus of *The Midsummer Marriage*. Miss Levy's comments on Aristophanic comedy must surely have crystallised the concept of the *agon* in Tippett's mind. She writes,

Fire in Summer: *the climax of* The Midsummer Marriage *at San Francisco. (Photo: David Powers)*

> The *agon* ... is generally fought between a humble and middle-aged citizen, and a boaster or pretender, the embodiment of *Hubris*, and is often a battle of words, with invective as the weapon. It is taken by the chorus divided into two bands on behalf of the opponents, and results in a reversal of the status of the protagonist, like the resurrection scene of the folk plays ... The sacrifice and its feast generally involve, after the crushing of various pretenders, some kind of metamorphosis of the old or middle-aged hero to personify a new order ... The *agon* was fought for no lady's hand but for some political or intellectual principle. The appearance of the silent and symbolically named partner (or partners), can only be attributed to the ritual, the Sacred Marriage which closed the fertility dramas.[6]

Within this frame, as described by Hanas, Harrison and Levy, Tippett has devised a story in which an initial 'conversation', an ageless struggle between the generations, is first mooted by the clash between the young Mark and his ally Strephon and the humble and middle-aged He-Ancient. With respect to this Aristophanic 'war of the generations' the Ancients and

King Fisher seem curiously to share common ground. On other levels of course they are pitted against each other, so there is a complex of different struggles, a series of miniature wars. All these culminate in the contest of power in Act III with Jenifer as the prize and Mark as the usurper of King Fisher's domain.

Acts I and III follow the Aristophanic pattern most clearly. The opening scene is set on Midsummer Day, traditionally an opportune time for significant changes in the life-cycle. Dancers come out of the temple and Mark demands from them 'a new dance' for his wedding day. The Ancients argue against this and warn that to meddle with tradition is dangerous. When he eventually celebrates his love for Jenifer (with 'a new song' instead) he is taken aback by Jenifer's entry; she is dressed for a journey and repulses him coldly. It is not love she wants but truth – 'For me the light, for you the shadow.' They go their separate ways, she up a spiral staircase, he into a cavern in the hillside whose gates close behind him. On a psycho-analytical level Jenifer must come to terms with her animus, which embodies the masculine principles of logic and truth, while Mark escapes into the subterranean caverns of mother earth to gain knowledge and understanding of his own inner femininity, his anima. When they return towards the end of Act I, both are partly transfigured and intoxicated by what proves to be a temporary reversal of their roles which must be resolved by a second 'rebirth', symbolised by her descent, his ascent.

Strephon (Jamie Cohen) at San Francisco. (Photo: William Acheson)

At the end of Act I she must now enter the gates, he must ascend the steps. In Act II we are made aware that the balancing of opposites must also be effected in the subordinate pair of lovers, Jack and Bella, the mechanic and the secretary. (This new aspect corresponds to the paranthetic role the second act assumes within the Aristophanic comedy which is the basis only of the outer acts.) By such a prolonged if dazzlingly impressive parenthesis the attention is taken away from the main characters to such an extent that we lose track of what is happening in their individuation process, which is presumably now reaching its summation off-stage. The drama which leads to the big climax in Act III is suspended and there is a corresponding interruption of the underlying pace of the opera. What compensates for this is the quality of the music, not just of the Ritual Dances but of the rest of Act II, Jack's and Bella's arias, unsurpassed in Tippett's music in sheer charm.

The four Ritual Dances take the form of a ballet in which the female is seen hunting the male (Strephon). There are three of these symbolic dances in Act II, grouped together and framed by duets for Jack and Bella. The fourth occurs at the climax of Act III where it suggests that the two pairs of lovers, although never having held the stage at the same time, present two complementary aspects of the same human problem. The Dances serve to indicate in a realistic manner important psychological phenomena and they do this in a mysteriously cosmic manner, for now Jenifer's and Mark's quest becomes explicitly what it had so far been only by implication; the hunter searches out the hunted, and there are psychic undertones to the animalistic representation by the dancers of a struggle in which the human protagonists are seen also as one with the animals. It is really a sexual chase, and in his search for vivid images to depict this, Tippett tells[7] how he was introduced to the Welsh romance of Taliesin by reading Robert Graves' *The White Goddess*. The gist of the romance is that Ceridwen, in her attempt to compensate for her son Afagddu's ugliness, boiled up a cauldron of inspiration and knowledge from which he would later imbibe. Little Gwion was put in charge of this and accidentally drank some of it, thus becoming informed intuitively of Ceridwen's plan to kill him as soon as his work was finished. Graves describes what follows:

> By use of the powers that he had drawn from the cauldron he changed himself into a hare; she changed herself into a greyhound. He plunged into a river and became a fish; she changed herself into an otter. He flew up into the air like a bird; she changed herself into a hawk. He became a grain of winnowed wheat on the floor of a barn; she changed herself into a black hen, scratched the wheat over with her feet, found him and swallowed him.[8]

Tippett uses the first three representations in 'The Earth in Autumn', 'The Waters in Winter' and 'The Air in Spring' respectively, and he must surely have been prompted to depict the bird hurrying out to peck a grain (see 'The Air in Spring') from the last part of the original idea, 'the grain of winnowed wheat'. This is incorporated into the harrowing scene of the hawk's attack on the unsuspecting bird.

These first three dances are dramatic images which assume the nature of a dream within a dream. The apparatus, while derived from early Welsh mythology, was given a peculiar modern relevance when Tippett read John Layard's *The Lady of the Hare*, a psychoanalytical study of the hare as an archetype existing in the deeper levels of the unconscious 'ready to spring forth into effective action (as a healing power) once the internal redemptive process is activated and begins to work.[9] This study of the healing power of dreams discusses the sexual symbolism of the hare, its abnormal fertility, its function as a 'love gauge', and its connection with Aphrodite, the Cupids and Bacchic mythical and ritual cycle. It is a happy modern confirmation of what Tippett saw to be the significance of the old Celtic mythology of the sexual chase. In each dance Strephon is hunted by a girl dancer as if to suggest that the feminine instincts must be allowed a full rein. In the first dance the two dancers adopt the role of the Hare and the Hound, but there is no dénoument as yet, implying that there is more to man than his carnal nature. A different metaphor, of the otter pursuing the fish, provides the additional image of 'wounding', symbolic of the sacrifice which must be made in the search for wholeness. Significantly, this wound is that we have already seen inflicted by the Ancients in Mark's 'new dance' in Act I, Scene 2 (there is musical confirmation of this). Similarly when, in the next dance, the Bird is almost killed by the Hawk we are reminded that psychic death is the basis of transformation. The bird escapes this time, for the moment of transformation has not yet arrived; for that we must await the reappearance of Mark and Jenifer and the renewal of the Ritual Dances in Act III.

In Act III, as the Fourth Ritual Dance begins, Strephon is no longer the hunted. He falls at Mark's and Jenifer's feet 'in the pose of a hieratic pedestal'. The Chorus sing ecstatically of 'St John's Fire', the traditional festive fire of the feast of St John the Baptist, the *Johannistag* of *The Mastersingers*, the Midsummer Night of Shakespeare's *Dream*. This last dance 'Fire in Summer' is appropriate as a physical representation of a great spiritual change. This is Mark's and Jenifer's moment of psychic transfiguration. As the ritual assumes a timeless metaphysical universality so does the symbolism imply in its apocalyptic manner the all-embracing nature of Tippett's religious position.

Mark and Jenifer:

> Sirius rising as the sun's wheel
> Rolls over at the utter zenith
> So the dog leaps to the bull
> Whose blood and sperm are all fertility.

The strange reference to the dog and its enigmatic function in the Persian legend of the overthrow of the bull by Mithras is a case in point. The bull is a legendary source of all fruitfulness, as Jung has pointed out in *Symbols of Transformation*[10] – 'fruits from his horns, wine from his blood, corn from his tail, cattle from his semen, garlic from his nostrils.' It was thought that the bull was the first creature of the earth and by killing him Mithras became the originator of life on earth. In the Mithraic sacrifice a dog is often shown leaping upon the injured bull. It is an act which is open to different interpretations, but here undoubtedly the dog is Mithras' co-operator.[11] By uniting this story with the reference to Sirius, Michael Tippett forges a link between two mythological cults. Sirius, the brightest star in the heavens, was connected with almost every religion in antiquity. The Egyptians saw in Sirius their guardian, because faithful and watchful like a dog, 'its heliacal rising never failed to indicate the anxiously awaited approach of the Nile flood'.[12] These two cults are thus united as a representation of the power of the myth working through the dream, a power which is oracular and religious in its implications.

But more significantly, in the Persian legend, Mithras takes the bull (or as the Egyptian hymn says 'the bull of his mother',[13] his love for his *Mater Natura*) on his back – an act which, according to Jung, is comparable with that of Christ carrying the cross. Jung defines this cross, or heavy burden which the hero carries, as 'the self', which is both god and animal, the 'totality of his being which is rooted in his animal nature and reaches out beyond the merely human towards the divine.'[14]

The operative words of the Chorus express vividly this duality with the self, carnal and divine:

> Carnal love through which the race
> Of men is everlastingly renewed
> Becomes transfigured as divine
> Consuming love.

The religious connotation implies the transformation of sexual love *eros* into the Christian *agape*, symbolised by the fire which now seems to consume the couple. At a distance the Ancients offer a loaded interpretation:

> From heavenly One the Two divide
> and Three as Paraclete can make
> Symbolic union with the Four,
> The messenger, the path, the door
> Between the light and dark, the guide.

This Jungian concern for number[15] is derived initially from the Pythagorean belief that the elements of number were the elements of all things. The Pythagoreans endowed individual numbers with symbolic qualities which had a numinous power, that same power which is referred to in the last verse of the thirteenth chapter of Revelations, 'Here is wisdom. Let him that hath understanding count the number of the Beast . . .' The clue to the doctrine of numbers, which was the Pythagoreans' main contribution to philosophy, was of the 'One going into the Many, and the Many losing themselves within the One . . . Here the tetraktys (the ten in a triangle of four) was the nucleus of all material form. From this all numbers proceed, as the fountain and root of ever-springing nature'.[16] Levy quotes Aristotle's observation on Plato that the self-animal is composed of the form of One, and this view was adapted by Jung when he pointed out that 'the self appears . . . in the form of a totality symbol'[17] as we understand by our symbolising of One, Two, Three, and Four. The function of the image here

67

is to express the numinous power of order (as expressed by number) in man and nature, religion, the law, science, and life in its all-encompassing universals. In this particular context the Four as a totality symbol is particularly apposite; Four completes the quartet of the seasons, the points of the compass, the humours, the temperaments and the elements. But of a more specific interest in the context of this opera is Jung's assertion that the animus and the anima also exhibit four stages of development. This was described in part three of Jung's symposium *Man and his Symbols* by one of his closest collaborators M-L.von Franz. The animus,

> first appears as a personification of mere physical power ... in the next stage he possesses initiative and the capacity for planned action. In the third phase, the animus becomes the 'word' often appearing as a professor or clergyman. Finally, in his fourth manifestation, the animus is the incarnation of meaning. On this highest level he becomes (like the anima) a mediator of the religious experience whereby life acquires new meaning.[18]

> Similarly the number four is also connected with the anima because, as Jung noted, there are four stages in its development. The first stage is best symbolised by the figure of Eve, which represents purely instinctual and biological relations. The second can be seen in Faust's Helen: she personifies a romantic and aesthetic level that is, however, still characterised by sexual elements. The third is represented, for instance, by the Virgin Mary – a figure who raises love (eros) to the heights of spiritual devotion. The fourth type is symbolised by Sapientia, wisdom transcending even the most holy and the most pure. Of this another symbol is the Shulamite in the Song of Solomon.[19]

The extent of the quadernity symbol is, of course, unlimited. It is perhaps no coincidence that there are four Ritual Dances in this opera and that many aspects of the work are paired to suggest always the dualities. But what is significant is that all elements become united at the end in a moral alignment of opposites which is very deep-seated. Jenifer's personal aim is realised on a far more elevated level now, for her triumph over metanoia creates for her a new situation in which 'truth is assumed in love so rich'. In understanding how we 'live each other's death, and die each other's life', she and Mark are initiated into a doctrine which is very ancient and not at all the mere product of those nineteenth-century evolutionary theories which we ascribe to Bergson or Butler. In *The Gate of Horn* Levy describes how Herakleitos of Ephesus

> proclaimed the doctrine that was the embodiment of Dionysian dynamism. He took away the moral stigma from Anixamander's Separation of the Many from the One by making them co-exist ... mortals and immortals 'live each other's death and die each other's life' ... He thus conceives of life as continually transformed by death, 'the ever-living Fire with measures kindling and with measures going out'.[20]

In a BBC television programme on 2 March 1975 Michael Tippett described the setting at the start of *The Midsummer Marriage* as 'a stonehenge', and how 'by magic the ruins have become pristine while inside are the Ancients and the Ritual Dancers'.

> We guess that this is a Midsummer Day which has slipped out of the calendar and that we are in a 'loop in time'. It is in this loop that marvellous and often frightening

adventures take place (sometimes during the night and leading to a great moment of illumination). But humans have to come out of these loops and therefore there must be a second dawn, the real dawn, the real marriage.

Strephon (Joseph Scoglio) in the Australian première of The Midsummer Marriage *at the Adelaide Festival, 1978. (Photo: Australian State Opera)*

Time can be suspended no more. When we reach the final scene and the allegory is come to an end, 'Was it a vision? Was it a dream?' ask the Chorus. Whose dream is it, we ask? When Mark and Jenifer meet in the wood in the final scene and the dream fades it is still Midsummer morning, as in the very opening scene! The vision has revealed itself instantaneously, but there is a new awareness as the young couple come out of their 'loop in time', and a new optimism characterises their preparations for marriage. It is left to the Chorus to echo a line from Tippett's essay 'Contracting-in to Abundance'. Here, referring to the concept of the whole man, Michael Tippett describes how the early Christians contracted-out of the Roman Empire into a new abundance. 'From this sense sprang the characteristic which most puzzled their contemporaries – their gaiety.'[21] It is this spirit which the process of individuation brings about:

> Chorus: All things fall and are built again,
> And those that build them again are gay.

69

This is a quotation from Yeats' poem 'Lapis Lazuli' which sums up Tippett's affirmation of the heroic victory of man's search for self-realisation. In the poem the aesthetic poise of the destructive and the creative is worked out around the central theme of 'gaiety', a quality defined in some detail, almost in a technical way by Yeats and others.

Incidentally, these lines recall Anaximander's utterance as noted by Gertrude Levy:[22]

> Things perish into those things out of which they
> have their birth,

but while this is a curiously Butlerian philosophic statement of order, of natural law, Yeats and Tippett make an assertion of joyous creativity. And in this final celebration there is the culmination of man's development towards wholeness as implied in the prefix to the opera. Here is expressed the Orphic doctrine of cyclic experience – man's fall into sin, and final escape from the constrictions of birth and death through union with divine life. Gertrude Levy also has described this cycle where souls return into the earth like seeds to be reborn. She mentions the Fall from Heaven and she, like Tippett in the prefix to the opera, quotes the Petelia gold tablet which is in the British Museum:

> 'I am the child of Earth and starry Heaven,' says the newly dead on one of the Orphic grave-tablets, 'but my origin is of Heaven alone?'[23]

Thus is effected a balance between the rational and the instinctive; the Dionysian frenzy is tempered by the reforming influence of Orpheus whose doctrine tends towards asceticism and emphasises mental ecstasy. By this it is hoped to achieve union with the god and thus to gain mystical knowledge not to be had otherwise. The Orphic passion for truth and beauty balances the pristine savagery of Bacchus so that the balance which results is a creative synthesis of the orderly and the unruly.

In his search for the right symbols and the most satisfactory metaphors and similes Michael Tippett became so involved in his own poetic world that his libretto ironically became, if anything, too rich in metaphors. Even he himself admits this and there is no doubt that as a result his attitude towards libretto writing changed significantly after *The Midsummer Marriage*. But without the enormous range of references here in the first opera it is doubtful whether the all-inclusive religious nature of the work could have made its real impact. For *The Midsummer Marriage* is indeed a uniquely all-embracing religious expression, and of an unusual kind. To begin with, in Tippett's experience the divine is synonymous with 'the collective'. He, like T.S. Eliot before him, accepts the Buddhist doctrine of the stream of consciousness. Thus, when King Fisher goes under he perishes into that thing out of which he has his birth. It is an ancient mythological progression, the hope for immortality through rebirth and the perpetual renewal of life permeated as it is by the *spiritus mundi*.

In a television programme[24] Tippett amplified on theories (accepted from

Buddhism, from Anixamander, Butler, Bergson, Shaw and Eliot) in an idiosyncratic and original manner. The idea of Michelangelo realising in stone a personal vision of the human form is not new; it was described by Tippett as a 'releasing of the figure' from the rock. This concept of Michelangelo's function as an artist is somewhat analogous with that of Tippett's. As a composer he sees himself as a vessel through which the divine message is revealed. This concept was expanded in a strikingly mystical way by comparing the calcium of Michelangelo's stone with the calcium of his own bones, thus suggesting a more fundamental cosmic unity than one would ordinarily expect. It is no coincidence that this should be both a very modern and a very ancient hypothesis; it looks back to the alchemists, is influenced by nineteenth-century evolutionists but is also, to a certain extent, forward-looking. Analysis will undoubtedly resolve the process of organic creation into an ever-increasing number of physico-chemical phenomena, but such a scientific progress does not as yet explain what Bergson believed to be the fundamental identity of inorganic and organic matter.[25] However, the evolution of life and the matter that precedes it do reveal at the very heart of their mechanisms the presence and action of a spiritual energy. The hypothesis of a hidden consciousness or of spirit in the heart of things is understandably a precarious one to many, but man and nature are seen undoubtedly to have something in common. Spirit above all has a unity, is an all-inclusive synthesis, and is monistic in its annihilation of individuality and in its affirmation of total unity. 'They but thrust their buried men/Back into the human mind again' is the message. For like Teilhard de Chardin, Tippett sees each one of us connected by all the fibres of his being, material, organic and psychic, with everything else around him.

We have seen that Jung plays a central role in Tippett's interpretation of man's 'inheritance' in the broadest, evolutionary meaning of this term. In turning to mythology (personal and collective) it is not surprising that it should be through music that that which is of timeless significance can be most successfully presented, for, like Jung, Tippett sees Man alienated from the mythopoeic substratum of his being. He parodies to a certain extent Jung's scientific procedure, but as an artist his main aim is to express those emotions that a man experiences when face to face with the ineffable. Thus, in his preoccupation with Hellenic optimism and the celebration of 'the purely human' Tippett stands in the great Romantic tradition whereby myth, while satisfying the intellect, also safeguarded the rights of the fabulous, fanciful world of dreams. *The Midsummer Marriage* was a moving attempt to provide hope at a time when Europe, in its progressive mutilation and disfigurement, was recovering from a Second World War. The 'dark side' he expressed in his not unoptimistic oratorio, but the 'light' shines dazzlingly only in his first opera, for here are united all the dualities, those dualities which are of such abiding fascination for Tippett. He writes:

I return to it again and again. I find it reflected in such seemingly contradictory figures as D. H. Lawrence and Blake. I may not experience the division and the copulation in Laurentian or Blakeian terms – I am neither a novelist nor a mystic; but I cannot escape

71

the special impact of any art which seems to be the product of a marriage. Lines of a Rilke sonnet haunt my mind . . .[26]

and these, translated, assert what may account for the impact both of *A Child of Our Time* and of *The Midsummer Marriage*, their expression of a rounded personal philosophy in moving works of art:

Only he who raised his lyre also under the shadows may with divining tongue sound the infinite praise.[27]

NOTES

1. In conversation with the author, 29 July 1974
2. *The Raw and the Cooked* (London: Jonathan Cape, 1970) p18
3. I. Kemp: *M. Tippett: A Symposium on his 60th Birthday* (London: Faber, 1965) p95
4. M. Hadas, ed: *The Complete Plays of Aristophanes* (New York: Bantam, 1962) p6
5. J. Harrison: *Themis* (Cambridge University Press, 1912) p331 ff
6. G. Levy: *The Gate of Horn* (London: Faber, 1948) pp320–1
7. In conversation with the author, 29 July 1974
8. R. Graves: *The White Goddess* (3rd Ed. London: Faber, 1952) p28
9. J. Layard: *The Lady and the Hare* (London: Faber, 1944) p23
10. C. G. Jung: *Collected Works*, V
11. M. O. Howey: *The Cults of the Dog* (Rochford: Daniel, 1972) p73
12. *Ibid*, p49
13. C. G. Jung: *Collected Works*, V, p302
14. *Ibid*, V, p303
15. *Ibid*, VIII, p456, for instance
16. G. Levy: *The Gate of Horn*, p308
17. C. G. Jung: *Collected Works*, VI, p460
18. C. G. Jung and others: *Man and his Symbols* (London: Aldus, 1964) p108
19. *Ibid*, p185
20. G. Levy: *The Gate of Horn*, pp306–7
21. M. Tippett(*Moving into Aquarius* (London: Paladin Books, 1974) p24
22. G. Levy: *The Gate of Horn*, p303
23. *Ibid*, p305
24. BBC/TV, 2 March 1975
25. *Creative Evolution*, trans. by A. Mitchell (London: Macmillan, 1911) Ch 1
26. M. Tippett: *Moving into Aquarius*, p132
27. *Loc. cit.*

BARBARA OLLEY

The Golden Age

Moving into Aquarius

This is the Age of Holy Breath
The Dove – full wingéd she
The Paraclete, the Comforter
To rescue man from Death.

'This is the Age of Aquarius'
When Cosmic music sounds
Vibrating through the Universe
Bringing harmony to earth.

This is the Age of Holy Grail
The sword of Truth reclaimed
And Arthur restored as King
Will awaken all Israel.

This is the Golden Age of Man
When all the Sons of Light
Surround the world with Love
Fulfils the Promised Plan.

dedicated in hommage to
Benjamin Britten
and
Michael Tippett
— masters of the native soil.

Robin Holloway
CLARISSA

opera in two acts

op. 30

after Richardson's novel

1976

ACT I
Part 1

Tippett rehearsing the English Chamber Orchestra for his 75th Birthday Concert at the Queen Elizabeth Hall. (Photo: Malcolm Crowthers)

PETER GARVIE

Magic and Irony

I F REALITY is that which is, magic is that which may be. It is reality's potential for change which requires something beyond itself for that change to happen. Reality seems stable because most of the time the force for change is not exerted. Magic does not work upon a void. It may seem to produce something that was not there, as in the magician's trick, when the object suddenly appears in his hand. But that, too, is a transformation – of the hand without an egg to the hand holding an egg. There would be nothing marvellous to us if a god's miracle had no relationship to our reality; it would be incomprehensible and irrelevant play. And there is no magic in a human being simply finding the right key on his key ring to open a door. The process of composition requires both the acceptance of the incomprehensible and the methodical work of trial and error.

The role of magic in Romantic art seems partly a gesture against a world too manipulable by keys, and a heightening of the human above a mere opener of locks; and partly – in Malinowski's phrase – a 'substitute activity', or godlike power in a universe without credible gods. The magic is in Isolde's potion and the fairy tales of Tchaikovsky's ballets, and in the articulate Nature of Mahler and Delius. Not always so. Bruckner's is a true, archaic God, while the realist Verdi has his characters play fairies in Windsor Forest only to make Falstaff become a more complete human being.

What may at first seem surprising is the persistence of magic and myth in the music of the twentieth century even when it seems set against its immediate past. The ballets of Stravinsky, late as well as early; all the stage works of Bartok; the legends of Sibelius and the fantasies of Ravel; much of Ives and Messiaen; even such a work as Berg's Violin Concerto in which a Bach chorale serves as the spell – all are transformations of the mundane into a world of music that exists only within its own rules in which we, the listeners, must in some sense believe. *Petrouchka* and *Bluebeard's Castle* tell us as much about being human as do *Wozzeck* and *Grimes*, though not in the same terms. Stravinsky's and Bartok's fairy tales could only be transferred to the other two operas as that which their heroes dream.

Much of this magic material, or its potential for the composer, was in fact not so readily available until about the turn of the century. It was then that the collector of folk material gathered and kept the songs and stories as they actually were. It was then that the anthropologists began to trace the hidden resemblances between disparate cultures and to sketch a sub-world held in common. And it was then that the psychologists began to find in legend some of the best instances of the motives in ourselves. All this became a credible and communicable kind of belief – less threatening as myth? – even while science was challenging the more literal beliefs of religion with its more demonstrable literalism. This is a convention of belief shared in the cause of the imagination. The magical is an agreed midpoint between literal scepticism and untenable faith. It is something that the imagination must do and witness as a substitute for what the gods were really believed to do, but not an activity presumptuous of their once-upon-a-time real powers. Here is the difference between magic and miracle. And the distinction must always be kept between what the characters in an opera believe and what we and the composer believe outside the magic, or convention, of the performance.

The distances of belief vary. In Britten's *Noye's Fludde*, for example, all the references are to what we in our usual experience and the Flood myth have in common. We are supposed to feel with – as – Noah. In Sibelius' *Luonnotar*, on the other hand, the Creation myth is narrated, and we respond to this particular telling of it. There is yet a further distance in Stravinsky, where we are not expected to identify with, say, Apollo as Leader of the Muses, but only to regard him. Which is not to say that the closing pages of *Apollo* may not seem as 'marvellous' to us in their abstract serenity as the union of gull and goddess that makes our universe in Sibelius, or the healing compact between Man and God that restores it in Britten.

Music itself seems marvellous in its power to communicate in comparison with the symbolism of word and sign. For they, even if we do not subscribe to the notion of art as imitation, draw a much more direct relationship between our experience and the meaning we give it than does music; if not literal, then as closer analogy. Tippett's music is a celebration of music (and dance). It is central to *The Midsummer Marriage*, where dance is specifically named a ritual. It is instrumental music, not words, that comes closest at two points to Saint Augustine's vision. It is Hermes' invocation of music that gives the sudden new dimension to the last act of *King Priam*. In both the Third Symphony and *The Mask of Time* the blues is sung against 'the blues'. The magic in which we believe is that of Orpheus, but the whole of his fable.

The idea of transformation is essential to our appreciation of Tippett's music. For, paradoxically, it is the equilibrium of a world of unstable contrasts. As an inclusive composer, he takes big risks on how much of experience can be transformed from what the alert sensibility is aroused by, to what the imagination can control. The intensity of his experience will not let him go. It must find its proper forms without falsifying its actuality. From his own testimony we know how often a work begins with a sudden, vivid apprehension. And how that is succeeded by a long period of gestation; at first dormant, then a preoccupation with measurement – length, proportion,

78

emphasis, shape. The actual notes come last. This is surely one reason for his increased interest in *accumulative* forms. And even in his finest, most completely realised works the end of the transformation is never without a certain tension. As Jung observed, the analyst may be transformed by the patient.

The conclusions of Tippett's works, therefore, are not of the once-and-for-all kind. The polarities of experience remain to enrich and torment and deride, whatever transforming balance the end of that particular work may have achieved as music. Transformation is metaphor. A is no longer just A, once its relation to B is observed; it is an A transformed. And the relation may be one of likeness or contrast. The coming into balance – not the resolution of one into the other – is achieved by the power of metaphor. The chords that end the Third Symphony are a good example. We hear them as the interaction of background and foreground. The declamatory violence is eventually quietened, but the emergence of the quiet music cannot be in this context pure. The balance, or transformation, is in the silence that follows the last chord. That this is where we must end does not remove the residual tension.

Tippett's preoccupation with opera seems inevitable. The theatre is a transformation of experience, so that it does not merely happen to the people involved, but signifies to others. And opera, as opposed to the spoken play in prose, is a magical medium because the presence of music works against the audience's expectations of realism. The strength of the modern realistic theatre has been its exploration of recognisable character which, of itself, must require a certain language. That language is most powerful when stretched to its limits, when it is trying to tell us more than we are used to. And especially so if it is intimating at what is usually unspoken or difficult to speak of: powers beneath or beyond our conscious selves – in some sense the magical. This is why silence is so important to good productions of Ibsen and Chekhov and the less realistic Beckett and Pinter. The past, which is more than the human characters onstage, is what hovers at the edge of that stage and in those silences; and in the different ways that the characters understand it, or fail to understand it.

If in the realistic play the magical must always be consistent with the actual, in Tippett's operas we can almost say that the reverse is true. *The Midsummer Marriage* is an opera wholly of transformation. *King Priam* in its very construction is about the Fate/Choice dichotomy, and its handling of time reminds us of it throughout. In *The Knot Garden* the unravelling requires more than is usually apparent in the people; the *Tempest*-charade is the access to change. Even in *The Ice Break*, which makes more use of contemporary naturalism, the characters are on the edge where identity slips into stereotype; and the central image of the title is not human, but more than natural in its ambiguous power: to release and to flood.

Forty years earlier it had been 'the moving waters' of spring that renewed the earth at the end of *A Child of Our Time*. The other vocal works have all in their various ways been preoccupied with the capacity for transformation. In

Boyhood's End it is the fear that the accord between the boy and nature – what makes the natural seem supernatural in its effect – may be lost to greater self-consciousness. *The Vision of Saint Augustine* attempts to record what cannot, finally, be described, only experienced, though music may take us closer than words. The *Songs for Dov* are less about him than about his magic journey. He is the involved witness as is the solo soprano in the Third Symphony.

The Mask of Time attempts an even more comprehensive journey than Dov's; through aeons as well as through almost every culture. Only *The Heart's Assurance*, written out of an individual loss in real life, may at first seem purely personal. Yet poems and music are not really in the first person singular, or about this particular instance, and the passionate rhetoric of the music serves a text whose imagery is that of myth. The cycle is more distanced than, say, Britten's *Michelangelo Sonnets*.

Magic is not, of course, always good. The Faust legend is western man's most persistent reminder that his wish to transcend himself may be self-destructive. The dark side of self may be understood and offset; it is not abolished. Nor is it always possible to tell the rightness of wish and intention or to interpret prophesy and consequence. Tippett reminds us of the wry and realistic comment of Euripides: 'Whatever else the gods are, they are power.'

Even in the enchanted world of *The Midsummer Marriage* the appearance and effect of Sosostris are hardly those of the usual *dea ex machina*. Her first 'appearance', in fact, is not her at all, but a practical joke. It is Jack, the earthy mechanic, who is disclosed. Her great aria proves her to be, ironically, the most fully drawn character in the opera:

> I alone cannot consult myself
> I alone draw out no dream
> To dream myself awake.
> I dream the shadows that you cast.
> I am a medium, not an end.

So in *The Ice Break*, Astron, thrown up from a Euripidean celebration of Dionysus as an answer to humanity's inability to be human, says coarsely:

> Saviour? Hero? Me!
> You must be joking.

It is almost as laconic a put-down as Dov's at the end of his song cycle, 'Sure, baby'. And the only music left out of all that which has swirled him around the globe is that single, least musical sound, a dismissive tap of the claves. A snap of the fingers dissolves that spell.

In other contexts, irony and reverence are shown to be two sides of the same coin. The last section of *The Vision of Saint Augustine* postulates the conditions under which such transformation of self into a momentary union with God may be possible. Then the chorus, speaking for us in our vernacular, not in the saint's Latin, whispers: 'I count not myself to have apprehended.' And apprehension, in the other sense, is part of the awe and humility that is one of those conditions. In *King Priam*, Hermes describes himself as a 'divine go-between', which does not seem much of a role. Yet he is not 'an old phantom tied to Troy'. He comes to represent 'A timeless music played in time', and death as a transformation of life. His great aria is placed in the last act just where Tippett placed Sosostris's intervention in the earlier opera. *The Knot Garden*, played on a more exclusively human level, so that *The Tempest* and a surrogate Prospero serve for the supernatural, ends with compassionate irony. It is less reverence than a coming to terms that Thea and Faber feel for one another, though without a limit set to those terms. 'The curtain rises,' they sing together as the material curtain falls to end the opera.

As *The Ice Break* explores the compulsions by which individuality becomes mass reaction, and how each person may recover his Self from the collective dark side, so the Third Symphony bears witness to our collective distortion of the world. Beethoven's Ninth Symphony is now no abracadabra to draw communion out of separate wilfulness; and given Tippett's special reverence for Beethoven, this is irony indeed. Only a single human voice, stretched to its limits, will serve this bleakest of his visions. There is no go-between divine messenger here; only the individual whose small magic must make of it what he can. Even if there is a god, he is likely to be manifest only in the whirlwind. And how likely? The most terrifying moment in all Tippett's music is when the soprano, just managing to ride the tumult of the orchestra like a white water rafter, sings 'Though he be answered;' and then follows it with the ironic shout 'Answered?!'

It is interesting to compare *The Midsummer Marriage* with a parallel in T. S. Eliot's *East Coker*. Both are set at Midsummer in the countryside, and both invoke the traditions of St John's Eve – its fires, its dances and the union of man and woman. In Eliot we must 'Wait for the early owl'. Then, 'If you do not come too close', it is possible to imagine the ceremony described by his ancestor – 'A dignified and commodious sacrament'. That it is in the past makes it almost a miniature. Eliot's music is that 'of the weak pipe and the little drum'. The observer is at the edge of the field, in a different time. And this vision is only one of many that the poem absorbs as it moves forward in a multiplicity of tones. The only glance back is to show the ceremony lost: 'The dancers are all gone under the hill.'

Tippett's vision is much more participatory. It began, as he has told us, with the image of a temple on a hill, and there is a certainty about beginnings – they assume a skill to carry them through. Beginnings are magic. We are there, and all that does not belong to St John's Eve is not, or is in process of transformation so that it may belong. Creatures, seasons and elements are part of an all-encompassing rite, and one so real that Bella shrinks from the pursuit of one creature by another, a fundamental logic of natural life. It is the last of the ritual dances that becomes a human allegory; pursuit is changed into conjunction. Tippett was surely aware of Frazer's conclusions about fire festivals: that they were not just an invocation of the sun or of the sexual drive, but of good magic to drive out bad magic.

It is possible to read *The Midsummer Marriage* as one dramatisation of a single psyche as *The Knot Garden* might be another. What is important is the myth as dramatic and musical form so that it is cogent *in the event*. (The problem with *The Mask of Time* is its heterogeneous length. To paraphrase Valéry, the myths only sometimes become a consonance.) Even an instrumental work can formally acquire a mythic character. The pounding, heroic C's that begin the Second Symphony, and were its origin, seem to be waiting just below the aural horizon through all the various music we traverse. When they are delivered up at the end, the 'gestures of farewell', in Tippett's phrase, seem to have included all else.

The province that Tippett's music claims as its own is perhaps best suggested by this passage from *The Greeks and the Irrational* by E. F. Dodds:

> Man shares with a few others of the higher mammals the curious privilege of citizenship in two worlds. He enjoys in daily alternation two distinct kinds of experience . . . each of which has its own logic and its own limitations; and he has no obvious reason for thinking one of them more significant than the other. If the waking world has certain advantages of solidity and continuity, its social opportunities are terribly restricted. In it we meet, as a rule, only the neighbours, whereas the dream world offers the chance of intercourse, however fugitive, with our distant friends, our dead, and our gods. For normal men it is the sole experience in which they escape the offensive and incomprehensible bondage of time and space. Hence it is not surprising that man was slow to confine the attribute of reality to one of his two worlds, and dismiss the other as pure illusion.

Beside this we may set another quotation from Valéry:

> It is the very one who wants to write down his dream who is obliged to be extremely wide awake.

In what sense can we speak of the actual sound of the music as 'magical'? When it depicts magic in operatic and other texts, obviously; and when that sound is carried over to another purely instrumental context and we make the association. The special glitter of celesta and piano together in the Piano Concerto, for instance, evokes the world of *The Midsummer Marriage*. But there is another sense too. Here responses are more than usually subjective, but three examples may be mentioned from three different centuries where the music miraculously suggests its opposites simultaneously.

In the slow movement variations of Mozart's B flat Concerto, K.450, there is a passage where the left hand continues a gentle forward motion, while the right hand suspends above it a series of rich chords. The effect is not to make the music static, but to enable those chords to register for what seems a much longer time than they actually occupy. A similar passage is the 'Panorama' in Tchaikovsky's *The Sleeping Beauty*. The music manages to comprise simultaneously both the movement of the Prince towards the Sleeping Beauty and the stillness that emanates from her. We are moving in stillness. A third instance is to be found midway in the first movement of Sibelius' Fifth Symphony. The music moves away from us, and we are unaware of it. Then we realize that we are in the *scherzo* section without having been conscious of the transition in which the music became swifter and lighter.

The magic moment, then, is not when the music perfectly fulfils its context, seeming exactly right, but when it suddenly opens up what we could not have guessed, when it transforms its context. And the strangeness does not in the least depend on the surprise of a first hearing. It is always strange, always somehow unanticipated, and indeed, for all we know, was so for the composer. And is never quite accounted for.

Tippett's music, as it were, 'believing' more than most in that other world, has many instances. The soprano's lead into the first spiritual in *A Child of Our Time* is always a surprise as the wordless single line introduces the solid harmonies of 'Steal Away'. The individual becomes collective in a music that is at once more popular and more formal than the rest of the oratorio. At the end of Part One of the Third Symphony the magic process is reversed. As the wide reverberations of the gong die away, surely conclusive, a tiny figuration on the harp still traces the pattern of celestial music. This distant compassion will much later enable the symphony to end, not in the furious and unanswered challenge to the gods, but in the equivocal hope of those juxtaposed chords.

The Third Piano Sonata offers a different example. The slow movement is a set of variations on a series of chords; all the calm of the vertical, if the appositions were not so elaborately ornamented. It is a synthesis of motion and stasis comparable with the Mozart and Tchaikovsky instances cited. The toccata-like finale is entirely horizontal – its palindromic form emphasises this – yet across it is thrown more than once a series of dissonant chords. The vertical now has a furious obstinacy, yet is borne off by the swift, light-textured counterpoint with an effect summed up by 'the myriad of mirrors' of *King Priam*. Nonetheless, the way those chords suddenly bite down always seems to leave the finale's capacity to go on in doubt for a few seconds, no matter how often we have heard the sonata.

Tippett's music conjures with space as well as with time and texture. In the opening movement of the Triple Concerto we are aware of solo violin, viola and cello individually busy up front. The first interlude is, by contrast, all background; muted, gentle, not the least insistent. When the slow movement begins, the three solo strings reappear, each one now a part of a united sonority, a warm tune, not quite of this earth, that fills the whole space. We may be reminded of *The Tempest* in which Shakespeare keeps his three groups of characters separate until the ambience of the island works its spell upon them.

Even more remarkable is the very end of *King Priam*. The last act of violence that will round out the story and complete the pattern, already foreseen, still comes with a physical shock to us, clangorous and decisive. Yet before silence there is that shift from Troy to us – we are the last victims of the gods' go-between – and the few quiet bars make our reaction audible to ourselves. As Tippett has said, they are the music of our tears.

King Priam may be his operatic masterpiece. Its libretto is free from archness. The score has none of those self-consciously 'with it' kinds of music that seem a substitute for characterisation. Its myth is clear, and magic and irony constantly reflect one another. Formally, everything is in the event. As we look back, the new style it is said to have inaugurated – of accumulation rather than development – seems less an abrupt change, more aptness of music to subject. And that may be why it has not always worked so well in later works so that they seem not so much *in* the event as *about* it. Craft is enormously important to a composer like Tippett because he is ambitious and inclusive, but it offers no guarantees. The deeply informed conscious skills must be aligned with the magic imperatives of the music's origin. He cannot write a shallow work, it may be said, but he may write a flawed one because of the scale of his risk taking. So his finest achievements are not mere successes, but worlds unto themselves in which, finally, the faith of the magician prevails over the doubt of the ironist. A vivid, but fugitive faith. As Samuel Daniel put it,

> Glory is most bright and gay
> In a flash, and so away.
>
> Feed apace then, greedy eyes,
> On the wonder you behold:
> Take it sudden as it flies,
> Though you take it not to hold:
> When your eyes have done their part,
> Thought must length it in the heart.

ANDRÉ PREVIN

Tribute

ONE OF the most extraordinary aspects of Michael Tippett's genius is his total reliance on his own voice. Almost without fail, 20th century composers have succumbed (at least during their formative periods) to one or the other of the almost inescapable influences. Whether these influences tend to be Stravinsky or Schoenberg or Bartok or Boulez is immaterial; what is important is that these gigantic predecessors of our own days have quite understandably marked the progress of all but a tiny handful of current composers. Certainly Tippett is a member of this elite group. Nothing and no one has seduced him temporarily, and his music is, and always has been, totally his own. Even visually his scores are unique. Often the printed page will seem prolix, even dense, but the results are always very beautiful and often miraculously ethereal. If musicologists, in their sometimes desperate search for labels, have to arrive at a conclusion, it would have to reach all the way back to Beethoven, and certainly that influence is philosophical as opposed to musical. I don't know of another composer currently creating whose output is such a mixture of applied intelligence and achieved beauty. His personality is irresistible; on the podium, intense and near messianic; in private, relaxed and blessed with a wicked sense of humour. At the age of eighty he seems half his age. His enthusiasms are unbounded, his energy seemingly limitless, and he is a generous and kind man. It is a privilege to wish him Happy Birthday. He has enriched all our lives.

For Sir Michael Tippett on his 80th birthday

86

YEHUDI MENUHIN
Tribute

IT IS perhaps no surprise that the two composers, Handel and Haydn, who more than all others embodied the concept of the good and the beautiful as indivisible, were honorary Englishmen. I was very impressed to learn that in the manner of great men of supreme integrity, whether scientist or artist, all permanent learners, Sir Michael submitted himself at the age of twenty-five to a year-and-a-half's course of counterpoint and fugue. In the very same spirit Ernest Bloch, at the age of fifty, proudly showed me in Paris a copybook containing a whole year's work in self-assigned contrapuntal and fugal exercises.

Sir Michael's constant preoccupation with learning and re-learning, with the grasping of the intangible, the embodying of spirit and sound, has kept him throughout his life in close contact with children. As music director of Morley College in the Forties, he made an outstanding contribution to London's musical life. I am forever grateful to him for visiting my School, taking time to guide and instruct and inspire our little community. Their enthusiasm comes of their intimate acquaintance with Sir Michael's music.

The School orchestra under Peter Norris has performed his *Little Music for Strings*, the *Fantasia Concertante on a theme of Corelli* and the Concerto for Double String Orchestra, beautiful works which I too have performed many times and recorded. The children have had the privilege of working with him on his Second String Quartet and his Second Piano Sonata. But it was on the occasion of his last visit to listen to and rehearse his *Fantasia Concertante* that a photographer took this wonderful photograph of him; having heard the pupils perform it, he took them through the whole work himself, conducting and rehearsing with unique energy and exuberance, and, as on each occasion, he spent time talking informally with the staff and students, his marvellous sense of humour, the tremendous breadth of his interests and his personal warmth always very much in evidence.

Perhaps what distinguishes the great English composer from his colleagues the world over is the somewhat old-fashioned concept, now often discredited by the over-sophisticated, cynical and brutal, that the good and the beautiful are broadly synonymous.

In the creator, the dream precedes reality, and perhaps for that reason the creator is always part child, not least because his hand is guided, whereas in the cynic, reality precedes the dream – usually an ugly dream. The danger with the dreamer is that he may oversimplify the paradoxical and complex aspects of the good and the beautiful, and the danger of the realist is that he may totally forget the beautiful and the good – less sugar-and-spice-and-everything-nice than people too easily imagine, but often, in fact, more realistic than it is assumed to be. Nor can the good and the beautiful be isolated from the ugly and the terrible. We must try as artists to infuse the whole community, including its ugliness and terror, with the beauty of our music, otherwise we too will die in isolation. When the dreamer is obliged to come to grips with reality and with the reality of symphonic sounds, with the structure and proportions of a living work and with the human beings who must perform and who listen to his works, we have, I believe, the highest human synthesis possible of the good and the beautiful: fact and fancy.

It is profoundly reassuring that we may pay tribute to you, Michael, with the prayer that you may long remain as hale and hearty and as youthful as you are today and continue to receive our love, reverence and devotion. I have had the honour eight years ago of presenting a great and a good man with the Gold Medal of the Royal Philharmonic Society.

Today the students of my School join me in congratulating him on his eightieth birthday, proud of our association with him and privileged in the enjoyment of his friendship.

Michael Tippett at the
Menuhin School, 1983.
(Photo: Mary Goodman)

For Michael Tippett.

Sir Walter Raleigh   FRAGMENT from LUCRETIUS   Iain Hamilton
(1984)

If all this world had no o-ri-gi-nall, But
things have e-ver been as now they are: Be-fore the siege of Thebes or Tro-yes
last fall, Why did no po-et sing some el-der warre?

© Iain Hamilton

NICHOLAS MORRIS

'Simply the thing I am shall make me live'
A Jungian perspective on *King Priam* and *The Knot Garden*

MOST ANALYSIS that has touched on the psychological side to Sir Michael Tippett's work has tended to concentrate on the verbal and dramatic symbolism. Tippett, like Wagner, is his own librettist and clearly the text supplies important information as to the inner meaning of a work. However, as Robert Donington has said of Wagner: in a form such as opera, '. . . it is important to realise that the symbolism is not only in the words, but in the music too.'[1]

This essay will attempt to unite some aspects of the libretti and music of Tippett with the psychology of Carl Jung.

Prior to the composition of *A Child of Our Time*, Tippett reached a nervous and creative crisis that culminated in a visit to the Jungian psychoanalyst, John Layard. A period of self-analysis continued and Tippett gradually learnt to appreciate the functioning of the psyche, particularly with regard to creativity. As a sensitive and humanistic artist, Tippett is obviously drawn to the interpretation of creative expression as defined by Jung. He says: '. . . maybe Jung is right, when he says that if once the artistic creator, leaving personal idiosyncrasies aside, gives expression to the archetypes of the collective unconscious, then he also speaks with the tongues of millions – as Einstein, or Jung himself, or Gandhi.'[2]

The need for a communication of human values collectively, and of inner growth individually, is a recurring feature in Tippett's life and work. Among the many influences on Tippett, such as Monteverdi, Purcell, Beethoven and Eliot, must be included Jung. It would be foolish to suggest that Jung was as great an influence on Tippett's composition as Beethoven, but '. . . it certainly seems true that Tippett's exploration of, and understanding of, Jungian ideas opened the way for, and participated in, the purely musical achievements which followed.'[3]

Jung asserts that the psyche is divided into two parts; the conscious and the unconscious. The system is in constant movement and is self-regulating. The psyche might be imagined as a submerged island which becomes partly visible at particularly low tides. The island is the ego, or 'I', and is the centre of consciousness. The 'seashore' is an area of semi-comprehension and repressed or forgotten memories. Jung calls this area the personal unconscious and it belongs to the individual. The collective unconscious is the unknown from which our conscious emerges and Jung viewed it as the source of the creative, and also destructive, spirit of mankind. As it is truly unconscious it is difficult to observe, but through the study of instincts, myths and dreams its presence can be concluded. It may be thought of as a collective bank of mankind's experience.

The emergence of recurring symbols from the collective unconscious suggested to Jung that mankind apprehends and experiences life in a way that is conditioned by the past. These prehistoric forms of perception, intuition and apprehension Jung calls archetypes. As archetypes are unconscious, we are only aware of them when they appear as mythological figures such as dwarfs and giants, or in abstract or geometric forms, such as squares, circles, wheels, characters or situations in dreams. Archetypes are also experienced as emotions in typical and significant human situations, such as birth and death, or triumph over natural obstacles.

The psyche is made up of opposing poles, components that are balanced by their complement, and Jung suggested a need for a careful equilibrium, or a 'Union of Opposites', as he termed it. Tippett drew upon this notion in *A Child of Our Time*, where the tenor sings what became the motto for the whole work:

> I would know my shadow and my light,
> So shall I at last be whole.

The goal of wholeness, which Jung calls individuation, has many pitfalls and has been likened to a journey: '. . . the traveller must first meet with his shadow, and learn to live with this formidable and often terrifying aspect of himself: there is no wholeness without a recognition of the opposites. He will meet, too, with the archetypes of the collective unconscious, and face the danger of succumbing to their particular fascination.'[4]

The matching of Jungian psychology to music can best be approached through the symbol. A symbol should not be confused with a sign. A sign is a substitute or representation of the actual event or thing, whereas a symbol carries a wider, psychic meaning which eludes a complete exegesis. If it is a genuine symbol our comprehension will not be able to grasp the whole, and mystery will still remain: 'A symbol attempts to express something for which no verbal concept yet exists.'[5] Our inability to account for the emotional and intellectual components in our art makes music a true symbol.[6] 'A symbol remains a perpetual challenge to our thoughts and feelings. That probably explains why a symbolic work is so stimulating, why it grips us so intensely.'[7]

Are there any archetypes in music? An ascription of extra-musical meaning in music is unreliable and often opinionated, and a syntactical analysis cannot adequately explain the emotional effect that music has upon us. Therefore music exists as a symbol. Works that are obviously symbolic cry out with a pregnant language that they mean more than they say. 'We can put our finger on the symbol at once, even though we may not be able

to unriddle its meaning to our entire satisfaction.'[8] Thus one may talk informatively on the mechanics of Beethoven's Fifth Symphony but still fall short of an emotional or symbolic solution, compounded of feeling and of intuition.

We may approach music as a symbol through many angles: for example, pitch, duration, rhythm, what has gone previously and our expectations for the rest of the work; but in this essay I propose to show how tonality and pitch reference is used by Tippett to articulate at a symbolical level.

Tippett's artistic interest in Jung can be located most easily in the operas, as we shall see in *King Priam* and *The Knot Garden*. What makes these works Jungian is their specific use of symbols in the manner that Jung identified through dream and myth analysis.

The path of individuation in Tippett's second opera, *King Priam* sees Priam, King of Troy, confronting his shadow and the archetypes of the collective unconscious. Priam, as a symbol of the Self, must account for the imbalanced aspects that are warring within him before any sort of self-realisation may occur.

To Priam is born a child which, it is prophesied, will cause Priam's and Troy's death, if allowed to live. The baby, Paris, is condemned by Priam but Fate plays her part and the child survives, unbeknown to Priam. The baby grows to a shepherd boy and returns to Troy to become the hero, Paris. The shepherd boy grows to a man whose adulterous love is a major factor in a

Priam (Rodney Macann) and Hecuba (Janet Price) reject Paris in his cradle as the Old Man (Richard Stuart) gives his prophecy at the opening of King Priam *in the Kent Opera production, 1984. (Photo: Malcolm Crowthers)*

93

A young shepherd-boy (Paris, who has survived thanks to the compassion of a young guard) talks to the hero Hector, his brother. (Nana Antwi-Nyanin and Omar Ebrahim). (Photo: Malcolm Crowthers)

war with Greece, the apex of which is the death of Priam. Paris and Hector are heroes, but heroes in different ways; Paris is the great lover while Hector is the great warrior. Priam's professed love for Hector is greater than that for Paris and this imbalance will be the King of Troy's downfall. Priam mistakenly believes that Hector's death was the price for the life of Paris, when, in fact, it was but one event in a chain. Priam withdraws to his inner self before the Greeks break into the city and Achilles' son fulfils the prophesy from Act I, Scene I.

Hecuba is Priam's wife, and shares her husband's royal pitch centre of D but also has a particular motif of running sextuplets in the violins, individual to her. When the motif appears with regard to other characters – for example, Priam's choice to have the baby, Paris, killed in Act I, Scene I – then it signifies the strength of her influence. Hecuba, who is also portrayed as the goddess Athene, represents the reasonable mother. Andromache, Hector's wife, also portrayed as the goddess Hera, represents the faithful. Both characters are partly divine though Helen, the wife of Paris, is more so. She had a divine birth and although Tippett portrays her as the passionate lover, Aphrodite, she is the only person who can communicate with Priam when he withdraws into his inner self. The fact that so little is known about her (as she says: 'I am Helen') makes her a dramatic symbol. Her relationship with Paris is shown musically by a juxtaposition of tonal polar opposites that suggests that Paris is a more earth-bound character, a pawn of Fate.

94

Paris (Howard Haskin) chooses Aphrodite (Anne Mason) in preference to Athene (Janet Price) and Andromache (Sarah Walker) with Hermes (Christopher Gillett) above.
(Photo: Malcolm Crowthers)

95

Other characters in the opera seem to be symbols of Priam's psyche. For example, Achilles would appear to be Priam's shadow; the confrontation with the Greek hero over Hector's mutilated body is a necessary part of Priam's individuation. The chorus of Old Man, Young Guard and Nurse represent the past, present and future. In particular, the Old Man is allied to the archetype Jung calls the 'Wise Old Man', a figure who encompasses meaning, wisdom and prophesy. Tippett allots the Old Man music that seems to well up from the murky unconscious itself.

A truly divine character is Hermes, winged messenger of the gods. He it is who provides a bridge between Priam's changing mental state with his 'Hymn to Music'. We are invited to feel the pity and the pain of the drama. He is also a link between the inner and outer worlds, a symbol of the link between the conscious and unconscious, which Jung calls libido.

Dramatically, Priam begins the opera strong and confident, with the qualities of leadership, authority and wisdom: an 'archetypal' king. While other characters tend to be static, a change in Priam's psychic situation can be seen clearly during the course of the opera. We see a change from a strong, confident king at the beginning of the opera to a dishevelled and uncertain mortal at the end – a change that is reflected in tonality. The death of a king in mythology, as Jung identified, is a recurring symbol of essential renewal within the psyche. It signifies a new beginning or an achievement of equilibrium within the psyche.

The characterisation of Priam is aided by the music. When he enters the opera, the accompanying material depicts him as confident and strong by a measured chordal tread and spacious scoring in the regal key of D major. (Example 1)

Tippett has made the impact of Priam's entrance to the opera particularly strong by a tonal preparation to the downbeat key of D at Figure 17. The work begins with a fanfare that strongly suggests the pitch A that becomes an upbeat to the entry of Priam. Clearly then, it is an important moment dramatically and musically.

The music is repeated and developed, still stressing a D pitch centre, implanting a particular pitch with a specific character and role, as for example Priam at Figure 22.

Achilles and Patroclus in the tent. (Neil Jenkins and John Hancorn). (Photo: Malcolm Crowthers)

97

A crucial moment arises; the child is a threat to Priam. 'Shall he die that I may live?' he ponders. It is not surprising to find a strong pitch centre of D at such an emotionally crucial moment. (Example 2) When, on the other hand, Priam is obliged to succumb to his wife's, Hecuba's, wishes to let the child die, Priam's earlier solid music is replaced by music associated with the queen. The pitch D is notably absent in Priam's part, though the accompanying violin sextuplets associated with Hercuba suggest the regal D of royalty. The implication through the music is that Priam's decision is not his sincere wish.

Scene 2 is a reunion between Priam and the son, Paris, whom he thought was dead; Fate has played her part. The strong pitch centre of D that characterised Priam in Scene 1 is lost to passing references as Priam considers this crucial moment. Eventually he accepts the 'trick of fate', and the pitch centre of D reasserts itself at Figure 132.

Act II has the war with Greece as its backcloth, the opening scene featuring a squabble between the sons Paris and Hector. When Priam enters to stop the quarrelling the regal music from Figure 17 returns, as does the pitch D. The combination of this pitch, and the particular scoring that depicts Priam as King, is so strong that when at Figure 240, for example, the material is concentrated into two repeated chords, the association continues. From this solid platform of music and character association we move towards the opera's culmination.

It could be suggested that Priam's uncertainty in the second scene of Act III is due to his already knowing that Hector, his favourite son, is dead. Priam's D sits above a dominant A on a single horn – an instrument associated with Priam. The tension of the moment is sharpened by woodwind clusters that inflect the pitch-reference of D which increasingly becomes the peak of Priam's phrases. Once Paris presents Priam with the news of Hector's death, the pitch reference to D becomes inflected by E flat and as the scene unfolds a sense of D gradually becomes less distinct. The psychic turmoil is quite evident; Tippett has written: '. . . if this did not unhinge Priam's mind, as Cordelia's death unhinged Lear's, it certainly faced him with a final confrontation of himself.'[9]

98

The death of Hector reaches the very core of Priam's psyche, shown by a weakening of the D pitch-centre's strength, and the destruction of his kingly music. (Example 3)

The Trojan women come in, one by one, but Priam will only see Helen. The music that recurs here strongly suggests A flat, a long way from Priam's earlier D. (Example 4)

The pitch reference to A flat becomes more prevalent, a phrase often beginning on D and then emphasising the tritone pitch. Tippett suggests that Priam is engulfed by his inner world, the personal unconscious, and we have found that this mental change has been followed by a change of tonal orientation, from D to A flat. A pitch reference to D is not entirely lost but is far less stable than a more positive A flat. From the imbalanced, outer world of the opera's beginning, Priam is transformed, through Hector's death, to an inner equanimity. The tritone would apparently symbolise this transformation so making a clear relationship between Priam's psychological breakdown and tonality as a symbol of that mental collapse. This technique of tonality as a symbol of psychological transformation Tippett pursues in the third opera, *The Knot Garden*.

The musical development that matches dramatic development in Priam is

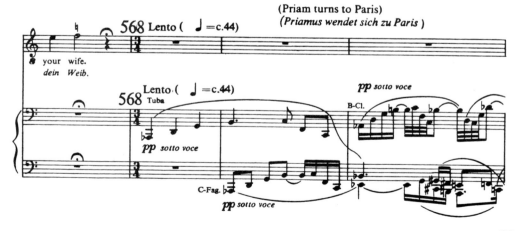

Paris, Hector and Priam . rejoice at the death of Patroclus. (Photo: Malcolm Crowthers)

lacking in the other characters since they have a more static role to play. The drama is concerned with Priam. The other characters revolve around him, and so do not require such intense musical development.

In *King Priam* we are concerned with one character's development; in Tippett's third opera we are asked to consider six, if one disregards the Prospero-figure Mangus.[10] The opera works like a crucible in which six individuals segregate, confront and purge the inner impurities within each of them.

Mel and Dov represent man's bestial and creative sides. Mel's quittance is through love which Jung says is one of the essential components of individuation. In both cases their music has individual traits that belong to particular sides of their personality, though Tippett draws this less sharply than for the other characters. Mel receives his quittance within the opera but Tippett had to go outside the work for Dov in the composition *Songs for Dov*.

Denise is the catalyst of so much in the opera. She has the noblest of souls, the will to fight for truth and right. Her psyche, however is naïve and unformed and she has to understand and appreciate man's physical and sexual side in the form of Mel to complete and balance her psyche.

Faber and Thea are immature people whose matrimonial discord reveals itself through Flora and their continual retreat within themselves, as is symbolised by the factory and the garden. The opera sees that discovery and the beginning of their maturation.

100

Faber suffers from an imbalance within his psyche due to an uncontrolled anima. The anima has a duality that corresponds to the contrasting sides of a woman; on the one hand, the pure and noble queen or goddess; on the other, the witch, seductress and prostitute. The anima is basically a personification of male erotic desire; an image which may become projected upon a real woman but which may have little to do with the actual nature of the real person.

Such is the nature of Faber. His uncontrolled sexuality sees him flirting with Flora, Denise and Dov; the blues that close Act I include a self-portrait of Faber as playboy. The anima as a pure and desirable maiden is projected onto Flora and indiscriminately onto Denise and Dov; the anima as witch is projected onto his wife, Thea, who actually physically attacks him, reinforcing her image of sorceress.

Thea is a symbol of the Earth Mother. This archetype also has a duality for it is associated with maternal sympathy, wisdom, fertility and love but also darkness, seduction, the poisonous and that which is inescapable. Nature typifies such a figure; 'Mother Earth' sends the sun to germinate the seeds but also the rain to sweep them away. She gives with one hand and takes away with the other. 'Anyone possessed by this figure comes to believe herself endowed with an infinite capacity for loving and understanding, helping and protecting . . . she can, however, be most destructive, insisting (though not necessarily openly) that all who come within her circle of influence are "her children", and therefore helpless or dependent on her in some degree.'[11]

Thea's connection with this archetype is seen in the obsessive cultivation of her garden, which is a symbol of her ego, and in her motherly protection of Flora.

Thea in the garden is accompanied by very distinctive music. Horns and a lilting $\frac{5}{8}$ suggest a pitch-centre E flat which is followed by upper strings playing triplets suggestive of A major. (Example 5)

SCENE 2
(Thea is coming slowly from the inner garden, stooping occasionally to tend the flowers.)

Thus the material at Figure 17 presents the two aspects of Thea's character which will be developed in the opera's course. The ensuing dialogue in Act I, Scene I, features the rich horn sound and the pitch of E flat, these being clearly associated with the garden and hence with Thea. Later she berates Faber for his half-real, half-imagined attack on Flora; the

'Earth Mother' attacks with strident music that lacks the warmth of the horns heard at Figure 17. When Thea's rhetoric involves the garden and its tending, (a manifestation of the 'Earth Mother') the E flat pitch and the distinctive scoring for horns is particularly strong whereas the A is neglected.

In Act I, the two specific and individual types of music are synonymous with different parts of her character and archetype. In Act II, these rigid elements are broken up. Thea's inability to truly understand Faber's relationship with Flora shakes the strength of her earlier solid pitch-centre of E flat.

The psychic storm of Act II, Scene 8, sees the instability and imbalance of Thea's inner garden. Mel's brief mocking outburst to Thea: 'Go water your roses', strikes at the core of her imbalanced psyche illustrated by the frenetic horns and strings. The attack is important for Thea as she is left alone in a sound world far removed from her warm horns and E flat pitch-centre, a psychic world of 'Briars and thorns'.

Act III sees the final confrontation for Thea in the Chess Game of Scene 7. When she throws the queen piece to Faber it is a symbol of the confrontation with her animus, which can then lead to self-realisation. The pitch of E flat is lost for a gentler and more stable A as she contemplates the 'strange enigma' of individuation. Her 'journey' towards wholeness includes a reprise of the music first heard at Figure 17: 'This morning my garden

The horrifying ceremony as Paris, Hector and Priam smear each other in Patroclus's blood. (Photo: Malcolm Crowthers)

102

seemed a sanctuary', making quite clear the relationship between the two. But this is lost and the music returns to the calming numinous A.

By the close of the opera, Faber, too has reached a similar point of self-realisation. He, like Thea, represents an archetype, that which Jung calls the anima.

For Faber, Thea is seen as the witch:

> A mother bitch!
> Who turns me to a cur.
> A Mother bitch!
> And yet my wife.

This image is intensified by Thea's physical attack on him in Act II, Scene 4.

In the game of chess that saw Thea's confrontation with herself, Faber and Flora are the physical players. Faber's sexuality is confronted when Flora upsets the board, stopping the game and thereby freeing herself of him, and thus him of her. The music that is associated with Faber and his sexuality is heard at Figure 30 when Faber enters the opera and in any following dialogue. (Example 6) The characterisation of Faber in Act I links his sexuality with this angular trumpet idea and a pitch-centre E. Faber, like Thea, must confront and resolve the imbalance within herself. The final association between the spiky trumpet motif and the pitch E with Faber

Priam visits Achilles to ask for the body of Hector, killed in revenge for Patroclus's death. (Photo: Malcolm Crowthers)

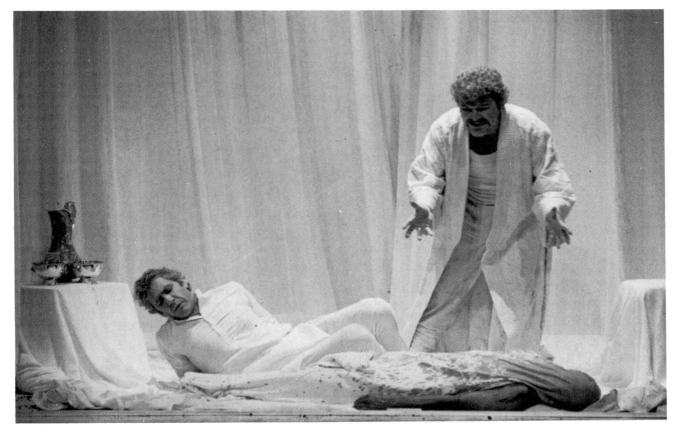

103

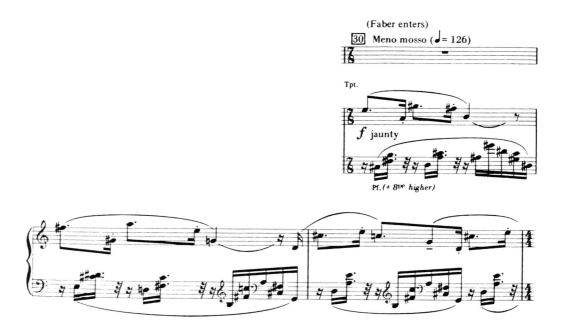

comes in the confrontation chess game of Act III. If Flora loses the game with Faber she symbolically surrenders herself to him.

In the following scene of self-realisation there is no reference to Faber's 'anima' music or the pitch E that symbolises his sexual indiscretions. The Epilogue is a place of introspection, and Faber's putting away of the factory papers shows his resolve to meet Thea instead of running 'wherever the partner cannot follow'. 'Our enmity's transcended in desire,' they sing; Faber's now controlled anima can be seen at 'desire', where a pitch reference to E reappears but the trumpet and the angular rhythms and contours are absent, controlled by an 'individuation' A.

According to Jung, individuation is usually the quest of mature people. Flora, it would seem, is not ready for this process. Her half-imagined, half-real anxiety over Faber is to some extent caused by her own immaturity. Flora is the Jungian archetype of the 'maiden', a helpless counterbalance to the stronger and older 'Earth Mother', hence Flora's name and interest in the garden. The helplessness of the maiden in mythology exposes her to the dangers of reptiles, dragons and sacrificial slaughter. In *The Knot Garden* this danger is symbolised by Faber.

Her neurotic state is depicted in Act I by fast semiquavers under a trill that expresses a pitch-centre of A. This sobbing, hysterical music is always heard in association with Flora's unstable psyche, for example, her fear of Faber's advances or the horror of the disfigured Denise. Dov is responsible for Flora's enlightenment, showing her a world contrasted to her own introspective and shaded life. Dov's world is the 'big town', 'high trees' and the 'Californian West', but also includes tenderness and real love. Flora's response is in the form of a Schubert song transposed from the original A minor to B minor. The reason for the transposition is two-fold. As one of the most beautiful and tender moments in the opera it fits into an overall

104

Priam withdraws in his grief.
(Photo: Malcolm Crowthers)

structure of B for the whole opera, and secondly it shows that Flora can develop away from her 'immature' A.

As symbols, the pitches A, E flat, E each have a duality that, due to their very nature, cannot be fully defined. Flora's A can be seen as another element in Thea's neglected psyche. Thea's pitch of A is a symbol of her counterbalance to the 'Earth Mother' archetype that dominates her psyche. Jung postulates that such an imbalance would create a situation where the neglected half can no longer be disregarded and bursts forth; and Flora is a symbol of this.

We have seen that overtly Jungian libretti are articulated musically in terms of tonality or referential pitch and we might expect other such aspects to be revealed. This suggests that the instrumental music can be seen in a new light. What of the 'birth-death' pieces, the Fourth String Quartet and the Fourth Symphony? What of the message of humanism that flows from the Third Symphony? Can the duality of themes in Part I and the juxtaposition of loud and soft chords that form the Coda be appraised in Jungian terms?

Perhaps Tippett has already supplied the answer in *King Priam*:

> O divine music,
> O stream of sound,
> in which the states of soul
> flow, surfacing and drowning,
> while we sit watching from the bank
> the mirrored, mirrored world within,
> for 'Mirror upon mirror mirrored
> is all the show'.
> O divine music,
> melt our hearts, renew our love.

NOTES
1. R. Donington: *Wagner's 'Ring' and its Symbols* (Faber & Faber, 1963) p26
2. M. Tippett: *Music of the Angels* (Eulenburg Books, 1980) p52
3. A. Whittall: *The Music of Britten and Tippett* (Cambridge University Press, 1982) p32
4. F. Fordham: *An Introduction to Jung's Psychology* (Penguin, 1953) p79
5. C. G. Jung: *The Spirit in Man, Art and Literature*, Collected Works, Vol. XV (Routledge & Kegan Paul, 1966) p70
6. Aaron Copland says: 'Is there a meaning to music? – My answer to that would be, "Yes". Can you state in so many words what the meaning is? – My answer to that would be "No". Therein lies the difficulty.' D. Cooke: *The Language of Music* (Oxford University Press, 1959) p
7. C. G. Jung: Collected Works, Vol. XV, p77
8. C. G. Jung: Collected Works, Vol. XV, p77
9. M. Tippett: op. cit., p229
10. Mangus could be said to achieve a sense of self-valuation too:–
    'Now that I break my staff
    and drown my book'.
He is the manipulator – but has to admit his inadequate psychic resources, a position for potential individuation.
11. F. Fordham: op. cit., p60

*Priam is killed by
Achilles's son, attended
by Greek guards.
(Photo: Malcolm
Crowthers)*

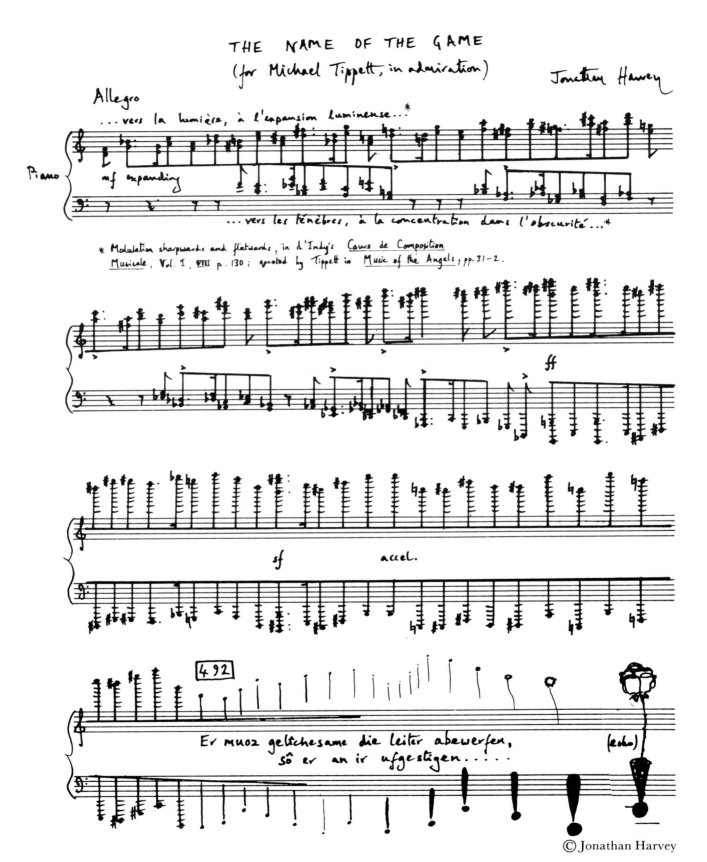

108

ARNOLD WHITTALL
Tippett and the Modernist Mainstream

L IKE MOST of the labels which historians and critics attach to cultural movements, 'modernism' is easily abused, and rightly treated with some scepticism. Certainly, it is more than likely that to call Tippett a 'modernist' would seem more abusive than complimentary to many music lovers, and more irrelevant than either. Tippett is Tippett, and the less critics seek to compromise his remarkable originality – even in the name of illumination – by inferring influences and implying associations, the better. But my purpose here is not to consign Tippett to the unwelcome category of being more modernist than original: it is to argue that there is value – a distinct, and permanent aid to understanding – in defining certain phenomena in twentieth-century culture as modernist, and in seeing Tippett in their perspective.

'Modernism' is usually employed in the most obvious sense, to mean a whole-hearted abandonment of tradition, seeking the new to replace the old, often at all costs, and usually with more destructive than constructive consequences. Tippett himself recognised this nuance when he referred to 'anti-art or Dada' as 'a third modernistic tendency' in opposition to both neo-romanticism and neo-classicism[1]. And although Tippett's own attitudes may well have developed and changed since that comment was made in 1965, it is notable that, in writing about Ives in 1969, he referred to that master as 'a pioneer' whose 'experiments can become uncouth'[2], but who evidently did not merit the label 'modernist' as a pejorative term. Of course, however the word is used, modernism is not normally thought special to the twentieth century: one era's modernism may be another's tradition. Yet it can be argued that what is most modern about twentieth-century music does mark an especially radical departure. Before the twentieth century, all styles and structures, however diverse, tended to serve the time-honoured aesthetic principle that, as Webern put it, 'unity is surely the indispensable thing if meaning is to exist'[3]; art was a matter of synthesis, of subordinating diversity to unity, the parts to the whole. Such a notion has not exactly vanished without trace since 1900: for example, Stravinsky wrote of composition as the 'search for the centre upon which the series of sounds . . . should converge', even though 'we can bring the poles together without being compelled to conform to the exigencies of tonality'[4]. But it has been strongly questioned. For example, Stockhausen has declared his intention 'to modulate one event with another without destroying it, really discovering those original qualities of something which are the most characteristic, and which are strong enough to be matched with the stronger characteristics of something else – leading to real Symbiosis'[5]. And one cultural historian has argued forcefully that what distinguishes twentieth-century modernism from all previous manifestations of the radical spirit is the strength of the 'urge to fragmentation'. This urge can lead to total, aleatory chaos, but may also foster the development of techniques for bringing diverse elements 'into the most intimate relationship with each other whilst at the same time preserving the validity of the contradiction between them'[6]. In other words, a new, freer coherence resulting from the balance of distinct, complementary elements may replace the old, hierarchically structured formal principles[7].

For a pre-Stockhausen statement of pure modernist intent, none is more striking than this: 'taking the place of the old fixed linear counterpoint, you will find in my works the movement of masses, varying in radiance, and of different densities and volumes. When these masses come into collision, the phenomena of penetration or repulsion will result. Certain transmutations taking place on one plane, by projecting themselves on other planes which move at different speeds and are placed at different angles, should create the impression of prismatic aural (auditory) deformations'[8]. Varèse, like Stockhausen after him, evidently rejects the notion of synthesis, resolution, convergence onto a centre, even though it might well be argued that Varèse's actual music – for example, *Déserts* – is by no means as unequivocally modernist as this manifesto might lead one to expect. The crucial point here is that no composer whose work still encourages consideration in terms of synthesis rather than symbiosis can be thought of as strictly modernistic. But that does not rule out the possibility of modernist phases, and modernist tendencies, in the careers of composers who, in the end, might be felt to have resisted the temptation to embrace modernism purely and consistently: such a career may itself encapsulate a neat symbiosis between modernist and traditionalist tendencies.

This matter should not be confused with the 'tonal' versus 'atonal' issue. Webern's twelve-note compositions are triumphantly and lucidly atonal, but in the way they use complementary motivic and contrapuntal strands to generate unified, integrated wholes, they are certainly not modernist. Stravinsky is a complex case, to be discussed more fully in a moment. But for a close contemporary of Tippett's whose modernism is as consistent as it is thrilling, we need look no further than the 'simultaneous oppositions' of Elliott Carter[9]. It is Carter who most unambiguously represents the 'modernist mainstream' today, with his inheritance from Ives, through Varèse and Stravinsky, and his transformation of the complementation techniques of Stravinsky (and Webern) into a powerful post-expressionist idiom.

* * *

Students of Tippett have never found it difficult to identify the appearance of something akin to an 'urge to fragmentation' in his work – from at least the Symphony No. 2 (1956-8) onwards, and perhaps reaching a climax sixteen years later in the Symphony No. 3 (1970-2), before the tendency of the later works to reassert – not without ambivalence – forces making for unity and synthesis. Such a broad interpretation at least has the value of questioning the automatic assumption that Tippett's own confession – 'I am . . . a disciple of Jung and a lover of Stravinsky'[10] – is an expression of belief that Jung and Stravinsky are significantly similar. Indeed, it might become possible to argue that Tippett's development has been determined to no small degree by the fact that while his principal non-musical inspiration stresses integration and synthesis, his principal musical inspiration was a master of what Elliott Carter has termed 'unified fragmentation'[11]. It is nevertheless more likely that both Jung and Stravinsky were similar in the sense that they gave Tippett a heightened sensitivity to the contrasting and conflicting elements of which 'wholes' are constructed, and that just as the palpable textural continuity of Tippett's earlier music may lead us to underestimate the nature and function of the contrasts within it, so the more evident conflicts and diversities of his later works may lead us to underestimate the forces making for – if not integration – then for coherence. In this respect, some further consideration of the Stravinskian achievement may be useful.

The richness and originality of Stravinsky's music stemmed in large part from an instinct – in which conscious anti-Wagnerianism certainly played a part – that it was possible to achieve satisfying formal coherence without succumbing to the seductions of 'endless melody' – to what Stravinsky saw as an amorphous organicism 'more improvised than constructed'. In Stravinsky's celebrated put-down, this Wagnerian melody denoted 'the perpetual becoming of a music that never had any reason for starting, any more than it has any reason for ending', and led to the notorious claim that 'there is more substance and true invention in the aria 'La donna è mobile' than in the rhetoric and vociferations of *The Ring*'[12].

If this polemic amounted to nothing more than a preference for separate numbers in opera as opposed to through-composition, it would be of little interest. What it actually creates is a powerful tension between the desire for anti-organicism on the one hand and the recognition of the superiority of what Stravinsky terms 'similarity' on the other. Thus the above statements about the respective merits of Wagner and Verdi might at first seem to be directly contradicted by other remarks in *Poetics of Music*, like the following: 'for myself, I've always considered that in general it is more satisfactory to proceed by similarity than by contrast. . . Music gains in strength in the measure that it does not succumb to the seductions of variety. . . Variety is valid as a means of attaining similarity'[13]. It will be evident that Stravinsky cannot be arguing that composers can somehow do without contrast in any shape or form. 'Similarity' is not the crude kind of repetition you get if you reiterate an unvaried ostinato ad infinitum: rather, it is the consistency which comes from the balance, and regularity, of comparable events. Two events can be similar in kind without resembling each other in their content at all, and the crux of Stravinsky's attitude would seem to be that it is only valid to compare events, and to determine the similarity of their contents, if those events are *ordered* – in particular, if they are closed-off cadentially – and not in some kind of endless present without adequate punctuation or phrasing.

Such considerations enabled Stravinsky to achieve an enhanced sense of the way in which contrasts can contribute to a formal process without positively preventing the final achievement of an overall coherence. Works like *The Rite of Spring* and *The Soldier's Tale* are emphatically not 'organic' in the Wagnerian sense. But their large-scale, anti-organic structures are not therefore to be characterised as fundamentally lacking in coherence. That coherence has been well defined by Elliott Carter in the paradoxical phrase already quoted (and first applied to *The Soldier's Tale*) – 'unified fragmentation'. Carter argues that what appear to be abrupt juxtapositions of unrelated elements contribute to 'an underlying continuity of material' in which 'all the brief, almost discrete fragments, however roughly they connect with each other, end up by producing a work that holds together in a new and very telling way'[14]. *Oedipus Rex* is very different in subject and style from *The Rite of Spring* or *The Soldier's Tale*, but Stravinsky himself evidently saw it in terms not seriously at odds with the notion of unified fragmentation: using the German word which Kurt Schwitters invented to describe his collages, Stravinsky called *Oedipus* a '*Merzbild,* put together from whatever came to hand'. But he went on to argue that 'I have made these bits and snatches my own, I think, and of them a unity'. The composer himself had no doubt that he was 'fusing different types of music'[15]; and we can accept that without needing to feel that the resulting fusion was a fully synthesised, unified structure in the classical – symphonic – sense.

*   *   *

All contemporary composers are able to choose (consciously or instinctively) whether (1) to view music in terms of a unifying centre which is diversified but never loses its ultimate control; (2) to view it in terms of polarities which are ultimately 'brought together' through a 'search for the centre upon which the series of sounds . . converge'; (3) to make symbiosis or opposition the central feature in a form which balances diversities without seeking to integrate them, to resolve their complementary or conflicting properties. In these absolute terms, it is the second category which fits Stravinsky most successfully – and, I would suggest, Tippett also. Indeed, I would argue that only a composer aware of the capacity for 'simultaneous oppositions' to become a self-consistent principle of style and form could have responded so imaginatively and variously to the frightening but fruitful no-man's-land between the absolutes of the Modern (in the sense of continuing the traditional aesthetic and structural emphasis on all-embracing unity), and the Modernist, as defined above.

Writing of *Les Noces* at the time when he was composing *The Midsummer Marriage*, Tippett commented that 'although *Les Noces* took Stravinsky longer to finish than any other piece of comparable length, it has an extraordinary unity. The notion of unity is one of the key notions in Stravinskian aesthetics'[16]. Tippett does not speculate further on what the other 'key notions' might be, but in any case it seems apt that he should be particularly drawn to what is undoubtedly one of Stravinsky's least fragmented compositions at that particular stage of his own development. Of all Tippett's earlier works, it is perhaps *A Child of Our Time* which conveys the least unified impression, but there is no evidence that the composer sought deliberately to portray contemporary social and political tensions by means of a *'Merzbild'* created from the juxtaposition and superimposition of diverse musics, as he might have, for example, from a 'random' polyphony of Negro Spirituals, or the effect of different Spirituals approaching and passing and receding like Ivesian marches. More realistically, the possibility for unmediated confrontation between the Spirituals and Tippett's own style of the time is positively avoided, for the obvious reason that the theme of the work is the need for reconciliation: the shadow and the light together form the whole.

This essentially Jungian notion does nevertheless provide a thought-provoking model for a music in which polarities are established and only gradually drawn into integration. It is often said that the most impressive aspect of both the Concerto for Double String Orchestra and *The Midsummer Marriage* is the glorious sense of goal-direction and attainment. (Only the Symphony No. 1 of the works of this period anticipates a more equivocal attitude to such confirmations of integration). The opera certainly does not eliminate the essential, comic gap between Inner and Outer, Ideal and Actual. Polarity is at its most palpable in the very different arias for Jenifer and Mark in the final scene of Act I. But this polarity, like others – the contrasts between Mark and Jenifer, and Jack and Bella; or between both couples and King Fisher – is expressed most basically through style, through musical manner, rather than through any more thorough-going structural devices. The way in which Tippett, soon after completing his first opera, became more aware of the possibility for juxtaposing contrasts without smoothing the path between them, is familiar enough, and was evident at least from the time when his comments on the Piano Sonata No. 2 were published, with their statement that 'the effect is one of accumulation – through constant addition of new material: by variation and repetition. There is virtually no development and particularly no bridge passages. The formal unity comes from the balance of similarities and contrasts'. The last sentence, in particular, may be construed as a clear statement of moderate modernism, and the music bears out the moderation, for not only are the contrasts more successive than simultaneous, but the music still relates – though obliquely, it is true – to the notion of goal-directedness and resolution. What the sonata reveals, as its progenitor *King Priam* had also revealed, is a double development. 'Formal unity' is no longer primarily a matter of evolutionary, developmental continuity, and the musical language is no longer governed exclusively by reference to the harmonic principles of an extended but still vital tonality.

Historians often comment on the particular significance of changes occurring during the mid-1950s – in direct reaction, it might almost seem, to the death of Schoenberg in 1951. Stravinsky's discovery of serial technique came not so long before Tippett's discovery of atonality, and even if the motivation for the latter is felt to be more a matter of responses to changes in the type of subject-matter which the composer preferred for his dramatic works, it cannot be completely divorced from the remarkable attempt – in Tippett's Symphony No. 2 – to provide Stravinsky with another Symphony in C at just the time when Stravinsky himself was casting C and all other tonalities aside. The neo-classical strengths of that symphony cannot exorcise the notably radical response to the 'finale problem' which it reveals. To describe the fourth movement as a 'fantasia in four unrelated sections' may itself be an attempt at wilful over-statement, but it shows the composer discovering that 'un-relation' is not a synonym for incoherence, and gives the relatively restrained use of the 'in my end is my beginning' technique at the very end a memorable ambivalence.

The years of the Piano Sonata No. 2 and Concerto for Orchestra (1962-3) are likely to go down as the years of Tippett's purest modernism, the years in which he could have confirmed a complete break not only with the kind of textural and formal continuities he had used in the past, but with any last lingering tonal connections. They were equally crucial years for his major contemporaries: in 1961 Carter completed the Double Concerto for Harpsichord, Piano and Two Chamber Orchestras, one of his most resourceful demonstrations of 'simultaneous oppositions'; Lutoslawski wrote *Venetian Games* in the same year, and Stockhausen began the first version of *Momente;* in 1962 Xenakis composed two of his most representative stochastic pieces (ST/4-1, 080262 and ST/10-1, 080262); in 1963 Messiaen composed *Couleurs de la cité céleste* – and it is probably to this last, most individual and idiosyncratic master, three years his junior, that Tippett is closest in the sense that the new extreme did not establish a new norm, but a point of departure from which further development, bringing elements of old and new into a new relation, became possible. As far as I am aware, no one has ever suggested that Tippett's unwillingness to follow Stravinsky not only into atonality but also into serialism may have had something to do with the general musical disorientations of the late 1950s and early 1960s. But if, as was clearly the case, Tippett did not 'need' serialism, he could hardly assume that he needed atonality either. And if some kind of tonality was still possible, he might indeed be led back to the notion of polarities converging onto centres – onto 'higher consonances'[17] – and to the 'balance of similarities and contrasts' as a means of achieving an adequate degree of formal coherence, through juxtaposition rather than superimposition.

Of course, the appropriateness, even inevitability of this development does not ensure that the music itself is any easier to write. In some later works, the Symphony No. 4 and the Triple Concerto, for example, it is possible to argue that the balance between contrast and continuity is not totally convincing. But in most compositions, and especially the Symphony No. 3, the success of the enterprise is so complete, so powerfully memorable, as to justify not only the enterprise itself but also any occasional failings. The Symphony No. 3 is so memorable, not least because the composer resists the temptation to force a fusion, a reconciliation, between polarities which cannot yet be merged. Tippett's Goethean strivings no longer dissolve into the radiance of the earlier works, and even when, as in *The Ice Break* and *The Mask of Time*, the ending is far from bleak or hopeless, 'a contemporary, ironic ambiguity' remains, for a reason the Preface to *The Mask of Time* makes clear: 'An abiding theme in the work is the polarity between knowledge obtained through intellectual processes (the knowledge of scientists) and that obtained from deep inner-sensibilities (the knowledge of creative artists). Sometimes in their divinations of the future, these different sources of knowledge coincide and complement each other.'

It is that possible coincidence, or convergence, which enables a degree of optimism to survive. Even in the earlier works, of course, ultimately optimistic resolutions were not achieved without struggle; but in the 1970s and 1980s, the still more searching tempering of optimism is the beginning of wisdom. Tippett's myths, poems and texts have set him challenges which his compositional technique has grown‧equal to, and the most challenging consequence of that technique has been his resistance to the possibilities of atonal saturation, whether through the complementary hexachords of the twelve-note system, or through the total emancipation of the dissonance which the post-expressionists have so triumphantly carried through. Tippett is, in general, more allusive, and more ambiguous, than these: but in choosing the middle path, he creates little sense of neutrality, still less of compromise. Tippett has not sought to commit himself to the 'modernist mainstream': but his points of contact with it, and his highly individual refinements of, and commentaries on some of its most fundamental features are nevertheless of far-reaching significance.

NOTES
1 M. Tippett: *Music of the Angels* (Eulenberg Books, London, 1980) p100
2 M. Tippett: *op. cit.*, p116
3 A. Webern: *The Path to the New Music*, ed. W. Reich (Bryn Mawr, 1963) p42
4 I. Stravinsky: *Poetics of Music* (New York, 1947) p39
5 Stockhausen: *Conversations with the Composer*, ed. J. Cott (London, 1974) p191
6 J. McFarlane: 'The Mind of Modernism', *Modernism 1890-1930*, ed. M. Bradbury and J. McFarlane (Harmondsworth, 1976) pp81, 88
7 For a fuller consideration of these issues, see A. Whittall: 'Webern and Atonality. The path from the old aesthetic', *The Musical Times*, cxxiv, December 1983 , pp773-6
8 Quoted in F. Ouellette: *Edgard Varèse* (London, 1973) p84
9 See D. Schiff: *The Music of Elliott Carter* (London, 1983) p13
10 M. Tippett: *Moving into Aquarius* (Paladin Books, London, 1974) p85
11 *The Writings of Elliott Carter* (Bloomington, 1977) p304
12 I. Stravinsky; *op. cit.*, p64. It should be remembered that, in its final written form, *Poetics of Music* is the work of Roland-Manuel, even though it surely represents the composer's actual beliefs with complete accuracy.
13 I. Stravinsky: *op. cit.*, p33
14 E. Carter, *loc. cit.*
15 I. Stravinsky and R. Craft: *Dialogues* (London, 1982) p27
16 M. Tippett: *Music of the Angels*, p93
17 For this term, see A. Whittall: *The Music of Britten and Tippett* (Cambridge, 1982) especially pp5-6, 287-91

Michael Tippett at the
1984 Brighton Festival.
(Photo: Malcolm
Crowthers)

FAYE ROBINSON
Tribute

Happy Birthday
Michael
W

Love, dear, sweet
Mom, who has
been an inspiration
to many through
your wonderful
music

ARIETTA

for Sir Michael Tippett
on 2nd. January 1985

DAVID BLAKE

York 1st. May 1984

118

ROBERT F. JONES
Tippett's Atonal Syntax

THE CHANGE from a fundamentally tonal harmonic language to a fundamentally atonal one is a common element in the creative evolution of many twentieth-century composers. Especially in the cases of those composers who had developed in their maturity a strongly personal tonal style, it is not surprising that they carried many characteristic stylistic features of these works into their atonal music. The continuities of technique, style, and personality between the tonal and atonal works of many of these composers have been documented in many studies. Yet to assess these continuities properly, one must also take into account the magnitude of the syntactical change brought about by the abdication of tonality and the necessary transformation of the functions of the constituent elements of music caused by this change.

In the case of Michael Tippett, the continuities (along with much else) have received excellent coverage in the studies by David Matthews (1980), Meirion Bowen (1982), and Arnold Whittall (1982). The present essay will focus on the structural principles of harmonic organisation at work in Tippett's atonal music by means of analysis of selected excerpts.

As a point of departure, one that will clarify the nature of Tippett's style change, I have chosen a pair of examples, one 'tonal', the opening stanza of the first song in *The Heart's Assurance* (1951), and the other 'atonal', the first section Tempo 4 from the Second Piano Sonata (1962). (See Examples 1 and 2.) These excerpts show obvious similarities of texture and of sonority, and both exploit the diatonic pitch class collection.

A deeper analysis reveals, however, a profound difference of structural organisation. The excerpt from the earlier work evinces a goal-directed tonal sense lacking in the later work. Example 3a presents a reduction of Example 1 from which much of the figuration has been eliminated. This clarifies the harmonic and linear outlines, making possible the further reduction shown in Example 3b, a quasi-Schenkerian graphic presentation of what I hear as the essential middleground progression.[1]

This reduction would be misleading if it were presented without qualifications. The apparently clear harmonic and voice-leading background shown in the sketch is blurred considerably at the foreground level by a

119

Example 1. 'Song' (The Heart's Assurance, No. 1): bars 1 - 15

Example 2. Piano Sonata No. 2: bars 15 - 22

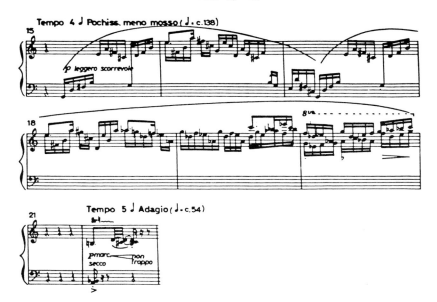

number of features. Firstly, the implications of tonal centre at the beginning of the song are ambiguous: the B minor I have shown as tonic is not at all obvious right away, as the repeated bass motion B – E suggests a possible tonal centre of E, with B as a modal dominant. In addition, some features, summarised in Example 4, point to a possible tonal centre of A, the ultimate goal of the song.

Secondly, the tonal functions are obscured by a number of harmonic substitutions, principally fourth-chords and 6/3 triads substituting for 5/3 triads built on the same bass note. Most notably, the B-minor tonic at the end of the passage is represented not by a B-minor 5/3 chord, but by a G#diminished 6/3 chord; the G# must be understood as a substitute for F#. Tippett uses the same cadential structure in A minor at the end of the song (see reduction in Example 5). Its appearance at the close of the first stanza helps to establish it as a norm.

Thirdly, the expansion of the dominant harmony uses so many A-naturals that its tendency to imply resolution to B minor is attenuated. The first appearance of the dominant harmony (third quaver of bar 6) is certainly strong enough, but the return to it after so much emphasis on A-based chords is very weak – not so much stated as suggested. (I have read, not with a great deal of confidence, the $f\#^2$ on the third quaver of bar 14 as implying a structural dominant. If this seems a dubious interpretation, one may prefer the alternative reading summarised in Example 6.)

In music as dense as this with non-triadic structures, there is naturally a good deal of room for disagreement about the details of the reduction. Regardless, though, of whether or not the reader agrees with all the details of my analysis, I think that the discant progression of Example 3b, as well as the underlying progression I – V [expanded] – I, are clear enough to support my argument about the passage.

121

Example 3a

We have seen that underlying the elaborately ornamental foreground of Example 1 is a simple tonal background. The passage from the Second Piano Sonata (Example 2) reveals no such use of functional tonal relations. As a starting point, one should observe that the passage moves from one diatonic collection to another. (See Example 7.) In Tippett's presentation of these collections one may distinguish pitch-class priorities (G for collection A and D^b/A^b polarity for collection B) as well as a hierarchical ordering of the functions of the remaining pitch classes. Within collection A, for example, we may distinguish four levels: the single pitch class G, which is the bass note and is heard as root and even, in a sense, 'tonic'; B and G, the remaining pitch classes of the G-major triad, which are treated as stable elements; F# and A (major seventh and ninth of G), which, while implying resolution to G, are 'frozen' (in Roger Sessions's term) to the triadic sonority; and the two remaining pitch classes, C# and E, which are always presented as dependent on the relatively more stable notes D and F# (see the dotted lines in the first 3 bars of Example 8). These motions, by introducing unstable elements and withholding their resolutions for varying amounts of time, serve to animate the underlying stable harmony and prevent a static effect from settling in.

123

Example 3b

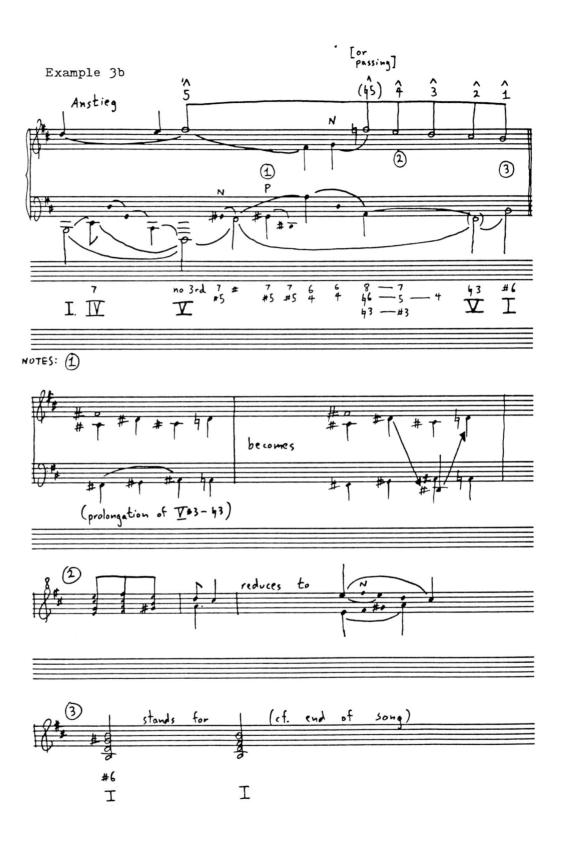

Example 4

B minor (?): I ——————— IV

E minor (?): V ——————— I

A major (?): II ($\hat{5}$ $\hat{4}$ $\hat{3}$ $\hat{2}$ ‖) V

Example 5

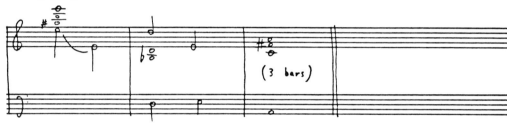

(3 bars)

Example 6

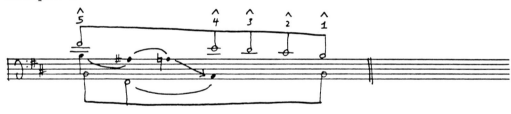

$\hat{5}$ $\hat{4}$ $\hat{3}$ $\hat{2}$ $\hat{1}$

I   V$^{\sharp3 - \natural3}$ I

Example 7

collection A   collection B

N.B. 2 common tones: G and C♯/D♭

With these distinctions in mind, the mechanism of the transition between the two collections becomes clear. The transition is triggered by a 'foreign' G# that introduces an ambiguous zone. (See Example 8, bar 18; the notes belonging to collection A are stemmed upward, collection B is stemmed downward.) Interpretation hinges on the shifting roles played by several pitch classes. Note the pitch-class succession A – G$^{\#}$ followed 5 semiquavers later by A – A^{b}. Initially the G$^{\#}$ is understood as a lower neighbour to A, but what follows the second statement forces a reinterpretation of the relationship: now the A-natural is unstable, an upper neighbour to the A^{b}. A similar reversal takes place of the relative stability of the pitch classes B and C$^{\#}$/D^{b}. The first C$^{\#}$ in bar 18 is heard as unstable, resolving to the following B. As the second pitch-class collection achieves stability, this B must be reinterpreted as a lower neighbour (C^{b}) to the D^{b}, the 'tonal centre' of collecton B. G, the tone centre of collection A, has become a passing note between the stable notes A^{b} and F by the 12th semiquaver of the bar. The only pitch class of collection A not submitted to a reinterpretation is D, left hanging in the register of middle C and picked up again in the first bar of Tempo 5 (bar 22).

The analysis presented so far may seem to be perversely 'picky' in its concentration on details of linear implication in a bar that lasts, after all, less than two seconds. A broader perspective, however, reveals similar procedures. The juxtaposition of the two pitch-class collections in this passage and the lack of functional relationship between them might lead us to consider one a neighbour harmony to the other. But which is the stable harmony and which the neighbour? Similar questions arise in consideration of just about any passage in the sonata and are typical features of Tippett's atonal language. While at the surface level, as Arnold Whittall has observed, 'very clear distinctions between "ornamental" and "fundamental" features may be detected' (Whittall 1982: 217), that is, it is usually possible to sort out 'non-harmonic' notes from 'harmonic' ones, further attempts at reduction – the hierarchisation of individual harmonies – often result with a pair of harmonies, each relatively stable with respect to the surface ornamentation, in a context in which their juxtaposition mitigates against our hearing either as stable relative to the other.

Tippett's exploitation of such harmonic devices correlates with his fondness for 'mosaic' form. Although some of the individual fragments are organised around tone centres, even centred on consonant harmonies, these tone centres have a merely provisional effect because of the lack of harmonic continuity between them. Tippett's 'mosaic' style has obvious similarities with Stravinsky's, and Edward T. Cone's study of Stravinsky's technique of 'stratification, interlock, and synthesis' (Cone 1972) may be used to provide a helpful perspective on Tippett as well.

Cone describes three phases to this technique. First, *stratification* ('the separation in musical space of ideas – or better, of musical areas – juxtaposed in time'); second, *interlock* (by which term Cone refers to the alternation of

Example 8

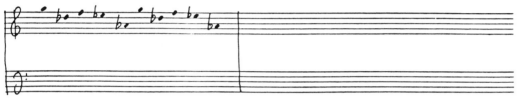

different strata); and third, *synthesis* (a process by which the conflicts are led to a final goal and resolved). Cone's term, 'synthesis', is a good one, and his description of the concept is worth quoting:

> Some sort of unification is the necessary goal toward which the entire composition points, for without it there is no cogency in the association of component areas. But it is seldom as explicit as the original stratification, and it almost invariably involves the reduction and transformation of one or more components, and often the assimilation by one of all the others. The diverse elements are brought into closer and closer relation with one another, all ideally being accounted for in the final resolution. (Cone 1972: 156–58)

Stravinsky's use of the technique typically (though not invariably) concludes with a final chord of resolution, generally a major triad (with or without added notes), that creates the effect of a resolution of the previous tensions in a single stable sonority, an effect no less than that of a conventionally tonal perfect cadence.

Tippett, in his later works, not being concerned with the 'semblance of tonality' (Berger 1972: 154) that figures so prominently in Stravinsky's neo-classic works, generally avoids resolving his mosaic structures in a single chord of resolution. Typical of Tippett's endings is a process of reduction by which conflicts are pared down to a single opposition (harmonies, textures, dynamics). The 'sense of an ending' is achieved not through arrival at a stable sonority but by creating the effect of a precarious balance between two forces that are incapable of further reduction.[2]

The ending of the Second Piano Sonata provides a particularly clear illustration of this technique. The sonata is an extreme example of Tippett's mosaic style, being composed of 38 sections in 8 different tempi. Although previous commentators have perhaps overemphasised the lack of connections between the fragments, the overall effect is, nevertheless, one of extreme disjointedness, with sudden and extreme disruptions of the musical continuity. As a means of increasing the tension towards the end of the work Tippett writes what he calls 'a kind of "climax" coda where the bits of addition and repetition are made very small and the resulting mosaic therefore more intense' (Tippett's programme note, cited in Mason 1965: 206). This leads, at bar 301, to a return of the opening music of the work. (See Example 9.) What is remarkable is that this very striking musical idea is the only one of the entire work that has not been subjected to repetition and fragmentation – its return at bar 301 is its first appearance since it was interrupted in bar 3. The central sonority is the whole-tone trichord C – D – E; the outer voices C and E suggest C major, with chords based on B^b and D used as neighbours. Rather than use this 'C major' as a chord of resolution, however, Tippett juxtaposes it with developments of the 3-note chromatic cell[3] that first appeared (explicitly) in bars 112–113. In the present context they act as disruptions, contrasting in dynamics (p espr. vs. ff risonando), harmony (chromatic vs. diatonic), and rhythm (flexible vs. rigid). The size of the interruptions decreases (9 notes, 9, 5, 2) until finally only one note is left – the f^3 of bar 315 played quietly after the last fortissimo chord. Tippett has reduced the conflict to the minimum and the resulting balance, however uneasy, is conclusive. A further statement of the fortissimo chord would be as unwelcome as an additional tonic chord at the end of Beethoven's Ninth Symphony.

Before continuing further, we may pause to consider some general features of Tippett's musical language before and after the great divide. We may follow Janet Schmalfeldt's useful distinction between 'vocabulary of pitch structures' and 'syntactical relationships' as interacting elements of a 'harmonic language' (Schmalfeldt 1983: 221–22). Our first two examples may be said to employ similar vocabularies at the service of radically different means of syntactical organisation.

The excerpt from *The Heart's Assurance* is, in spite of its small scale, representative of Tippett's use of tonality in his earlier work. However tonally ambiguous some passages may be (and one must admit that, especially in the larger works, Tippett may conceal the harmonic goals for considerable lengths of time) processes of clarification – harmonic, melodic, and rhythmic – ensure that the goals, once reached, sound like resolutions. It is this mastery in the handling of large-scale harmonic and voice-leading progression that gives the lie to Ian Kemp's facile remark about 'Tippett's indifference to functional harmonic progression' (Kemp 1978–79: 146).

The study of 'syntactical relationships' in any atonal music is, in many respects, still at a somewhat primitive stage, so it is not surprising that few

Example 9. Piano Sonata No. 2: bars 301 - 316

attempts to analyse systematically this aspect of Tippett's later harmonic language have been made. Arnold Whittall, whose recent book on Britten and Tippett deals in more depth about more aspects of Tippett's music than any previous study, is extremely cautious on this issue, falling back on the concept of the 'instinctive rightness' of Tippett's handling of degrees of 'tension and repose', although he remarks also that 'only very rarely . . . might one form the opinion that the vertical aspects of Tippett's texture are devoid of all harmonic significance' (Whittall 1982: 300, 217, 6).

★   ★   ★

The remainder of this essay will be taken up with attempts to understand

Example 10

(registers simplified)

syntactical principles underlying Tippett's later music through the analysis of excerpts from *The Ice Break* (1973–76).

The opening scene affords an appropriate starting place. Several points are worth noting.[4] First, although the entire scene is in a single tempo (crotchet = 72) and, for the most part, a single metre (54 bars of $\frac{3}{4}$ changing to $\frac{4}{4}$ for the last 6 bars), Tippett uses much the same sort of mosaic techniques as in *King Priam* and the Second Piano Sonata. It has often been observed that, in spite of the fragmentariness that a superficial examination of his mosaic-style scores might suggest, Tippett projects a sense of growth and development through the patterns of juxtaposition. As Whittall observes about *The Vision of Saint Augustine*, 'Although the table of fourteen distinct tempos set out at the beginning of the score might seem to imply a highly sectionalised form of juxtaposed "blocks", it is the evolutionary interaction rather than the contrasted juxtapositon of materials which dominates.' (Whittall 1982: 217).

In the first scene of *The Ice Break* the most obvious technique of providing a sense of ongoing development is the linear organisation of the bass. Abstracting the prominently emphasised bass notes from the first 48 bars of the scene gives us the line presented in Example 10.

This sequence of notes, considered by itself, certainly suggests a clear tonic of C. Indeed, many other aspects of the music support the notion that the scene is 'in C'. Many of the bass notes given in Example 10 support what Whittall has called 'higher consonances', chords whose registral layout (and orchestration) 'give some priority to triadic elements' (Whittall 1982: 5). In the typical 'higher consonance' one can readily hear a 'root' but not necessarily a harmonic function. It is striking, therefore, that at several crucial points in this scene, Tippett uses sonorities that, in tonal music, are virtually unambiguous in their tonal functions. The C-based chord in bar 19 (C, E, G, B^b, D^b), for example, is a dominant of F (V^{b9}), and – even more striking – the arrival back at C in bar 46 is preceded by the dominant seventh chord G, B, D, F. The crucial structural role of this arrival is underlined by the restatement of the opening 'ice break' music at this point.

In spite of these unmistakable references to a tone-centre of C, other factors act against such an interpretation. An air of instability hangs over the C-based chords. We have already noted that the C-based chord of bar 29 (the first return to C) has the chord construction of a dominant of F (V^{b9}). When C returns in bar 46, a firm sense of cadence is avoided by its being set so obviously at odds with the solo voice part. It arrives in the middle of the vocal phrase, and the voice part is constantly involved in semitone clashes with the orchestral harmonies. Even the return of the 'ice break' music at this point is

130

an ambiguous gesture: rather than creating a sense of stability, it initiates a return to a far from unambiguous harmonic situation.

The 'ice break' music itself is worthy of closer examination. Taking a narrowly strict tonal perspective as a point of departure, we may observe several peculiarities. How are we to understand the functional relation between the opening dyad C – E^b (which strongly implies a C-minor harmony) and its successor B – D$^{\#}$ (which, with its anacrusis F$^{\#}$, presents a B-major harmony)? At the very opening of the opera we are plunged into the tonal world described earlier in which two potentially stable harmonies undermine each other by sending out contradictory tonal signals.

The 'ice break' music recurs at three later points in the opera: when Nadia and Lev are reunited and embrace (Act I, Scene 7: beginning 2 bars before Fig. 68), as the dying Nadia recalls the sound of the frozen river ice breaking in the spring (Act III, Scene 4: beginning 2 bars before Fig. 341), and as Yuri, after his operation, takes his first faltering steps and embraces his father (Act III, Scene 9: beginning 2 bars before Fig. 441). At all three of these appearances, Tippett weighs the ambiguous harmonic relationship in favour of resolution to E-minor, explicitly in the first case (I/7: Fig. 70) and by implication in the two instances from Act III (the music is interrupted just at the moment corresponding to Fig. 70 in I/7; i.e. III/4 Fig. 344, III/9 Fig. 443). In none of these cases, however, is the E-minor treated as anything other than a temporary goal.

★   ★   ★

The function of long-range stepwise motion in a non-tonal context presents a problem for the analyst. In tonal music, of course, step movement is used for either neighbour motion (a relatively stable note embellished by a step-related unstable one) or passing motion (a gap between two relatively stable notes filled in with unstable passing notes). If pitch-class priorities are established in an atonal context, then it is easy to understand how the concept of neighbour notes can be applied. Similarly, if individual harmonies can be established as having even a provisional stability, then step motions can be used as passing notes to connect notes of the stable harmony. The analysis of Example 2 presented above relied on both these concepts.

These neighbour motions and small-range passing motions function essentially in the same way as they would in tonal music. With longer range step progressions, however, especially when each degree carries a different harmony, the situation is very different. In tonal music, the harmonic functions of the boundary tones establish a stable frame on which the passing notes are dependent, even though they may support their own harmonies. In the absence of a tonal context, the end of a passing motion will have to be defined by other means.

As an example, let us consider the passage accompanying the preparation for Yuri's operation in Act III, Scene 7, of *The Ice Break* . Between Figs. 412 and 419 the top voice can be heard as an ornamented ascent, by half and whole steps, from f^1 to e^3. In the bar before Fig. 420 this line is picked up an

Example 11a

Example 11b

octave lower (f², g^{b2}) and led, at Fig. 420 to g², at which point a descent begins. This basic line is shown in Example 11a.

Without a doubt this ascending line generates a sense of increasing tension over its 36-bar span. But what does Tippett do to control this build-up, to give it a sense of specific purpose, to avoid an effect of arbitrariness when the ascending line changes direction?

Several things suggest themselves. Let us consider first the role of the pitch class F. As first note of the progression it automatically commands a certain amount of emphasis. Its importance is reinforced by the accent mark and by the embellishment with a lower neighbour figure. The ascent of the first octave (f¹ to f²) takes place with deliberation: the process is spread over 28 bars split up into 3 and 4 bar units and there is much backtracking (some of it shown in Example 11b). When the f² is reached at Fig. 418 it is supported by almost the same harmony as at its first appearance (see Example 12; note that 5 out of 6 pitch classes, including those of the outer voices, are identical). It might be expected that this octave ascent would produce a sense of return to stability when the higher F is reached, but Tippett undermines this tendency. Comparison of the harmonies supporting the two F's reveals that the one changed pitch class, coupled with changes in spacing, effects a striking

Example 12

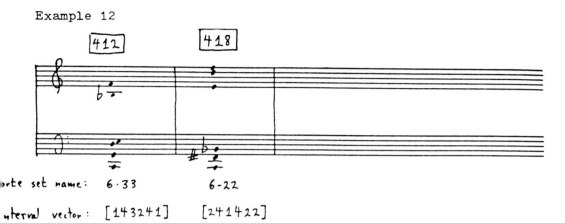

increase in tension. Attempts at formulating exact quantification of relative degrees of chord tension are, it seems to me, doomed to failure – so many factors other than the pitch content exert powerful influences. Nonetheless, several factors contribute to increased tension in the second chord. The change from G to F # has removed the obvious triadic basis of the first chord and, as comparison of the two interval vectors reveals, it adds another semitone and another tritone to the total interval-class content.

The increase in harmonic tension at Fig. 418 forces the line to continue its ascent. The rate of ascent is drastically increased; only 4 bars are required to take the line up a major seventh to e^3. In additon, the regularity of the segmentation into 3 and 4 bar isorhythmic units is broken. Just at the moment when the line is on the verge of achieving f^3, Tippett interrupts the ascent with 3 bars of rests in the orchestra. This interruption serves as a dramatic articulation of the break in the line caused by the return to a lower register in the bar before Fig. 420. The pitch class F is deprived of its status as a goal and becomes part of a passing motion leading to g^2 (Fig. 420). The movement down from E to E^b in the bar before Fig. 419, as well as the E^b on the downbeat in the voice part of the bar before Fig. 420, prepare this change of role for the pitch class F.

Several factors interact to confirm the structural importance of the arrival at g^2 (Fig. 420). We have already noted that this is the point at which the line changes direction. The harmony at this point, a 'higher consonance' built over an A-major triad, serves to pull the line down: with the G sounding like the seventh of an expanded dominant seventh chord, a downward resolution is implied. In addition, we should note the changes in tempo, meter, orchestration, and melodic motive that occur here.

★   ★   ★

The natural tendency of musical patterns, once established, to perpetuate themselves until interfered with by other phenomena is an important compositional resource, one richly exploited by Tippett. Although an abstract description of the process can make it sound mechanical, in practice the use of variation as well as the combination with other elements can serve to avoid any tendency towards total predictability.

In the passage we have just been considering, for example, the ascending line, once established, has a tendency, in spite of several detours, to continue upward until a combination of factors conspire to change its direction. The organisation of the passage in terms of rhythmic motives has similar features.

The passage opens with 4 statements of a 3-bar rhythmic figure:

(a)

followed by a variant that extends the figure to 4 bars:

(b)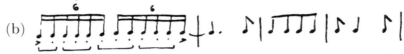

The increase in activity in the first bar of the variant parallels the rise in pitch level; the following statement, lower in pitch, returns to the early form (a). At Fig. 416, we return to the pitch level of Fig. 414 and return as well to rhythmic motive b. At Fig. 418, the pitch level is even higher, but as the line at this point achieves the higher octave of its starting note, we hear the rhythmic figure again. Rather than leading to another figure beginning in its 4th bar however, it is extended for three more beats:

(a extended)

The breaking of this pattern is, as noted above, one of the contributing factors in making the ascending line change direction. Thus we see that in the early stages of the passage the two patterns, melodic and rhythmic, support each other's continuing development; at the end their interaction helps to propel the musical argument to a new stage.

★ ★ ★

We turn now to a complete scene. Act I, Scene 5, is ideal for our purposes; it is short (29 bars) and very transparent in texture. Example 13 presents a transcription of the scene with the unpitched percussion instruments omitted. The boxed numbers are the rehearsal numbers from the score; the corresponding bar numbers (which will be used for reference in the following discussion) appear in brackets.

Immediately obvious is the use of repetition as a patterning device. The scene consists of three parallel 10-bar phrases. The second phrase is a slight variation of the first; the third – while corresponding in many respects – introduces more significant changes.

The pitch-class priority of C is firmly established at the beginning of the scene by means of the pedal note in the lower strings. The second note, D, is understood in its context as an upper neighbour to the C. In the second part of

134

the phrase this neighbour motion is embellished in different registers with secondary neighbour and passing motions involving $C^\#/D^b$ (Example 14).

In the second phrase, this structure is repeated with a few changes of detail. The third phrase, however, presents a contrast. Whereas the first two phrases can be understood as prolongations of a single pitch class, the third introduces the element of linear progression. The new bass note, E, in bar 25 changes the significance of the previous D from neighbour to passing note and the continuation, $F^\#/C^\#$, establishes a new pattern: the whole-tone scale.

The whole-tone scale, like many other symmetrical scalar and harmonic configurations, has a tendency to self-perpetuation. Overt statements of the whole-tone scale are rare in Tippett's work (although *The Ice Break* does feature one important motive based on it [see I/2: 5 bars after Fig. 29]); less rare is its use as an underlying patterning element.

Several factors interact to increase tension in this phrase. Notes foreign to the whole-tone collection occur at the ends of the first vocal phrases (Nadia's A and F, Yuri's D^b and G). The 8th bar of the phrase is transposed up a major third. The general level of loudness increases (note the off-stage cheering noises that begin in bar 23 and the direction that Yuri's last line be sung 'half-shouting') as does the tempo (*agitandosi un poco colla voce* is directed beginning at bar 25). The regularity of the patterning into 10-bar phrases is broken by having the next scene begin in the 10th bar (overlapping Yuri's last word). Note also that in each of the three phrases the first vocal entrance occurs earlier (on the 19th beat of the first phrase, the 17th beat of the second, the 15th beat of the third).

These are all, of course, general tension-raising devices. As with the ascending line from Act III Scene 7 that we examined above, an important question arises as to what features point to a specific goal for the passage.

I would suggest the following. Throughout the scene the major C – D in the bass has been followed by a $C^\#/D^b$ in a higher register. In the analysis presented in Example 14 we have explained this note as neighbour and passing note. This is certainly its principal function in the first phrase. In the second phrase, however, another perspective takes shape. In Bar 16 Nadia's D^b is introduced simultaneously with the C/D dyad. The resulting harmony is the chromatic trichord (Forte's set 3–1). The D^b functions here less as a 'non-harmonic' note (as in the first phrase) than as the final element in a gap-filling process: the musical space between C and D is filled in chromatically with the intervening pitch class.

This process is continued in the next phrase. As the bass line rises the voices supply the pitch classes that convert the whole-tone dyads of the bass into chromatic trichords (Nadia's F in bar 26, Yuri's G in bar 27; see Example 15). The chromatic build-up is continued by the brass on the third crochet of bar 27 (G – A – B^b).

These developments are interrupted at bar 28 by changes in register, dynamics, and harmony. The most prominent sonority in this bar is the 'fourth-chord' C# – F# – B (set 3–9). Example 15 shows the transformation of the whole tone from the bass of bar 27 into the fourth-chord sonority of bar

135

Example 13. The Ice Break, Act I Scene 5

N.B. Each system of this page continues on the next page.

137

Example 14

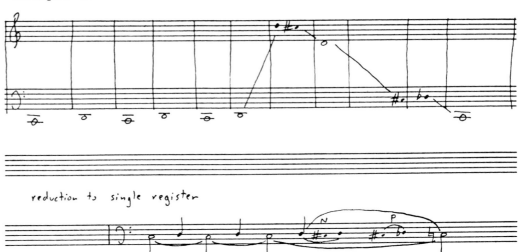

reduction to single register

28. Tippett has begun a process that will stabilize the pitch class $C^{\#}/D^b$. In the first two phrases this pitch class was dependent (in some sense) on C and D. In the opening bars of the next scene, $C^{\#}$ clearly has pitch-class priority. The modulatory process is triggered by Yuri's D^b in bar 27. The accompanying $F^{\#}$ and $G^{\#}$ produce the fourth-chord set 3–9 at that point. The D^b (the highest note of the bar) is continued in the same register in the next bar to become the bottom note of the fourth-chord. The trombone D (marked with an asterisk in Example 15) clashes against it. Ambiguity results as to the relative structural importance of the $C^{\#}$ and the D: the D is foreign to the $C^{\#}$ fourth-chord but – as it makes a B-minor triad with the upper two notes – perhaps the $C^{\#}$ should be understood as the 'non-harmonic' note. This conflict continues in bar 29 (with the $C^{\#}$ transferred an octave lower). In the following bar (the first bar of Scene 6) Tippett adds an E^b (doubled at the octave) beneath the $C^{\#}$ and D producing another statement of the chromatic trichord 3–1. In the 'modulatory' passage (bars 21–30), Tippett exploits the conflict and interaction of segments from three symmetrical pitch structures: the whole-tone scale, the chromatic scale, and the cycle of fourths (As complete collections, of course, the chromatic scale and the cycle of fourths have identical pitch-class content; when divided, as here, into smaller segments they may be easily distinguished.) The first chord of Scene 6 (the last chord in Example 15) may be related to each of these three pitch structures: its total pitch-class content represents the chromatic trichord, the lower interval $E^b/C^{\#}$ is both a part of the whole-tone scale and the outer voices of a three-note fourth-chord.

What is crucial in weighting the ambiguous balance between C # and D in favour of the C # is the appearance of the low E^b in bar 30, which converts the D into the middle element of the chromatic trichord. That this 'modulation' is completed only at the last moment may be demonstrated by substituting a low C for the E^b. This instantly resolves the C #/D conflict in favour of the D

138

Example 15

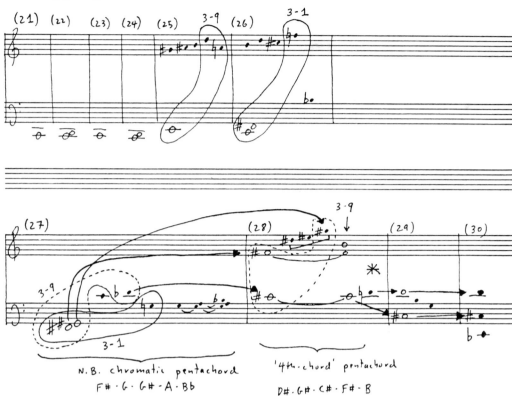

N.B. chromatic pentachord
F# · G · G# · A · Bb

'4th-chord' pentachord
D# · G# · C# · F# · B

(and incidentally destroys the sense of harmonic progress beween the two scenes).

★   ★   ★

Our last example will be taken from the final bars of *The Ice Break*. The opera concludes with a return to the sequence of four chords associated with Lev's quoting from Goethe's *Wilhelm Meister*. (See Example 16.) In Act I, Scene 8, we hear the first of these chords accompanying Lev's first quotation (Fig. 77); the complete sequence of four chords underlies the quartet ensemble that opens Act II (the complete progression is heard from the beginning of the act to Fig. 140; this passage is repeated between Figs. 143 and 148; the first chord appears again at Fig. 156). At the end of the opera the complete sequence returns with the basic harmonies separated by soft three-note chords in the electric organ ('as though in the far distance "the horns of elfland faintly blowing"' [Tippett's stage direction, 1 bar before Fig. 449]; these organ chords are shown in brackets in Example 16).

The basic progression consists of four chords identical except for transposition level. Although each contains 10 notes (9 different pitch classes), Tippett's spacing and orchestration divide them into three easily distinguishable layers. The root-position major triad at the bottom gives a solid underpinning and sense of root to the chord not shaken by the conflicting elements placed above. The top layer is a dominant seventh chord built on the

Example 16

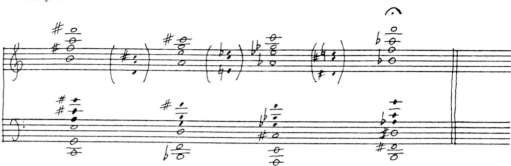

major seventh of the bass note and whose highest note (the major third of the V^7 chord) is the minor third of the bass note. This can be understood as a reference to the ambiguous relationship of the C/E^b and B/D# dyads of the opening 'ice break' music discussed above. In the 'ice break' music the two dyads were stated successively; in this chord they are stated simultaneously (Example 17).

The middle layer cannot easily be analyzed in such 'traditional' terms. (Interpretation of it as a major seventh chord built on the major sixth of the bass note would seem to be pointless.) Its lowest note mediates between the two outer sonorities: it can be understood as a major sixth added to the major triad of the bass, it is also a double of the seventh of the treble V^7 chord. The two remaining notes conflict with both of the outer harmonies. The prominence of the perfect fifth makes possible the interpretation presented in Example 18: the fifth in the bass is stated simultaneously with fifths a semitone higher and lower.

The chord is a typical 'higher consonance'. In terms of its possible tonal implications what is worthy of note is the avoidance of notes that would imply a dominant function: B^b in particular, but also D or F, could suggest that the chord is a highly coloured V of F. Tippett is thus free to use it as his final sonority.

By this reasoning, though, any of the four 10-note chords of Example 16 could have been used to conclude the opera. Why the fourth one? How does Tippett create the sense of an ending? Two obvious factors, whose obviousness in no way diminishes their effectiveness, are the prolongation of the final chord through repetition and the fact that the complete progression

Example 17

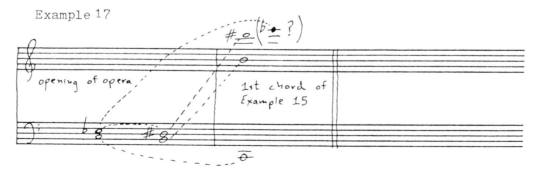

Example 18

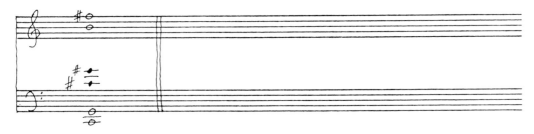

of four chords has been heard twice before in the opera. In addition, we should note that there has been a certain amount of emphasis on B as tone-centre throughout the opera: the reader is reminded of the C/B conflict in the recurring 'ice break' music (last heard only a few pages before the end) and referred to the transparent B-minor of the opening of Act III, Scene 6.

One further feature of the ending calls for attention. The bass line of the progression, the line that clearly acts as leader, pulling along the other voices in parallel motion with it, leaves a gap between C and B$^\flat$ in its descending motion. After reaching A it returns to fill in the gap with B. This process involves a motivic element as well: the descending whole tone, C/B$^\flat$, is answered by an ascending one, A/B.

★   ★   ★

For music to reveal anything significant to the analyst it must be taken on its own terms. Tippett's music, with its rich variety of structural means, demands a correspondingly wide analytical perspective. The eclectic approach of the present study reflects the wide range of technical resources displayed by Tippett. The concentration on detail stems from the conviction that the details of composition, the individual notes in their specific contexts, are the elements that propel the musical argument, even in music as grand in gesture as Tippett's.

The visionary character of Tippett's music is a quality often stressed, a quality that might seem to contradict the desirability of detailed technical analysis. But Tippett himself, in describing his 'true function' as a composer, has stressed two sides of the process of artistic creation: 'to create images from the depths of the imagination and to give them form' (Tippett 1974: 155–56). The form-giving side of the process is the only one that can be studied by the music analyst, but without it Tippett would have been powerless to communicate anything at all.

NOTES

1 A footnote is obviously not the proper place in which to enter into a thorough discussion of the appropriateness of using Schenkerian concepts to analyse music not conventionally tonal. The reader is referred to the excellent survey of several contrasting views of the subject in James M. Baker's 'Schenkerian Analysis and Post-Tonal Music' (1983). My own position should be implicit in my analyses; I would add only the following: I agree with Baker's premise that 'if one is to discover the extent to which a piece is tonal, one must begin as a "strict constructionist", examining every possibility for interpreting the structure in conventional terms'; I do not, however, follow his

further conclusion that, 'since prolongations are effected by means of operations on functions of varying structural weights, the analyst must establish the existence of a closed system of such operation and functions in order to be able to posit a multi-leveled structure' (Baker 1983: 168). Just as multi-leveled structures can be understood in the diminutions of much 'pre-tonal' music in spite of the absence of a 'closed system' of operations, I do not see why the lack of a completely 'closed system' in 'post-tonal' music should necessarily deny the presence of multi-leveled structures.

2 This discussion is not meant to imply that this technique is original with Tippett (cf, for example, the conclusions of Stravinsky's *Petrouchka* and Berg's *Wozzeck*) but rather that, given the harmonic and formal concerns of Tippett's mosaic-style works, it is the appropriate way to conclude. Furthermore, not all of Tippett's later works have similar endings: both The Knot Garden *(1966–70)* and the Third Piano Sonata *(1973)* end with Stravinskian 'chords of resolution'.

3 Less perhaps a 'cell' than a 'motive' as it appears with changing pitch-class set content but always with the same melodic shape.

4 Because of their length, it would be impractical to print these excerpts here. The reader must refer to the score.

REFERENCES

J. M. Baker, 'Schenkerian Analysis and Post-Tonal Music' in *Aspects of Schenkerian Theory*, ed: David Beach (New Haven: Yale, 1983)

A. Berger, 'Problems of Pitch Organization in Stravinsky' in *Perspectives on Schoenberg and Stravinsky* [rev. ed], ed. Benjamin Boretz and Edward T. Cone (New York: Norton, 1972)

M. Bowen, *M. Tippett* (London: Robson, 1982)

E. T. Cone, 'Stravinsky: The Progress of a Method' in *Perspectives on Schoenberg and Stravinsky* [rev. ed.], ed. Benjamin Boretz and Edward T. Cone (New York: Norton, 1972)

I. Kemp, 'Rhythm in Tippett's Early Music', *Proceedings of the Royal Musical Association*, 105, 1978–79

C. Mason, 'The Piano Works' in *Michael Tippett: A Symposium on his 60th Birthday* ed. Ian Kemp (London: Faber, 1965)

D. Matthews, *Michael Tippett: An Introductory Study* (London: Faber, 1980)

J. Schmalfeldt, *Berg's 'Wozzeck': Harmonic Language and Dramatic Design* (New Haven: Yale, 1983

M. Tippett, 'Poets in a Barren Age' in *Moving into Aquarius* [2nd ed.] London Paladin, 1974)

A. Whittall, *The Music of Britten and Tippett: Studies in Themes and Techniques* (Cambridge University Press, 1982)

Opposite

© Tippett in 1981, with score of Quartet No. 4 (Photo: Ron Scherl, San Francisco).

143

Magnificat

144

GEORGE GUEST

Magnificat and Nunc Dimittis

S T JOHN'S College, Cambridge, was founded in 1511, and so celebrated the 450th year of its existence in 1961. It was decided to mark this event by commissioning three choral works – by Robin Orr, Herbert Howells and Michael Tippett. Tippett, at that time, was on the point of completing his opera *King Priam*, yet he readily agreed to write a setting of the Evening Canticles for St John's.

The first performance of *Collegium Sancti Johannis Cantabrigiense* took place on Tuesday 13 March 1962, at a recital given by the College Choir in Chapel to mark the anniversary. It is a work totally different from any other using the same text, and has subsequently come to be recognised as one of the most significant choral works of its kind to have been written this century.

The words of the Magnificat are punctuated by rising fanfares ending in a high tone-cluster on the *Trompeta Real*, a loud reed stop of Spanish origin on the St John's organ, which greatly excited Tippett. I well remember, too, the occasion when Tippett posed the question: 'Which is the most important word in the Magnificat?' A difficult question to answer, perhaps, but the composer was in no doubt; his answer was the word 'for' – 'for' meaning 'because'. In other words, the only reason that Mary's 'soul' was now 'magnifying the Lord' was *because* He had done so many things that caused her so to sing. And this is the reason for so many heavy accents on the word 'for'. The Gloria is a splendid jumble of sounds, asymmetrical choral entries, glorious discordant clashes, and all bound together by an exciting organ part which seems to have little connection with the voices – indeed, a characteristic of the organ writing is that it is *not*, primarily, music for an accompanying instrument but, as Tippett put it in his programme note, 'the solution . . . was not to match the choir with the organ, but rather to let each speak proportionately'.

Tippett regarded the Nunc Dimittis as a 'song of renunciation'. There are three elements; the men's voices singing simply the words 'Lord, Lord' – does one think here that, in his physical extremity, Simeon was incapable of articulating anything else? The organ, as Tippett puts it, 'in contrast to the display of the Magnificat is reduced to primitive onomatopoësis of the thunderings of God' – does one think here that Simeon realised that he was shortly to give account of his life, and was therefore full of awesome and solemn anticipation? And what of the high treble soloist, who enunciates the words of the Nunc Dimittis? Is it too fanciful to suggest that Simeon conceived them, was too weak to utter them, but that they were plucked out of his brain (by an angel?), and articulated?

Whatever the truth of that, it is a superb work, one which is widely sung, and one which demonstrates Tippett's uniquely personal approach to any composition.

147

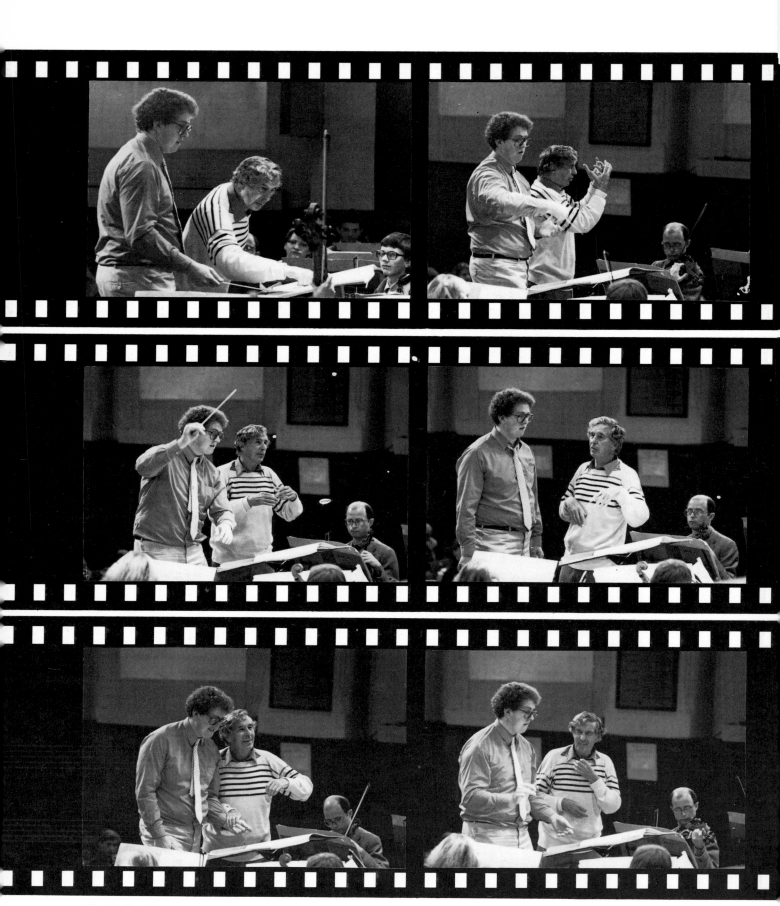

Sir Michael Tippett rehearsing his 4th Symphony with Graeme Jenkins and the Orchestra of the National Centre for Orchestral Studies at the 1984 Brighton Festival. (Photo: Malcolm Crowthers)

Michael Tippett, his Mystery

Tempo giusto : misterioso ($\text{♩} = 108$)

150

DESMOND SHAWE-TAYLOR
The Visionary Experience

UNTIL THE appearance of the full-length *Mask of Time* in 1984, *The Vision of Saint Augustine* was the largest of Tippett's non-operatic compositions; and it is likely, I think, to prove – together with the gloriously fertile and lyrical Triple Concerto – the richest and most profound of them all. I make this prediction with some confidence, although the scale and complexity of the piece have discouraged frequent performances, so that it has not yet made its way firmly into the affections of the musical public. Moreover, and most unfortunately, the RCA recording under the composer's direction has been unavailable for some while; a new one would be most welcome.

Tippett has never lacked confidence, and *The Vision of Saint Augustine* is among his most ambitious works. It is ambitious, not so much in its length, which is approximately that of a Brahms symphony, as in its complexity of lay-out and texture, and in its subject-matter, which is nothing less than a mystical vision of eternity. Strictly speaking, two visions are involved. The first (really the auditory equivalent of a vision), that of a child singing the words *tolle, lege* ('take up and read'), is merely alluded to *en passant* by the chorus during the first part of the tripartite cantata, and its introductions might well be called confusing – except that it adds another strand to the rich layering of thought upon thought, impression upon impression, by which the composer has set out to achieve his aim, and does so.

The main subject of all three parts is the second vision, shared by Augustine with his mother St Monica shortly before her death, while the two of them were standing in the window embrasure of an inn in Ostia Tiberina, looking at the inner garden and talking together 'very sweetly' of the life of the blessed in Paradise. In the second part a mystical exaltation descends upon them; in simple and searching words Augustine recounts how, as they were contemplating the notion of eternity, they soared in thought and 'went beyond' their own souls: 'and while we were thus talking of eternal life and panting for it, we touched it for a moment with a supreme effort of our heart.' In the third part, which consists of a single long and cumulative conditional sentence, son and mother reflect on the mystical experience they have just had, and perceive that, if only all the distractions of the world 'and the very soul too' could be silenced and that momentary exaltation of spirit sustained, then they would indeed have entered into the joy of the Lord.

All this – difficult enough for singer and listener to comprehend in any case – is set forth by the baritone soloist in the character of St Augustine, and consists of three paragraphs drawn almost verbatim from the original Latin of his 'Confessions', each paragraph forming one part of the musical scheme. A large chorus (there were about sixty at the first performance) sings also in Latin, sharing much of the saint's narrative and also interspersing it with biblical quotations in the text of the Vulgate and with the famous hymn of St Ambrose, 'Deus, Creator omnium'.

'We touched it for a moment': there lies the essential challenge to the composer who would tackle this great and formidable subject. Shall he keep the antecedents and sequel of the vision itself deliberately low and colourless, staking all on the moment of ecstasy? That would be to risk a general flatness, and even the further danger (after so much preparation) of a sense of inadequacy at the point of climax. Or shall he invoke and distil recurrent intimations of ecstasy from beginning to end of his work? The corresponding risk here is one of formlessness, of the composer's overplaying his hand, even of his contradicting the essential idea of the text.

Wisely, in view of his naturally lyrical and expansive temperament, Tippett has preferred to face the second of these risks – indeed, he may never even have contemplated the alternative. Within a few pages of the opening, at all events, the baritone soloist is already pouring out a paean of ecstatic ornamentation that grows increasingly florid to the end. Moreover, the layers of multi-coloured orchestral polyphony and interlocking choral commentary are in themselves richly complex. Was there not here a further danger, it may be asked, characteristic of this composer – that of needlessly complicating an idea that might be considered essentially serene and even simple? A danger, no doubt, but one that has been circumvented by his sure-footedness and fidelity to his own natural language.

Each time I have heard this piece, I admit, whether in live performances or in the recording, I have felt that the Ambrosian hymn, 'Deus Creator omnium', set to its own melody, supplies a less firm and indeed audible bass line to the complex passages in which it appears (it is first heard, '*poco f, cantabile*', on page 6 of the full score) than the composer must have intended. But pretty well everything else in the score has cleared up, so to speak, with repetition, and resolved itself into a marvellously strong, direct and meaningful statement.

Though the lay-out is so bold and so elaborate, the musical style will be instantly recognisable to those who know Tippett's earlier music. There is what he here specifically calls *glossolalia* (the inarticulate babbling of those who 'speak with tongues'), in his case a florid vocal style that stretches back to the wordless, dancing melismas of *Boyhood's End*. There is the rapturous profusion of notes in the high treble register that we specially associate with the first movement of the Piano Concerto. There are the glinting and magical celesta and woodwind sounds of Strephon's music in

The Midsummer Marriage; the sombre, thick, gentle criss-crossings and close harmony of the lower strings that we find in the slow movement of the Concerto for Orchestra; the fierce Achilles-cries and climbing martial trumpets of *King Priam*; the soft, mysteriously unresolved horn chords of the 'Ritual Dances' from the earlier opera. All these and many other elements of Tippett's familiar language are turned to new uses, worked together in new combinations and new perspectives. Through it all, the invention remains rich and vital.

The continuously repeating 'loops' in the solo baritone line near the beginning of Part 2, where the music gradually rises from the depths to the heights, that is from earthly to celestial and super-celestial contemplation, describe a curve (on the word 'erigentes') that is both elegant and profoundly eloquent; while the point of ecstatic climax is represented, not by the sudden profound stillness that might have been expected, but by the *glossolalia* of the chorus' 'joyous and ecstatic' cries of 'Alleluia'. The stillness comes thereafter, in the soft and lightly swaying choral setting of Augustine's wonderful circular phrase 'O aeterna veritas et vera caritas et cara aeternitas!' ('O eternal truth and true love and beloved eternity!').

Both the first and the second parts conclude, with solo and choral voices silent, in orchestral codas which carry us, so to speak, beyond the human into the impersonal sphere. In Part 1 we have leaping, ecstatic $^6_8$ figures that find their resolution only in softly muted brass chords; in Part 2 a purely instrumental recurrence of the 'depths to heights' idea, soaring at last into soft flourishes for piano and celesta and isolated notes for high woodwind and solo violin, dying away into nothingness.

It might be supposed that Tippett had left himself scant fresh possibilities for his third part; but here his brilliant idea of introducing the Psalmists's 'Lift up your heads, O ye gates, and be ye lifted up, ye everlasting doors' provides a wonderful, entirely apposite and musically tremendous conclusion. Or rather a quasi-conclusion; for the poet-composer has one more revelation to show us. There is a sudden hush; and the chorus first sings in Greek, then speaks in the vernacular of the performance, St Paul's 'I count not myself to have apprehended'. It is Tippett's humble apologia for essaying such high matters; and it may also serve as ours for attempting to trace his footsteps. When further apprehension comes, we may decide that he has here excelled himself in expressing a lifetime's concern with new sound-worlds and visionary perceptions.

Fragment of a Cadenza...

for Michael –
with all best wishes
and much affection
fra Jly.

154

PAUL DRIVER

The Knot Garden

*T*HE KNOT *Garden*, like *The Tempest*, begins with a magic storm. Unlike *The Tempest's* it is only half-real; it is half psychological or symbolic. Mangus, professional analyst and would-be Prospero, has conjured it as a display, for his own satisfaction and the audience's, of his magical or hypnotic power. He sits, at the centre of the whirlwind, on the couch of his profession. But then, 'at a gesture from him, the couch disappears'. The magic was not unreal.

The opera's setting is our modern urban world. The existence of the transcendent is no more excluded from this world, however, than it was from the timeless, allegoric world of *The Midsummer Marriage* or from the ancient mythological world of *King Priam*. The transcendent shadows and glints through the confused doings of the modern men and women presented, and takes them dimly by surprise. A clear perception of its significance is not permitted them; they are merely to be bewildered by it into a provisional and partial cognisance of broader scope to their lives.

What happens to them in the course of the opera may be compared to what happens to Alice in her two books of surreal adventures. Only *The Knot Garden* is a bitterer comedy; experience bites on the characters with a sharper tooth; the music that embodies them and entertains us is always 'music that's bitter-sweet'.

Mangus' storm at the outset has something of the formal function of the fall down the rabbit-hole at the beginning of *Alice in Wonderland*. Once down it, once swept by Mangus' magic, you do not find that events, however ordinary they may seem, are altogether accurate. They are liable to bump into each other, be suddenly curtailed, lack the expected definition, lose sight of the logic that brought them into being, or just 'dissolve'. The characters' environment has a corresponding instability – an urban garden can turn into a maze; a 'fabulous rose garden' materialises because of a song, and fades once the song is over. The setting is zany, yet recognisably modern; the opera is magical yet sobering.

It is true that in *The Knot Garden* the supernatural is not capable of the grand interventions it makes in the two preceding operas by Tippett. But in a more puckish way it can strike at any moment. And it is a serious mistake of production to attenuate its role, for example, by omitting the opening storm as did David Freeman's altogether domesticated (though frequently impressive) version recently performed by the Opera Factory, using Meirion Bowen's chamber-orchestral arrangement of the score. None of Tippett's operas, not even *The Ice Break*, can be regarded as 'secular'.

The next thing that happens in Act 1, 'Confrontation', of *The Knot Garden* is the appearance of Thea, coming slowly from 'the inner garden', which as her conversation with Mangus makes clear is her own inner world, wherein 'I touch the tap-root/ To my inward sap'. With a slightly Humpty-Dumptyish petulance she informs Mangus: 'Only I may prune this garden . . . Pruning is the crown.' Or, to change the metaphor, we are in the *Looking-Glass's* Garden of Live Flowers; and promptly in runs one of them, Thea's adolescent ward Flora, with an 'Ah-ee, ah-ee'. Thea's husband Faber follows, and is given *Hamlet*-ish advice by Thea to 'cut the offensive action', his supposed flirtations with Flora. The tensions in the garden are manifest, the knots tightly drawn. Faber is almost speechlessly exasperated. He withdraws 'to the factory', and Thea sinks deeper into her garden. Mangus sees life exploding as the result, unless the 'priest-magician' intervenes.

Flora is also Alice, an Alice grown out of her childhood serenity, more susceptible, but no less alert and inquisitive. Presently she has an encounter with Tweedle-Dee and Tweedle-Dum, American and Englishman, writer and composer, Caliban and Ariel, 'black earth' and 'white roses', Mel and Dov. Like everyone in the opera, they are 'acting a scene'. Thea, bearing a tray of cocktails, disparages them as 'children at play'. But Mangus knows that 'adults too play later'.

All must act because all have lost their own selves. When Faber returns to discover Dov howling, 'like Ariel's dog' on all fours, and asks: 'Who in hell are you?' he means it literally. When Mangus comes on carrying a mass of coloured costumes for charades, he intones: 'We be but men of sin. So sounds the accusation.'

The long, intensely beautiful formal aria of Thea's freedom-fighter sister, Denise, extols a world of tortured integrity beyond the masks and game-playing of 'the beautiful and damned'. But the blues ensemble ending Act 1 immediately bombards her 'true' song with lacerated parody of negro tribulation. Whether she knows it or likes it, she too is involved in this *Alice* world; she, too, has a fuller self to discover at the end of a labyrinth.

She and her sister are the first to be whirled into that 'Labyrinth' which is the second act. And it is her collision with Mel in the middle of it that brings the most heartfelt music of the opera, a richly harmonised, cantabile melody for strings, remembering the tune of 'We shall overcome'. As Mel sings: 'A man is for real,' and Denise: 'Should I not follow such a man?' the cliches almost dissolve into the truth.

What actually stills the tumult of the act is the strange meeting of Flora and Dov. They are blown together, two delicate flowers, to rest on each other. Dov asks her whether she likes music. She replies with a verse from a Schubert song, which Dov then 'musingly' translates: '. . . my love's so fond of green.'

156

He answers with a 'different song', a modern pastoral, 'I was born in a big town.' The refrain of this marvellously transformed rock-number is 'Play it cool, play it cool' – perhaps gentle advice to Flora herself. By the end of the song, the 'fabulous rose-garden' mentioned in the last line, and which has been gradually forming under the influence of Dov's music, has completely appeared (a proper production would represent it, Freeman's did not): 'the enclosing walls, the fountain, the girl, the lover, the music.'

It is the equivalent of Prospero's masque in Act 4 of *The Tempest*, and in the same way the beautiful illusion is shattered. Just as Prospero was brought news of Caliban's fresh misdeeds, so here 'a shadow enters the garden' and 'taps the lover on the shoulder'. It is Mel; 'I taught you that', he reminds Dov. And the garden fades, leaving, like Prospero's apparition, not a wrack behind.

One marvels at the skill with which this scene has been musically enacted. The Schubert melody is able to float into the texture with no disturbance of tone, and a perfectly magical evocativeness. The throbbing jazzy figurations of the electric guitar, bass clarinet and lower strings in Dov's song seem a natural, if new, item of Tippett's vocabulary; the seriousness and formality of the aria are unmistakeable, even if the operatic genre has been sea-changed. The theatrical poise of the scene is no less impressive. It grips the attention and complexly clinches the act. At the same time, one may let oneself be reminded of those occasions in the *Alice* books when Alice is asked to recite something, only to be interrupted by a long recitation of the questioner's own.

The 'Charade' third act moves swiftly and with brilliance. The allusiveness of the opera, which colours what Ian Kemp finds to be the work's 'expressionism'[1] is here at its most extreme and challenging. As Mangus tells Thea, 'The play has bewildering moments.' An elaborate re-enactment of *The Tempest*, in which scenes sometimes go awry, leads the characters gradually out of their muddle and darkness into daylight sobriety (though the opera ends in a 'vast night') and a modest submission to love ('If for a timid moment . . .').

All sorts of peculiar confrontations occur, as when Faber-as-Ferdinand-as-a-jailor brings on Dov-Ariel in handcuffs, speech-singing with a Cockney accent: 'He's gone off his food./ His wings are drooping./ He used to sing before.'; or when Dov-Ariel unduly belabours Mel-Caliban, going beyond the script, 'As I shall always do;' or when Flora-Miranda furiously upsets the chess-board on which she has been playing with Faber-Ferdinand (and the diaphonous accompanying music also), protesting his real-life falsity, provoking him to reply, 'That scene went wrong!' and Mangus-Prospero to return, 'That scene went right!'

What we are witnessing seems part mimesis of contemporary 'family-therapy', and part reminiscence of the anarchic trial scene at the end of *Alice in Wonderland*.

A dramatic signal that the therapy is working comes with the reprise halfway through the act (just after the chess-playing scene) of the opera's opening glissandoed 12-note theme. Taking it for accompaniment, Thea sings an aria of eerie beauty, declaring: 'I am no more afraid.'

Dov as Ariel, Mel as Caliban in Act III (Charade) of The Knot Garden. *(Photo: Malcolm Crowthers)*

The emotional fullness of her reunion at the end with her husband Faber will be signalled in like manner by an analogous gesture, an uprushing scale-passage that nearly saturates chromatic space. Adapting words from Virginia Woolf's *Between The Acts* the couple sing 'The curtain rises'. It has risen for them, and for Mel, who has somewhat found himself in Denise, and for Flora, no longer an Alice but a private woman (she departs 'alone, radiant, dancing').

Dov remains benighted. He will live further and find himself better in the *Songs for Dov* which Tippett conceived as a pendant to the opera.

The magical metaphor is not omitted in the closing scenes of *The Knot Garden*. All characters join to sing lines adapted from a poem by Goethe which apparently were inspiration for the opera from the earliest stage of its conception: 'We sense the magic net/ That holds us veined/ Each to each to all.' Though, by this time, Mangus has already broken his staff, drowned his book and told the audience that 'Prospero's a fake'. We remember the opera's epigraph, from the mouth of the rogue Parolles in *All's Well That End's Well*:

158

'. . . simply the thing I am/ Shall make me live.'

The achievement of *The Knot Garden* is remarkable on literary grounds alone. In his review of the first performance of *Songs for Dov* (which was premiered just before the opera in October 1970), Andrew Porter described Tippett's poem for *The Knot Garden* as 'one of the best librettos I know, as firmly structured for the theatre as *Hay Fever*, but as delicate, poetic and perceptive in its play of characters as Virginia Woolf's *Between the Acts*'.[2]

Other literary models and sources were skilfully incorporated into the text, for instance Bernard Shaw's *Heartbreak House*, T. S. Eliot's *The Cocktail Party*, Edward Albee's *Who's Afraid of Virginia Woolf?* and Christopher Fry's *A Sleep of Prisoners*. The latter, exploring the dramatological idea that characters might dream each other's dreams (a notion represented, we recall, to Alice by the Red King), was particularly influential on Tippett's second and third acts.

The pure verbal felicity of the libretto is everywhere in evidence. Not a word too many is used; not a quote but draws the fabric of the meaning

Dov (Nigel Robson) and Faber (Tom McDonnell) in the Opera Factory production of The Knot Garden. *Photo: Malcolm Crowthers)*

tighter; not an utterance that cannot be crisply set to music and gain its proper purpose there. The deployment of colloquialisms, 'blues' expressions and Shakespearean pastiche is always skilful and to the point. They are intended to stick out and be anachronistic; though criticism hasn't always recognised as much. The libretto is the only one possible for this opera; nothing else and no-one else's would do. *The Knot Garden* is an original work.

Cosi fan tutte, which is brought into a similar relation to *The Knot Garden* as *Die Zauberflote* was to *The Midsummer Marriage*, should probably be counted as a literary more than a musical analogue. There is little that is Mozartian about Tippett's music for either opera. But *The Knot Garden* music, while marking a new brashness and volatility in Tippett's style, does look back over the bony shoulder of the preceding opera, *King Priam*, to *Midsummer Marriage*'s outpourings of lyricism; and is a triumphant exercise in the synthesis of contradictory manners.

The major work that came before *The Knot Garden* in Tippett's oeuvre was *The Vision of Saint Augustine*, another synthesis of his early ecstatic lyricism and later declamatory brilliance. The oratorio's preoccupation with time and eternity is distant from *The Knot Garden's* ostensibly mundane concern. But in the new choral-instrumental *The Mask of Time*, at once zany and transcendental, we can begin to perceive what the *Vision* and *The Knot Garden* might actually have in common.

The brashness, bristling inventiveness and kaleidoscopic orchestration of *The Knot Garden* make it Tippett's most immediately effective theatrical work, and the chamber version of the opera now available makes a direct communication more direct still. It confirms the work as 'music theatre' – that pre-eminently 1960s genre of which *The Knot Garden* may even yet come to be seen as the most successful and moving example.

NOTES
1. Ian Kemp, Tippett: The Composer and His Music. (Eulenberg Books), pp 401
2. *Financial Times*, 14 October 1970.

RAYMOND FURNESS

Goethe and Tippett

Lila and The Knot Garden

'THE FIRST German I ever spoke was the German of Goethe. Of his time I think I am more conscious than of any other in Germany.'[1]: this quotation comes from Sir Michael Tippett's *Moving into Aquarius* (1959), more specifically from that chapter entitled 'Persönliches Bekenntnis', *Bekenntnis* meaning a confession of faith, an acknowledgement of his indebtedness to the great figures of the German cultural tradition. Tippett's knowledge of German literature is profound (perhaps there has never been such a literate composer since Richard Wagner); *Moving into Aquarius* refers to Brecht, Peter Weiss, Hoffmann, Kafka, Kokoschka, Thomas Mann and Schiller, and there are quotations from Hölderlin, Rilke and George. The later collection of sketches and essays, *Music of the Angels* (1980) is likewise rich in reference to German literary figures, including Ödön von Horváth. But references to Goethe and his genius predominate: *Moving into Aquarius* speaks of Goethe as scientist, as traveller, as creator of *Iphigenie* and *Faust*, of Goethe and his relationship with Beethoven, of Goethe as extoller of that 'ewiges lebendiges Tun!', that endless vital activity which refreshes and remoulds the rigid into pulsating life. And the second collection of essays, appearing some twenty years later, will likewise contain substantial references to him: the influence of the 'Prologue in Heaven' from *Faust I* on the sketches for *A Child of Our Time*, for example; the power of *Götz von Berlichingen*; Goethe and Schopenhauer and, most moving of all, Tippett speaks of that luminous scene from the end of *Wilhelm Meisters Wanderjahre* where Wilhelm, gazing down at the naked body of his son, wounded after the fall with his horse into the river, speaks those mysterious words: 'Wirst du doch immer aufs neue hervorgebracht, herrlich Ebenbild Gottes! Und wirst sogleich wieder beschädigt, verletzt, von innen oder von außen' ('Yet you will always be brought forth again, glorious image of God, likewise to be maimed, wounded afresh, from within and without'[2]) – the closing scene of *The Ice Break* is here, whose androgynous Astron seems an exemplification of the Goethean reconciliation of opposites. In this present article, however, I am concerned above all with that fascinating and little known work by Goethe, *Lila*, a *Singspiel* which could also be called a psycho-drama (see J. L. Moreno's use of the term in *Gruppentheorie und Psychodrama*, Stuttgart 1959[3]), a strikingly modern exploration of the cure of mental derangement; in Goethe's own words 'eine psychische Kur, wo man den Wahnsinn eintreten läßt, um den Wahnsinn zu heilen' (to Graf Brühl, 1.10.1818). Group therapy, music, dance and the externalisation of the patient's neuroses in differing shapes and forms will effect a remarkable cure of pathological melancholia: the relevance of this to one of Tippett's works I hope to prove.

Lila, if referred to at all, is normally held to be little more than a gallant offering, performed in 1777 in Weimar to alleviate the pronounced introspection of the Duchess Luise; it is forgotten that the original protagonist was male (that is, Baron Sternthal), a figure somewhat akin to the hero of Jean de Rotrou's *L'hypochondriaque ou le mort amoureux*. In this first version the part of the Doctor-Magus was played by Goethe himself, but there is much of Goethe in Sternthal, the introspection, self-laceration and melancholy, for example. Or, rather, it is true to say that Goethe is both – the wise counsellor who advises action *and* the introverted victim. It became apparent that Goethe was dissatisfied with the work, and the second version, dating from the following year, demonstrates a significant shift of emphasis. Goethe was well aware of the dangers of morbid introspection: he had visited Plessing in Wernigerode in November 1777, feeling partly responsible for the young man's 'Empfindsamkeitskrankheit', but a greater tragedy made him aware of woman's plight – the suicide of Christiane von Laßberg on 17 January 1778, whose body was found in the river Ilm not far from Goethe's 'Gartenhaus'; it was claimed that a copy of *Die Leiden des jungen Werthers* was found in her clothing. A mind darkened, deranged and ultimately self-destructive: the sorrows of young Werther, that paradigm of narcissistic solipsism, had wrought much confusion in the minds of young people, and Goethe sensed that some expiation or, at least, salutary guidance, was necessary. The protagonist is now Lila herself, not her husband. False news of his death has thrown her into an extreme state of depression: unable to grasp the fact that he lives and is well she persists in believing that he is in the grip of a fearful demon, and shuns her family and friends. The Doctor-Magus realises that a cure can only be brought about by acting out the story of her madness before her, by bringing her into the action as an active and responsible agent, to help her to 'free' her husband and return him to her. Relations and friends act the various parts – fairies, spirits and the ogre; by attempting to understand her fantasies, by a form of group therapy, Lila's isolation is overcome and she is restored to mental health. And music therapy is also most important here: this is a psychodrama but also a *Singspiel* for which music was provided by F. L. Seidel and also Karl Seckendorff (who also wrote the music for other minor works by Goethe, for example *Jery und Bätely* and *Der Triumph der Empfindsamkeit*). It should be remembered that music plays an important part as healing agent in *Der Zauberflöte zweiter Teil* (where Tamino and Pamina are saved from melancholy by Papageno's playing the flute), that Egmont's slumbers are charmed by music, and that music (again the flute) renders violence unnecessary in Goethe's *Novelle*. Gentleness and music are essential in this cure, yet shock-treatment is also not ruled out – the Doctor-Magus sees that the sight of the ogre must needs stir Lila's powers of determination when a relapse into depression seems imminent. She must not simply defy the ogre, but must identify with his 'victims'; a sick imagination gives way to an active imagination, and solipsism gives way to understanding, contact and involvement. Lila sees that her guilt lies in her isolation, her delay and her morbidity; the ritual dances, embraces, participation, – group therapy, in fact, – cure her. An ice-break, if you will.

The third version dates from Goethe's first visit to Italy; in 1788 he re-worked the second version and included a second pair of characters, Graf Friedrich and Marianne, Graf Sternthal's sister, whose affection, in good *opera buffa* style, acts as a light-hearted counterpoint to the potentially tragic relationship between husband and wife. This version was first printed in volume six of the Göschen *Gesammelte Schriften* of 1790 (the same volume, interestingly enough, contained *Torquato Tasso*, another portrayal of a figure prone to delusion, misanthropy and potential derangement): the title-page bore as a vignette the drawing by H. Lips of *Die gefesselte Psyche*, Psyche in chains.[4]. This is entirely appropriate for, in the words of Gottfried Diener, 'die gemütskranke, vom Dämon des Wahnsinns gefesselte Lila ist eben die leidende Psyche . . .':[5] this remarkable *Singspiel*, then, becomes an anticipation of certain preoccupations of German expressionism, a psychodrama which portrays the inner workings of a human mind under stress. By externalising Lila's hallucinations the Doctor-Magus (or 'auxiliary ego') brings to the surface and exorcises the latent fears which could well prove destructive: ballet, mime and song complete and enhance the ritual cleansing.

To return to Michael Tippett: his opera *The Knot Garden*, first performed at Covent Garden in 1970, bears striking resemblances to Goethe's *Singspiel*. In Tippett's work a group of characters, directed by a fatherly analyst, are made to act out the fantasies of their inner lives in a process of self-development; in the words of Martin Cooper an expressionistic 'in depth' drama is enacted and sung before us, aimed at 'a general catharsis'.[6] The knot-garden (an Elizabethan term, denoting a maze) is an externalisation of the knot of tied-up souls who seek resolution and peace; with Tippett there are three couples, with Goethe two, with the husband-wife relationship the dominant one. In Tippett the shifting shapes of the maze reflect the lability of their personalities; in Goethe the park gives way to a 'Rauher Wald, im Grunde eine Höhle' ('a wild forest, with a cave in the background') when the shock-treatment is necessary. Thea, in *The Knot Garden*, has retreated into the private world of her garden, much as Lila persists in wandering 'an der hinteren Seite des Parks [. . .] sie schläft des Tags in der Hütte [. .] vermeidet alle Menschen und wandelt des Nachts in ihren Phantasien herum'[7] ('on the furthermost edge of the park . . . she sleeps during the day in the hut, shuns everybody and wanders about at night in a dream world'). It is for Mangus the analyst to come to Thea's aid, to restore the marriage between her and Faber to health, just as he must help the adolescent ward

Ariel's flight in Act III of
The Knot Garden,
*with Flora (Janis Kelly)
and Mangus (Philip
Doghan).
(Photo: Malcolm
Crowthers)*

Flora, Thea's sister Denise, the writer Mel and the musician Dov. It has been claimed that the name Mangus 'derives from Boss Mangan in *Heartbreak House';*[8] it would surely have been more plausible to remember Goethe's Magus (that is, Dr Varazio), who stage-manages the different events. He is the one who knows: 'Wenn wir Phantasie durch Phantasie kurieren könnten, so hätten wir ein Meisterstück gemacht'[9] ('fantasy cured by fantasy would indeed be a masterpiece').

The references to *Heartbreak House*, however, should make us pause. Tippett himself explained the literary traditions behind his opera in a talk given before the first performance in 1970, and certainly mentions Shaw's play, a play about a set of characters gathered together somewhat arbitrarily in a house and garden where they play out a pattern or game of cross-relationships. Yet Mangan is not singled out in any way as being the prime catalyst. Tippett also refers to Albee's *Who's afraid of Virginia Woolf*, where the cross-relationships are reduced to four people, where the older couple know that they are playing out the ritual game. Most important: Shakespeare's *The Tempest* provides many of the games for the last act, games centred on forgiveness and reconciliation. Mangus will play Prospero, and 'put them all to rights' – there is no reference to Goethe. But this does not invalidate the present argument: Tippett's talk was meant to clarify the possible influences for an Anglo-American audience, and references to Shakespeare, Shaw and Albee are more appropriate; his essays and sketch-books are more suitable places for recondite allusions.

164

Thea in her garden, Lila in her park, the enchained Psyche longing for release, for that 'Exit from the inner cage' which Tippett speaks of in his final ensemble in *The Knot Garden* – it is love, gentleness and understanding that can release them. In Tippett's opera it is husband and wife who achieve the most durable reconciliation and reach an almost archetypal status; the other couples, we know, are not so blessed. The work is open-ended, whereas *Lila* is not. Yet *Lila* has no facile solution: although the heroine and her husband are reunited there had been relapses on her part, particularly at the end of Act Two, where she laments that love and goodness 'fließt mir wie klares Wasser durch die fassenden Hände',[10] (that they 'flow through her grasping hands like crystal water'). It is of interest that *Lila*, as has been stated, appeared in the same volume as *Torquato Tasso*, an analysis of confusion and suspicion which is likewise open-ended: is Tasso saved or not? Neat solutions do not appeal to the twentieth-century mind, and Goethe is remarkably modern in the way in which, especially in his late work, his attitude to form becomes curiously nonchalant. *Wilhelm Meisters Wanderjahre*, for example, quoted by Tippett as we know, is an aggregate of highly disparate pieces – *Novellen* (one of which is not even by Goethe, but a translation from the French), aphorisms, anecdotes and poems which Goethe did not even select himself: he placed before Eckermann certain bundles of papers and asked him to sort out sufficient material to pad out the novel. Tippett's *The Knot Garden* is likewise a montage, the libretto ranging from blank verse in the manner of T. S. Eliot, through prose

Ariel's flight, showing London Sinfonietta conducted by Howard Williams. (Photo: Malcolm Crowthers)

165

dialogue to slang and contemporary jargon which is strangely juxtaposed with quotations from *The Tempest*, whereas the musical language comprises dodecaphony, traditional harmony, Charles Ives, blues and an obvious allusion to Schubert: Flora's singing of 'Mein Schatz hat Grün so gern'. Acquainted as he was with Goethe's great novel, 'a novel which is quirky, strangely beautiful, remote, sometimes theoretically dry but again often as startlingly direct in physical impact as the later quartets of Beethoven',[11] Tippett knew that the most incongruous elements can exist side by side; he must also have been struck by the simple and yet profound aphorism from the section entitled 'Aus Makariens Archiv', the last of the *Wanderjahre* before 'Schillers Reliquien': Man wird nie betrogen, man betrügt sich selbst.'

One is not deceived, one deceives one's self. Is this not Lila's situation, finally? Is not perhaps all mental illness self-deception? The news of her husband's death was false enough, yet her constant refusal to admit his existence, the relegation of which, as well as of the whole of the surrounding world to 'Schattenbilder, und von den Geistern unterschobene Gestalten'[12] (to 'shadowy forms, shapes which the spirits have substituted') – her paranoid schizophrenia, in fact – is a self-delusion that can only be cured by a development or enrichment of these illusions. Through music and a fantasy world Thea and Faber are saved; Lila is restored to Sternthal. That art, the supreme illusion, that music above all enhances, controls and transfigures, is a knowledge that links Germany's greatest writer to a supremely talented twentieth-century English composer.

NOTES
1. M. Tippett: *Moving into Aquarius* (Paladin Books, London, 1974) p118
2. *Music of the Angels. Essays and Sketchbooks of Michael Tippett*, Ed. Meirion Bowen (London: Eulenberg Books 1980) p208
3. On J. L. Moreno see *Goethes Lila: Heilung eines Wahnsinns durch 'Psychische Kur'* by Gottfried Diener, Frankfurt a.M., 1971, to which I am much indebted.
4. See Diener: *op. cit.*, p258, for the illustration.
5. Diener: *op. cit.*, pp26-27
6. In *A Man of our Time* (London, 1977) p94
7. Goethe: *Sämmtliche Werke* (in 30 vols) (Stuttgart, Cotta, 1858) vol 8, p143
8. D. Matthews: *Michael Tippett. An introductory study* (London, 1980) p83
9. Goethe: *op. cit.*, p146
10. Goethe: *op. cit.*, p155
11. See R. T. Llewellyn's article: 'Parallel Attitudes to Form in late Beethoven and Goethe', in *Modern Language Review*, April 1968, Nr. 2, p408
12. Goethe: *op. cit.*, pp139-40

CHACONNE
– in homage to Sir Michael Tippett

Jeffrey Lewis

168

JOHN McCABE
The Third Symphony

MORE THAN most composers, Tippett seems to be able to specify precisely when the inspiration for his major works occurred, or at least to point to the moment when the basic idea crystallised in his mind. One thinks of the pounding bass Cs in a Vivaldi work that prompted the Second Symphony, or the Gieseking performance of Beethoven's Fourth Piano Concerto that impelled him to write his Piano Concerto. In the case of the Third Symphony he admits to an equally specific occasion, a performance at the Edinburgh Festival in 1965 of a modern work in which, as he says, he was hearing 'a very "motionless" modern music: it hadn't a harmonic or rhythmic or any other sort of drive that I could hear . . . I kept saying to myself . . . "I don't see how I could ever use this kind of thing for expressive purposes unless it were part of a piece based upon sharp contrasts".' (The work in question was *Pli selon pli*.)

The symphony as a whole is divided into two parts, each of two movements, and built out of the idea of contrast. In the fast opening movement of Part One, this is clearly the difference between two sets of ideas, the chordal brass and percussion material marked 'Arrest' (burgeoning out as the movement develops into fanfare-like figuration), and the faster, rhythmically more complex block marked 'Movement'.

The two blocks alternate, with greater length and developmental sophistication each time, until finally they are combined in a section whose growing tension and juxtaposition of previously disparate ideas seems to be leading to a cataclysmic explosion. Suddenly the music turns a corner – the cataclysm is reserved for the famous quotation from Beethoven's Ninth Symphony at the start of the second movement of Part Two, and instead – the sharpest and cleanest contrast one could have – there begins a 'nocturnal' slow movement of the utmost beauty. No preamble, no linking, no cinematic fade – just the direct opposition of two types of music.

This 'nocturne' (a useful handle to describe a superficial approach to the movement, but not really a satisfactory name for it) comprises a different kind of contrast, between high and low. Again, two blocks of material are alternated: music of the night and the stars which is mostly fairly high, and music of the deep sea, the tidal wave below – a very slow contrapuntal-cum-

169

harmonic ascent from the lowest strings, starting at Figure 115. In the whole of this symphony, throughout which Tippett's acute and subtle control of harmonic colouring is consistently at its finest, there is surely no more moving or delicately poised a series of harmonies as in this string section, slowly rising and becoming more impassioned as violins and increased woodwind doublings add to the richness of the music. There are typical examples of string scoring – the high violas, on top of the texture instead of in the middle even when the violins are taking part, remind one of the imaginative sound-world created by Tippett's highly individual sense of string balance in the Concerto for Orchestra's slow movement with its high, elaborate cello part, for instance. There is something very *Tempest*-like about this movement and it is indeed no surprise that Tippett has written music for a production of the play – one that means a great deal to him, as he has demonstrated, most notably, in *The Knot Garden*. Like Sibelius, whose *Tempest* music shows an uncanny sense of the play's heightened imaginative world, Tippett has a natural sensitivity to this kind of positive magic.

Whereas the first movement seems to be 'developing' towards a climactic point (which is, as I have said, abruptly side-stepped or postponed), the second movement of the symphony does not, although it uses similar methods of development by constantly shifting juxtaposition of the two blocks of material. True, it seems to be moving towards a greater intensification of the contrast between the blocks, but even this does not really come to a head, and the music fades out delicately into nothingness – a lovely, hauntingly melodic, static movement. The contrast in the 'scherzo' which forms the first movement of Part Two is the most traditional kind – simply a more 'thematic' contrast between various ideas, defined both by their melodic or harmonic identity and by their instrumental sound-world. Jubilant, virtuosic horns (reminiscent of the scintillating writing in the Sonata for four horns), galumphing cellos and basses, brilliant scurrying semi-quavers on the violins, a resounding and strongly etched chordal theme in the woodwinds, and a long-breathed, almost concerto-like theme for the piano are the elements in what the composer has called a 'play of five different musics . . . that hardly change at all in themselves but do change in their relationship with each other'. Here again, the juxtaposition of different materials is Tippett's method of building, but this time the mosaic-like handling of individual themes, rather than more complex blocks of ideas, reminds one of the Concerto for Orchestra (especially, in view of the music's tremendous energy, its finale) more than the first two movements of this symphony. The music testifies not only to Tippett's ability to refer back to a work of nearly a decade earlier and use its techniques with complete freshness, but also to the influence of Ives on him – at the scherzo's peak, the complexity of sound is due to the fact that the five 'musics' are sounding simultaneously, like the several bands in Ives' *General Putnam's Camp*.

As this movement reaches its climax, we seem once again to be approaching a major climactic point in the whole work, and after a sharp cut-off and a brief pause it turns out to be a cataclysm – the one delayed from the first movement. It is the strength of the work as a convincing entity that the impact of this moment is enhanced by this long delay and by the richness of the music which has intervened. At any rate, what bursts out into the symphony, and what astonished and puzzled many listeners when the work was new, is the dramatic and violent presto opening to the finale of Beethoven's Ninth Symphony. There are nine bars of it, as suddenly halted as it was begun, and replaced, in a touching yet powerful contrast, by a sad phrase in the divided violas redolent of loss, agonised tenderness, mercy. Rachmaninov used to say that every work had one pivotal point on which the whole turned, not necessarily the loudest bit, or the final climax, nor indeed inevitably placed towards the end. It seems to me that the confrontation between these two powerful, directly communicative musical images and the significance of the contrast between them is the fulcrum on which this symphony rests, and it makes a perfect point from which the music can go on (again with no linking passage but, as so often in this work, with the equivalent of a clean, cinematic cut) into its vocal finale, a set of four blues numbers for soprano and orchestra to Tippett's own texts. The blues idiom is captured immediately, with a flugelhorn solo (inspired by the Bessie Smith/ Louis Armstrong record of *St Louis Blues*, and maybe also by Miles Davis' rather more gnomic flugelhorn playing, so rich in implied gesture) starting even on the first chord. Two sharp contrasts in style (the Beethoven and the sad viola phrase) could easily in themselves be confusing. To add an immediate change to yet a third style – for the jazz idiom is a major new element in the makeup of the music – could throw the symphony off balance. Indeed, one is aware that there are listeners who feel that it does. For me, however, the point now reached is perfectly balanced by the confrontation discussed above, and the blues style seems an utterly natural direction for the music to take.

Quotation from other composers and deliberate use of a wide variety of styles can bring their own dangers. There is sometimes a feeling that composers who consciously 'use' the work of others in this way are bolstering up their own music by feeding parasitically off others, that they have lost their way and cannot find it without relying on this kind of self-conscious reference to other music. There is even the danger that the composers could be accused of not being able to say what they want to say in their own music, that their limitations are so great that they have to rely on Elgar, Schubert, Beethoven or whoever, to say it for them. But if a composer of Tippett's stature uses this device, especially one whose career is marked by a strong interest in other musics, then its significance must be taken to be serious and unselfconscious. It is, after all, not the first time he has done such a thing – in *Songs for Dov* and the opera to which both that and this symphony relate, *The Knot Garden*, he uses direct classical references, and one can think back to his use of the Negro spirituals in *A Child of Our Time*, which he makes so much his own.

So we arrive at a vocal finale, influenced by the symphonic element inherent in Mahler's *Das Lied von der Erde*, in which the symphony's last and most difficult conjuring trick is performed, that of balancing several different

171

styles and making them cohere into one unit. The four blues pursue a course taking us from the sensual and sexual pleasure of the first two, a slow, hauntingly beautiful number and then a more acerbic, fast 'walking' blues, through the richly compassionate warmth of the third, to the great vision encompassed in the final *scena*. It is worth commenting, by the way, on the manner in which Tippett not merely uses another 'music' and makes it his own, but also uses its clichés, uses their resonances to create, as it were by a reverse image, a completely new significance for them. It is a process akin to that in films of using type-casting to create a shock – cast Henry Fonda, such a natural *Young Mr Lincoln*, as an out-and-out nasty in *Once Upon a Time in the West*, and this 'reverse' casting uses the resonance of the typical Fonda character to make the new identity even stronger. So it is here in this symphony – the wonderfully fluid flugelhorn solo above bluesy chords in the first number uses some familiar types of jazz phraseology in a way that gives them complete newness.

The Beethoven presto introduction recurs once more as a *tutti*, and later in a more fragmented form. After the *tutti* reappearance Tippett then quotes (partly canonically) the cello/bass recitative theme from the Beethoven finale to lead into the fourth and final blues number. It is here that the philosophical contrast underlying the work is laid bare, and it is the text that makes it as clear as possible – the *Ode to Joy* was a chimera, men are not brothers, it is not possible, after the horrors of this century, to have the same kind of belief that Schiller/Beethoven showed:

> They sang that when she waved her wings,
> The Goddess Joy would make us one.
>
> And did my brother die of frost-bite in the camp?
> And was my sister charred to cinders in the oven?

Tippett's handling of these opening four lines is especially remarkable. In the vigorous, dynamic music for the first two, the enormously wide-ranging thematic and rhythmic material is underpinned by the constant presence of the famous main tune of the Beethoven '*Ode to Joy*', impregnating the texture and becoming, despite its direct quotation, pure Tippett by association. The third and fourth lines (another direct confrontation between types of music) are given the context of another quotation, this time from the night sky music of the 'nocturnal' second movement of this symphony. It is an extraordinary moment, for this music, so magical and hypnotically evocative in its original place, is suddenly given a completely different significance and meaning by its association with the text – Tippett can take even his own music, just as he takes the Beethoven or the blues idiom (or even the Negro spiritual), and somehow make it different by placing it so securely in a different context.

The allusiveness of Tippett's music is, as always, reinforced by the equally referential nature of his texts. Tippett's own libretti have always given trouble, even to his admirers, especially in the works following *The Midsummer Marriage* (which to my mind has a magnificent text), and it might be true to say that he is not so fine a writer of words as he is of notes. But his words

172

usually seem to me exceptionally well integrated with the music, as ought to be the case when the writer of both is the same person, and certainly they provide, in a sense, a kind of music of their own which becomes an essential part of the music of the whole. In this, as in other texts, one can spot all kinds of influences, including Blake, Martin Luther King ('I have a dream'), the surrealism of such writers as Arp and Schwitters ('O, I'll go prancing with my toe-tips/Flying'), and Eliot. The words of these blues have, despite the disparate influences, a rare cohesion, and a visionary power which matches precisely the gradual build-up of philosophical and musical tension during this movement.

Tippett has long been a composer concerned to express and explore paradox – 'I would know my shadow and my light' (*A Child of Our Time*) could almost sum up the completeness of his insight into the essential paradox of human nature. So in this work he explores, perhaps as wide-rangingly as he has ever done,[1] the same theme, from stylistic symphony, to the various kinds of paradox in this last movement's text. Nowhere is his compassion more clearly felt than in the third blues, with the ineffably moving setting of the third verse:

> I found the beautiful moronic child.
> His smiling eyes shone bright; he said:
> Nothing; for his mind is lost.

The confrontation between the belief of Schiller/Beethoven and the reality of the twentieth century carries us to the central dilemma at the heart of Tippett's art: what can we believe in? His answer, as always, is an affirmation of life and of compassion, and the argument pursued in both words and music of the final blues whirls us to the conclusion:

> We sense a huge compassionate power
> To heal
> To love.

Right to the end the confrontation between musics persists, strong brass chords related to those at the start of the work alternating with soft, gentle strong chords. It is the low strings who have the last sound, a reminder that compassion and mercy have their own quiet strength. So much of Tippett's music, including a great deal of this work, has a life-enhancing positiveness of thought – like so many of the endings of his pieces, this conclusion is, as it were, merely a sign that the dialogue is ended in a formal sense but will go on in the air about us. Above all else, what is so moving about this symphony, apart from the sheer exuberance of the thought, is that Tippett conveys so vividly, as few composers since Beethoven have been able to (Vaughan Williams and Nielsen spring to mind as exceptional), his understanding of both sides of humanity, and his understanding that both are positive aspects of the life-force.

NOTES
1. Prior to *The Mask of Time*, anyway.

Tippett acknowledging the ovation following the European première at the Proms of The Mask of Time, *conducted by Andrew Davis.*

PETER DENNISON

Tippett and the New Romanticism

THAT THERE have been fundamental shifts of emphasis in society in general, and in the arts in particular, since the mid-1960s is now widely recognised. After the Second World War, there was an overwhelming demand for stability, and throughout Western society this ushered in a new reign of order and authority, a rigorous uniformity in political and social expectations, and in many spheres of the arts. This amounted to no less than a new authoritarianism which stood as powerfully for reconstruction as it stood against the bogey of Communism. It was characterised by the dictates of McCarthy and Adenauer, and a passive acceptance of Korea and the nuclear build-up. The 1960s witnessed a sharp reaction against this world. Whole new sets of values surfaced with an explosion of diversification within Western society: a revitalised and powerful popular culture, the rise of active 'minority' groups, blacks, women and gays, the assertion of the young in the student revolts towards the end of the 60s, and finally the anti-war movement that culminated in the withdrawal from Vietnam. These changes welled up from deep within society, and it was inevitable that the arts, which continue to interact intimately with the basic impluses of society, should erupt in changes no less radical.

Such basic reorientations are not new to Western society, and a number of commentators have proposed that throughout the course of modern history there has been broadly an alternation of periods when the classical values of order and stability have been uppermost, and periods when diversity and change, values identified with the romantic ideal, have prevailed. Writing in 1980, John Warrack implicitly recognised this dichotomy when he identified a romantic period as one in which there is 'an apparent domination of instinct over reason, of imagination over form, of heart over head, of Dionysos over Apollo'. Each of Warrack's first features is as characteristic of the artistic climate since the mid-60s as it was of the early nineteenth century, and each of the alternatives is as characteristic of the two post-war decades as it was of the late eighteenth century. In June 1983, the New York Philharmonic mounted a festival with the theme 'Since 1968, a New Romanticism?', and in its six concerts, its forums and literary articles, the artistic director, Jacob Druckman, made a powerful case for the identification of a recognisable new Romanticism in music.

The principal impluse of much art music composed since the mid-60s has been towards a rediscovery of the self, and with it the capacity of music to express the deepest concern of the self, and to transport the self to new thresholds of experience. Within the new aesthetic, music has become a medium through which the composer has sought to communicate a heightened artist's response to the world, and to elicit a sympathetic emotional response from his listener. The stimulus might be an aspect of nature, the interactions of men, social and political phenomena, or some interaction of all of these. The new music reflects a conspicuous value placed on the instinctive, the suprarational, and on the probings of psychology. A further characteristic has been an exploration of the power of the associative. Many composers have appropriated passages of pre-existent music with demonstrably extra-musical communicative intention. The appropriated music can range from mere fragments which act as a brief reminiscence, to whole episodes or even a whole movement which can be subjected to complex reworking. Some composers have taken musical styles from non-Western cultures, and their intention has often been to propose some renewal of our society by the introduction of the art of another which may be in some way more whole. Behind the implicit belief in music's capacity to arouse the emotions there has been among some composers the assumption that music possesses an ethical power capable of alerting individual men to social and political issues. These factors constitute the essence of the new aesthetic of music that has prevailed in the last two decades, and confirm its identification with the Romantic ideal.

The new Romanticism found a distinctive musical expression particularly among a group of composers who, in 1965, were still in their thirties. With hindsight, one can recognise in such otherwise distinctive composers as Berio, Crumb, Takemitsu, Meale, Penderecki and Maxwell Davies, a similarity of artistic intention and communicative means that has done much to define the new Romanticism in music. Although the consolidation of the new aesthetic has tended to be gradual, and in the case of some composers spread over more than a decade, it has now matured with sufficient significant works to confirm the common basis of the movement. It is recognisable as a common denominator in works such as Crumb's *Echoes of Time and the River* (1967), Takemitsu's *November Steps* (1967), Berio's *Sinfonia* (1968–69), Penderecki's Violin Concerto (1976) and Second Symphony (1980), Maxwell Davies' two symphonies (1976 and 1980), and Meale's *Viridian* (1979) and Second String Quartet (1980). Over and above this basis, each of these works bears the distinctive stylistic imprint of its composer, and a uniformity of style is no more to be found in this music than it was in the greatest music written in the rich decade prior to the First World War. Nevertheless, much of the music of the new Romanticism shares some common technical orientation. The search for new thresholds of experience has led to an exploration of the sensual, the mysterious, the ecstatic and the terrifying. These have been sought through a renewed interest in the soothing and disturbing capacities of orchestral timbre and evocative harmony, in melody and lyricism, and in the energetic capacities of counterpoint. Composers have also explored the emotive potential of long,

176

cumulative episodes which have a gathering propulsion towards a recognisable goal. The aesthetic basis of the music of the new Romanticism, and its technical foundations represent a radical change from the music of the post-war, post-Webern avant garde. There, in the work of Boulez, Babbitt, Xenakis and Carter, an extreme rationalism and rigorous formalism became a means of transcending the imagined limitations of subjectivism in music that sought no rationale external to itself.

In 1965 Michael Tippett turned 60, and although he was twenty years older than Berio, and almost thirty years older than Maxwell Davies, from the mid-1960s his music also began to show significant stylistic and technical changes that bear a recognisable affinity with the impluses of the new Romanticism. A new sensuality replaced the uncompromising neo-classicism of the previous decade, and this became more prominent with almost each successive new work. The changes in Tippett's music stemmed from modifications in his musical language, a language that had been restlessly evolving throughout his entire composing life. These changes in his creative means implied, however, no alteration in his creative intentions or artistic philosophy, both of which had been determined decades earlier, and had been confirmed by his subsequent hard-won experience.

The essence of Tippett's artistic philosophy had always been his concern for the human condition, and with it the discovery of the self. He has constantly articulated the search for the real self through the metaphors of Jungian psychology. 'I would know my shadow and my light / so shall I at last be whole,' he affirmed in Part III of *A Child of Our Time* (1939–41), and the quest for wholeness through self-knowledge lies at the heart of *The Midsummer Marriage* (1946–51). In 1951 Tippett wrote of 'our prolonged catastrophe',[2] and clarified his meaning with the metaphor of 'moving into Aquarius'.[3] Externally he was alluding to the wholesale dislocations of people that had taken place in Europe during the previous two decades, but he was also reacting to an art (and he cited Picasso and Joyce in particular) whose absolutes were uncompromising pure abstraction, and soulless dislocation. He saw art at that time going through the death-throes of the age of Pisces, 'of ideological purity and fratricide',[4] but believed that this would yield to the birth of the age of Aquarius, 'of compassion and attempted union of the opposites'.[5] He went on to affirm his belief 'that modern man can find his soul is true. That art will speak again entire is as sure as the Zodiac'.[6] Tippett made his own role, and with it that of the artist, in the birth of the new age clear: 'That I (and my betters) belong body and soul to [this] artistic midwifery . . . is our pride.'

Tippett's appeal to the inner world of the self and subjective perceptions has been made, in the spirit of Jungian psychology, through the creation of images; he believes that 'it is only through images that the inner world communicates at all'.[8] Writing in the mid-60s, he elaborated on the nature of those images in a passage that could well serve as his artistic manifesto while it almost uncannily anticipates the communicative aspirations of composers identified with the new Romanticism over a decade later. 'Images of the past, shapes of the future. Images of vigour for a decadent period, images of calm for one too violent.

Images of reconciliation for worlds torn by division. And in an age of mediocrity and shattered dreams, images of abounding, generous, exuberant beauty.'[9]

These words, written when a substantial number of avant garde composers were going through a decade and a half of extreme formalism, were both courageous and prophetic. They also demonstrate that despite the constant evolution in Tippett's musical language, his artistic philosophy of humanism has remained steadfast even through times when it was out of step with prevailing aesthetic currents. Almost a generation older than many of that avant garde, Tippett has seen the tide turn, and many of the artistic values that he so eloquently and so singly upheld in a previous age become, in his latter years, adopted by many of the most significant composers of a younger generation.

After the musical luxuriance of *The Midsummer Marriage*, Tippett's musical style and technique moved towards a more astringent economy of means, a more violently disjunct melodic and harmonic language, and a concern for formal symmetries that gave it an affinity with neo-classical practice, and with Stravinsky in particular. This was anticipated in the Second Symphony (1956–7) which emulated the neo-classicism of Stravinsky's *Symphony in Three Movements* and *Symphony in C*. Tippett's neo-classicism was given a sharper edge through the influence of Stravinsky's *Agon* which he heard in 1957, and this culminated in *King Priam* (1959–61) where his astringency was at its most powerfully uncompromising. He was consciously aware of this, and concerning *King Priam* he wrote in 1967: 'I found this style change immensely stimulating and exciting.'[10] This style found further expression in the Second Piano Sonata (1962), and the Concerto for Orchestra (1962–3). Such uncompromising neo-classicism appears at first sight to be contrary to Tippett's avowed aesthetic. However, he was appropriating only the techniques of neo-classicism in which he saw a means of concentrating and intensifying his communicative intentions; the latter remained unassailed, and distinctly different from those of the principal neo-classicists. 'Whereas Stravinsky used classical forms to highlight the objectivity of his music and Hindemith to demonstrate their relevance to a contemporary climate,' wrote Ian Kemp, 'Tippett was far more subjective, using them to express his personal belief that music symbolised a dramatic flow in the psyche and that dynamic musical forms representing both duality and singleness were paramount.'[11]

Tippett's next significant shift of stylistic emphasis, and that which is the principal concern of this study, was precipitated by his first visit to the United States in 1965. The much greater social and political diversity that he encountered there together with 'the candour, vitality and friendliness',[12] and the tensions that these diversities generated, must have served as an immediate challenge to his own social and artistic ideology. To a feted visitor, the States could still seem a land of golden promise, but in 1965, in the wake of the assassination of President Kennedy and amid the escalation of the war in Vietnam, growing sectors of American society were on the brink of a turbulence which Tippett's artistic perceptions cannot have failed to recognise. In the

178

course of return visits to the United States in subsequent years, he must have been confronted with issues that were erupting in protest and violence, and this can only have confirmed and vindicated his belief that wholeness in man lay in self-knowledge, and compassion.

Tippett's preoccupations with the multiple dynamics of personal interactions among people who all bear some scars of a diverse and fractured society were powerfully articulated in the first major work that followed his first visit to the United States, *The Knot Garden* (1966–9). He began the opera with a libretto dense with metaphor and illusion drawn from urban popular cultures of twentieth-century America, and as if to affirm how basic these were to the human condition, he fused into these characters, with the utmost illumination, personifications of archetypes drawn from *The Tempest*.

The Knot Garden did not exhaust the potential of its subject matter, and hard on the heels of the opera came the cycle *Songs for Dov* (1969–70) scored for tenor and reduced orchestral ensemble. In the opera, Dov, the homosexual singer, was one of seven characters engaged in complex counterpoints of personality. In the cycle, which follows him after the action of the opera, he becomes a personification of the romantic wanderer in search of his creative self, and these three songs trace the artist's pilgrimage at a crucial stage of his career through, in Tippett's own words, 'illusion and disillusion, innocence and experience . . . to reach what maturity [he] may'.[13] Tippett has acknowledged that there is a good deal of himself in Dov, and has suggested that Dov's pilgrimage is indeed his own.[14] *Songs for Dov* objectifies the artistic dilemma in which Tippett found himself towards the end of the 1960s, and it represents a crucial turning-point in his career.

Like Dov, Tippett was by the mid-60s, experienced enough to recognise the nature of his origins and his identity growing out of them. His dilemma lay in his recognition that at this particular juncture a whole new world of experience and choice lay before him. This grew out of his artistic response to the new social and aesthetic currents that were burgeoning at that time, and to the liberating experience of his own discovery of America. It lay further in what initially seemed to Tippett to be the irreconcilable nature of rhetoric and poetry.[15] By rhetoric he seems to have meant the capacity of art to act as a persuasive ethical force alerting men to the harsh realities of truth, and by poetry he seems to have meant the inclination of the artist to create from deep within his inner self works of alluring beauty. Throughout Tippett's text for the cycle, these conceptual opposites become metaphorically localised in the particular dichotomy of urban and rural living.

The cycle takes *The Knot Garden* as its starting point, and its first song is that which Dov sings to the troubled Flora at the end of Act II of the opera. It is structured on the musical pattern AAB, and its first two stanzas expose the artist's dilemma couched in the urban-rural metaphor. In the first stanza Dov establishes his urban origins, and in the second embarks on his journey of discovery 'to the warm south / or the golden Californian west'. Even here there is an immediate resonance of the 19th century Romantic aspiration that many northern Europeans felt for the south in general and Italy in particular. In the third stanza it becomes clear that when he begins his journey Dov is expecting to find eternal youth and love, his own version of the great American dream. This first song expresses boundless, untempered idealism, a modern song of innocence which serves as the point of departure for the cycle in more ways than one. As in the other songs, its text is peppered with American popular jargon although this is largely of an age earlier than the 60s, and it confirms that Tippett is seeking to reach a wider, more heterogeneous audience than in any work since *A Child of Our Time*.

The second song follows the artist's journey, and is made up of three stanzas, each with different music, and each followed by a recurrent refrain. In each stanza, Dov is confronted by a different challenge, and the experience of evaluating these brings him closer to self-knowledge. Each stanza begins with a musical and verbal quotation which particularly illuminates the nature of the challenge to Dov. At Fig. 31 Tippett quotes from Beethoven's song 'Kennst du das Land', Mignon's serenade of a distant land of unalloyed bliss. Tippett begins with an exact quotation from Beethoven, and the remoteness of this musical language from Tippett's own emphasises the unreality in contemporary terms of the ideal. The second stanza is introduced at Fig. 51 with the beginning of the first of Tippett's own *Songs for Ariel* (1962), 'Come unto these yellow sands'. The lure is to the land of 'gold sand and beaches', and by implication to the hope of eternal youth and love, but Dov journeys on. The third stanza begins at Fig. 70 with the seductive words of the Sirens from *The Odyssey*, and music drawn from *King Priam*, at the point where Paris, having invited Helen to join him, is left alone to ponder the fateful choice that confronts him. He can either satisfy his deepest desires by possessing Helen, or he can save Troy from the otherwise inevitable carnage by relinquishing her. This is a turning point for Paris, and so it is for Dov, and by implication for Tippett himself. Unlike Paris, Dov has by now developed through experience the insights that allow him to see that he has to reject the Sirens, but he does consider taking from them that which he did find of value, their song.

The third and most complex song returns to the urban-rural, rhetorical-poetic dichotomy, and explores something of the unfolding of experience after a crucial choice has been well made. As the artist completes his odyssey travelling 'full circle west', he is confronted by the reality of the rural ideal, and finds this to be far from the idealist's dream. In finding that 'the living language of our time is urban', he uncovers a reality that provides the ultimate solution to his dilemma. Through the experience of his journey, Dov has discovered that those opposites that seemed mutually exclusive, city and country, rhetoric and poetry, truth and beauty, can in reality be complementary, and have the capacity to enrich experience through their own particular attributes. Thus from the city the distances need not lose heart nor the earth feel lonely. The destination provided Tippett, in effect, with a renewed, but reconsidered affirmation of Keats's Romantic credo 'Beauty is truth, truth beauty'.[16] He recognised that what had previously seemed irreconcilable could serve as powerful complementary poles, which could generate between them creative currents capable of nourishing his work with renewed life in times to which his temperament found itself particularly attuned. Above all, he recognised with clarity that his art could proclaim ethical truth while creating 'images of abounding, generous, exuberant beauty'.[17] The 'union of opposites'[18] that Tippett resolved in *Songs for Dov* opened a whole spectrum of new creative vistas which he was to realise in the following decade and a half. In the course of this odyssey of creative renewal, Tippett explored a number of new musical techniques (some had originated in *The Knot Garden*) which he pursued further in later works, and which became particular imprints of his style while in many cases playing their part in defining the new Romanticism.

In both the music and text of *Songs for Dov*, Tippett appropriated pre-existent material as a potent communicative weapon. He had drawn on pre-existent music before, most notably the spirituals in *A Child of Our Time*, and in the *Fantasia Concertante on a Theme of Corelli*. In the former he had particular extra-musical intention while in the latter his rationale and treatment were intrinsically musical. Allusion in both *The Knot Garden* and *Songs for Dov* became more germane to the composer's dramatic intention, and from this time it became a significant facet of his work. The practice emerges from about this time as a powerful communicative device in a diversity of other music from Berio's *Sinfonia* to Penderecki's Second Symphony, and its rationale is closely associated with the aesthetic of the new Romanticism. In *Songs for Dov* the quotations from the opening of *The Flying Dutchman* first at Fig. 46 in the second song, and from the opening of *Boris Godunov* I, at Fig. 125 in the third song, prompt passing eternal association. On the other hand, the use of Beethoven's song and Tippett's own songs illuminate the choices facing Dov with multi-layered significance, and they become forceful agents in his odyssey. Such appropriation of music assumes an even more central role in Tippett's next major work, the Third Symphony, and verbal allusion reaches a level of complex subliminal counterpoint in the text of *The Mask of Time*.

The vocal writing in *Songs for Dov* is characterised by florid melismas which amalgamate idioms that Tippett elaborated from Purcell with aspects of Stravinsky's style of setting the English language in the 1940s and 50s. It could still be uncompromisingly disjunct, relying heavily on the intervals of the seventh and ninth. Amid the largely gaunt propulsions of much of the orchestral texture, there are some anticipations of the later, more sensuous and effulgent style. In each of three stanzas of the second song, the word 'sang' occupies a pivotal position both expressively and structurally. At Figs. 36, 55 and 77 it is introduced by a sweeping, rising glissando on strings and piano that creates an alluring aura which the voice takes up. The beguiling melisma that sets 'sang' has a similar contour at each statement; it accelerates rhythmically, and is accompanied by tensile tremulo octaves in the strings.

Taking its cue from *The Knot Garden*, *Songs for Dov* assigns a new prominence to complex rhythmic combinations of percussion instruments. The first two songs open thus as does the recurrent refrain in the second song at Figs. 44, 63 and 84. The percussion and jazz kit are prominent in the boogie-woogie episode in the third song at Fig. 118. This greater role for the percussion was explored further in the Arrest motives of the first movement of the Third Symphony, in

The Ice Break, the Triple Concerto and in *The Mask of Time*. In the cycle, however, it was the idiom itself that was appropriated, not specific pre-existent music, and in so far as this represents the enriching of Western art music with popular elements, it is a further symptom of the new Romanticism. Tippett went on to explore idioms of jazz more fully in his Third Symphony.

Songs for Dov marks a turning point in Tippett's artistic development. On one hand it is an allegory of the creatively liberating experiences of his discovery of America in the mid-60s, what he described as his 'Private Mayflower',[19] and on the other it is the actual labour through which he came to recognise the complementary nature of what had hitherto seemed opposites. Furthermore the solutions to spiritual and compositional problems that it provided contained the seeds of musical potential that Tippett explored with a surge of creativity in the major works that lay ahead.

Each of the major works of the period that began with *Songs for Dov* takes up from its immediate predecessor specific extra-musical concerns, or compositional issues, and sometimes both. Thus there is between these works a pervasive aesthetic and musical bond which is a product of the extreme concentration of Tippett's mature creativity together with the singularity of his desire to communicate with an ever wider public. Although first thoughts of the Third Symphony date from 1965, Tippett did not begin sustained work on it, and probably could not have done, until 1970 after he had gone through the experiences of *Songs for Dov*. After that watershed, it is significant that he threw his creative energies first into the altogther greater complexities of the Symphony, and completed it in March 1972.

Like *Songs for Dov*, the Third Symphony created, and then solved its major technical issues as it took shape, and these all grew out of Tippett's explicit ethical purpose. The goal of the work is the finale in which Tippett returned to the ideal of a universal brotherhood under a benign godhead celebrated by Beethoven with Schiller's *Ode to Joy* in the Ninth Symphony towards the beginning of the last Romantic period. Tippett questions whether, in the face of the wholesale inhumanity of man to man which the twentieth century has witnessed, Beethoven's ideal could validly be sustained. In ultimately rejecting that ideal, Tippett proposed alternatively for this age an affirmative celebration of man himself utterly independent of any godhead, and able to achieve wholeness through self-knowledge, and 'a huge compassionate power / To heal / To love'. In assigning unaided man the central role in determining his own destiny for good or evil, Tippett's vision represents a powerful statement of the new Romantic aesthetic and its concern with the centrality of the self. This concern lies at the heart of the entire Symphony.

The first three movements are, as in Beethoven's Ninth, purely instrumental, yet their style and techniques disclose constant affinities with the new Romantic aesthetic. The first movement makes an ingenious regeneration of the sonata principle of exposing two opposites, exploring their developments and culminating in some species of triumphal reconciliation. Here, however, the two opposites are not the tonal polarities of earlier practice, but two diametrically opposed temperaments designated by Tippett as 'Arrest' and

182

'Movement'. These he described in the score as being metaphorical indications of, respectively, a compression and an explosion of energy. Raising two such concepts which can readily be identified with human conditions, to function as structural polarities thus creates an intimate interaction between the form and expressive content of the Symphony from the outset, and immediately identifies its Romantic impluse. The exposition alternates episodes of Arrest and Movement. There are three distinct musical motives associated with Arrest episodes and these are heard at the beginning of the movement, and at Figs. 11 and 28. Each of these is in duple metre, each is scored for brass and percussion, and each makes a prominent use of the interval of a fourth both harmonically and melodically. Five distinct motives are associated with the Movement episodes, and these are heard first at Figs. 1, 2, 14, 16 and 20. These also have a degree of unity in that each is in triple metre, each is scored for strings, usually multiply divided, winds, piano and tuned percussion, each is dominated by explosive semiquavers, and in each the intervals of a seventh and a ninth are prominent melodically. The development beginning at Fig. 38 is made up of six episodes of expansion, contraction and transformation of motives from the exposition in the most exacting symphonic manner. All of these develop the Movement material except the extended fifth episode, Figs. 59 to 80. The polarity of the two temperaments is resolved in the recapitulation beginning at Fig. 87 where they are ingeniously combined while each retains its identity of metre, scoring, linear shape and harmony. At the beginning of his Third Symphony, Tippett has created an imposing movement of powerful symphonic rhetoric such as was essential to match the impact of his finale.

The slow movement, which completes Part 1 of the Symphony, epitomises the sensuous, evocative expressiveness that lies at the heart of the new Romanticism. With extreme economy of means, Tippett creates episodes of motionless beauty, of mystery, and of ecstasy. The first section of the movement seems to take as its starting point the spirit of Bartok's night music, and introduces two themes whose apparent simplicity belies their crucial importance in the last movemet. The first at Fig. 104 (Ex. 1.1) is a hypnotic arpeggio pattern on a muted solo viola outlining the interval of a major ninth, and the second at Fig. 105 is a short phrase low on four solo violas in which the interval of a fourth is decisive both melodically and harmonically. The prominence of these two intervals associates each theme with the motives of the Movement and Arrest episodes respectively in the first movement. At the centre of the slow movement beginning at Fig. 115, there is an expansive episode which begins softly on divided lower strings, and rising through the violins and winds gradually grows into an ecstatic, radiant outpouring of effulgent lyricism and harmony. Even after the violins enter, Tippett continues to assign the top line to the violas creating an altogether more astringent beauty. In seeking to describe the two principal episodes of this movement, Tippett had recourse to extra-mural metaphors of 'the windless night sky and the tidal wave below',[20] and in doing so gave some notion of the Romantic impulse that lies behind the music.

Part 2 of the Symphony begins with a driving scherzo. Here five distinct thematic textures are offset in an Ivesian mêlée, and each is sharply defined by its scoring for horns, lower strings, upper strings, winds, and piano respectively. In the first and fourth textures (the latter beginning at Fig. 148) the interval of a ninth is prominent, and in the second texture beginning the bar before Fig. 142, the falling fourth is prominent. The sustained prominence of these two intervals here forges a symphonic affinity between the scherzo and both the first and second movements.

As the first movement was suddenly arrested by the second, so the headlong drive of the scherzo is dramatically terminated the bar before Fig. 182 by the fourth movement. This immediately defines entirely new symphonic parameters by quoting and extending the fanfare which opens the Finale of Beethoven's Ninth Symphony. This in its turn is cut short at Fig. 184 by a short episode scored for divided violas, cellos and basses whose musical and spiritual intensity recalls the slow movement. This serves as a potent antidote to the rhetoric of Beethoven's bombast, and reappears at a crucial stage later in the movement where its expressive intention is clarified by a text.

These preambles introduce the soprano soloist with the first of four songs. Tippett's vocal culmination for his Symphony had a powerful precedent not only in Beethoven's Ninth, but also in Mahler's *Das Lied von der Erde* as he himself acknowledged. In his first three songs Tippett returns to idioms of jazz, his musical vernacular. The first song, beginning at Fig. 187 and designated Slow Blues, is structured in the simple strophic pattern AAB. It is scored for lower brass and winds with a flügelhorn obbligato that Tippett acknowledged was inspired by Louis Armstrong's playing. The second song, beginning at Fig. 197 and designated Fast Blues, returns to the boogie-woogie idiom found in *Songs for Dov*. Whereas in the latter the boggie-woogie episode from Fig. 118 was built on a comparatively simple 10-bar bass with the pattern I-IV-I-V-I stated four times, the ground in this second song is much more stylised and further removed from the basic prototype. Its bass is 11 bars in length and is stated six times every second of which begins on a different degree of the scale. This allows the texture a greater harmonic variety than was possible in either *Songs for Dov* or in popular boogie-woogie examples. The soprano's music recurs after two cycles of the recurrent bass, that is each time the bass begins on a different degree. The third song beginning at Fig. 218 returns to a Slow Blues, but is a more complex strophic structure with the pattern AAABA. It too is built over a simple recurrent pattern in the bass which can begin on different degrees of the scale. The climaxes of each stanza at bars 360, 374 and 388 are spoken by the singer 'distinct and hard'. Tippett had used this device in the third song of *Songs for Dov* for the two statements of the vital line 'The living language of our time is urban' at Figs. 127 and 135, and for the ultimate and elusive 'Sure baby'.

The fourth song is in reality a dramatic scene in which Tippett confronts and resolves his central ethical issue. It is introduced at Fig. 234 with the return of Beethoven's fanfare extended and reworked by Tippett to embrace the cello recitative and the principal *Ode to Joy* theme from the finale of the Ninth as Tippett's soprano soloist exuberantly recalls Beethoven's ideal. In this episode the material which Tippett has appropriated is subjected to radical recomposition in his own most uncompromising style in order to expose Beethoven's vision of the 1820s to the most rigorous scrutiny in terms of the values of the 1970s. Here Tippett has made a much more extensive transformation of pre-existent material than he made in, for example, *Songs for Dov*, and the greater extremes of the techniques in the Symphony were dictated wholly by the urgency of his extra-musical purpose. The reworking of Beethoven is abruptly interrupted at Fig. 245 by a grim reminder of the 20th century inhumanity accompanied by the theme for four solo violas heard first towards the beginning of the second movement at Fig. 105. The next stanzas recount the bitter truths of contemporary experience that make it impossible to endorse the innocence of Beethoven's ideal today with episodes that alternate violent energy and intense introspection. The last of these at Fig. 266 returns to the darkly expressive episode for lower strings first heard at Fig. 184 as an antidote to Beethoven, and Tippett confirms his expressive intention with the text: 'It is our agony / We fractured men / Surmise a deeper mercy; / That no god has shown.' The movement culminates in an episode beginning at Fig. 269 which becomes the crux of the entire Symphony, and its text opens with an allusion to Martin Luther King's prophetic words of 1968 'I have a dream'. The soprano's setting of these words from Fig. 272 radically transforms the solo viola theme from the head of the slow movement at Fig. 104 which outlined with arpeggios the interval of a major ninth, and rose to a pungent foreign note at the end of each phrase (Ex. 1.1). The derivation at Fig. 272 is clearest in the flutes' line (Ex. 1.2). The upper strings accompany the soprano from this point with a striding unison line spread across two octaves. This expands the identical texture of striding unison strings spread over two octaves that accompanied the climax of the third of the *Songs for Dov* from Fig. 138 (Exs 1.1 and 1.2).

Towards the conclusion of the movement, Tippett gathers motives from earlier in the Symphony as if to confirm the extra-musical, ethical associations of the instrumental movements. At Fig. 283 he accompanies 'What though the dream crack! / We shall remake it' with the second motive of the Arrest group from the first movement at Fig. 11, and follows this with 'Staring with those startled eyes at what we are', accompanied by the theme for four solo violas from the head of the slow movement at Fig. 105. But now, after the harrowing experience of the last movement this is scored instead for four solo cellos. The final lines of text offer Tippett's solution that wholeness lies in a 'huge compassionate power / To heal / To love.' The melismas that set the words 'heal' and 'love' are each governed by a central thread of descending fourths (Exs. 2.1 and 2.2).
This pattern lay at the heart of the crucial melodic lines at Fig. 248 (Ex. 3.1), 249, and 250 (Ex. 3.2) earlier in the movement.
Such musical affinities are forged to serve dramatic affinities, and they afford examples of the closely-knit musical unity which pervades the whole Symphony, a unity that is as finely wrought as in any more conventional twentieth-century symphony.

No sooner had Tippett completed the Third Symphony than he began work on the Third Piano Sonata. He had originally thought that this would afford

comparative compositional respite, but as it took shape in the years 1972–3, it became another piece of substantial proportions. Although it was the first major work since the Concerto for Orchestra (1962–63) that had no avowed extra-musical intention, it did draw on many of the techniques of heightened expression that had been evolved in its immediate predecessors. It grew out of the Third Symphony specifically as it explored yet further Tippett's creative obsession with the music of Beethoven. But whereas in the Symphony he had appropriated Beethoven to confront and ultimately to reject the validity of Beethoven's ethical ideal for the 1970s, in the Piano Sonata without appropriating any pre-existent material, Tippett made a mighty act of homage to Beethoven the musician in the most absolute of musical terms. Tippett has referred to the work as his 'late Beethoven sonata', and in it he has recreated in vividly contemporary terms the spiritual breadth of Beethoven's late piano sonatas, and in particular the *Hammerklavier* Op. 106. This could have been possible only after he had achieved new spiritual and technical plateaus in the immediately preceding works.

The Sonata is cast in one continuous span, but falls into three clearly-defined movements. The first is a taut sonata-allegro in which the two subject groups are contrasted primarily by mood and temperament as in the first movement of the Third Symphony. The first subject contains three distinct motives beginning in bars 1, 2 and 5, and each is made up of two driving contrapuntal lines imitated in near-inversion at opposite extremities of the keyboard. This disposition together with the pivotal importance of the trill recalls the Beethoven of the *Hammerklavier*. The second group also contains three distinct motives. The first beginning at bar 23 breaks the incessant drive of the first paragraph with an almost static texture of dense clusters of sensuous chords in the centre of the keyboard which rely heavily on sevenths and ninths. The second motive begins at bar 38 (Ex. 4.3), and the third follows at bar 56 with a jagged dotted rhythmic figure which is imitated in inversion between each hand, and which expands by interval and rhythm as it generates its own extension. Beethoven had made insistent generative use of a similar dotted figure in the development of the *Hammerklavier's* first movement from bar 133. Tippett built much of the fourth section of his Fourth String Quartet (1977–78) from Fig. 84 on a similar dotted figure, and he developed this also in imitation by inversion. This instance suggests a particular resonance of the fugue subject of Beethoven's *Grosse Fuge* Op. 133, and in this case Tippett described his act of homage as 'quoting a gesture rather than notes'; this could equally well describe his debt to Beethoven here in the Third Sonata. The development begins at bar 80 by pitting the dotted figure against driving semiquavers derived from the second motive of the second subject. The recapitulation beginning at bar 111 intensifies much of the first subject rhythmically, and the second group is recapitulated from bar 134 consistently a tone higher than its pitch in the exposition.

As in the *Hammerklavier*, the longest section and the emotional centrepiece of the work is the slow movement. This is made up of gathering complexity on a 19-bar theme. In contrast to the relentless counterpoint of the Sonata's outer

187

movements, the theme is homophonic, and is built up from a succession of 17 broken chords which are compounded largely of sevenths and ninths. Each of the variations is 19 bars in length as was the theme, and each begins on a note a minor third higher than its predecessor bringing the fourth variation back to G flat, the first note of the theme. The first variation beginning from A at bar 211 maintains the homophonic texture of the theme with richly expressive harmonies in which sevenths and ninths are prominent. The second, beginning on C at bar 230 develops the theme by imitation in inversion between the hands separating in contrary motion. It maintains the sensuous harmonic texture while introducing, through contrapuntal elaboration, an exploration of the breadth of the piano's register. The third variation beginning on E flat at bar 249 lightens the texture, decorating melodic fragments from the theme with flourishes from which the original chords materialise. The final variation beginning on G flat at bar 268 expands the harmonic spectrum of the original chords by tracing two of their component intervals through near-parallel writing across much of the chromatic scale. This variation becomes the emotional and technical goal of the entire slow movement through an extreme concentration of the most expressive harmony.

The final movement returns to the two-part counterpoint and driving semiquavers of the opening. Its two generative thematic cells in the first bar (Ex. 4.1) are both derived from the first movement. The first figure in the left hand is a rhythmic intensification with octave transpositions of the left hand's figure in bar 1 (Ex. 4.2), and the first figure in the right hand is derived from the semiquaver pattern beginning the second motive of the second subject in bar 38 (Ex. 4.3). These correspondences were almost certainly not consciously calculated by Tippett; they are much more likely to have been a consequence of concentrated subconscious associations in a master at the height of his creative powers. The last movement is ternary in design, and its middle section, bars 356 to 417, repeats the first section, bars 287 to 348 in strict retrograde. It is a breathtaking feat of technical ingenuity which Tippett appears to have calculated entirely in his head. There seem to have been no sketches, and in the autograph manuscript in the British Library[21] this palindrome is not written out. In 1951 Tippett had been apprehensive about the artistic value of the palindrome in the third movement of Berg's *Lyric Suite*.[22] By 1972–3 his doubts had been resolved, and he proved here that the technique could become a means of rarefied and concentrated artistry. He would also have known of, and was perhaps paying homage to Beethoven's rather shorter palindromic episode in the fugue of the *Hammerklavier* Sonata at bars 153 to 174. After Tippett's palindrome, the first section is repeated almost exactly with a cumulative coda that hurtles precipitously onto two widely-separated chords in the last bar, each of a major ninth: the chord which generated so much substance in his Sonata.[23] Like *Songs for Dov* the Third Piano Sonata achieves a resolution of opposites. It is foremost a work of absolute musical values with no ethical or illustrative purpose, yet at the same time Tippett has been able to create a work of spiritual depth that touches whole realms of human experience through his music's immediate communicative and Romantic impluse.

With these three diverse works, one an artist's odyssey, the second an ethical statement and the third a work of absolute musical values, Tippett forged and consolidated his last major changes of stylistic and technical emphasis. These opened up new thresholds, and made possible the flood of creativity in the following decade which produced an opera, a symphony, a string quartet, a concerto, and an oratorio. Each of these pursues lines of development initiated in their three or four immediate predecessors, and confirms the spiritual and artistic homogeneity that underpins these works of an otherwise distinct individuality.

The Ice Break (1973–6) brings the claustrophobic world of *The Knot Garden* out into the open, and examines the alienations and reconciliations of nine heterogeneous characters against a setting of the international tensions of the mid-1970s. In a note prefacing the score, Tippett specifically mentioned his intention of evoking through the music both fear and excitement. The emotional extremities of fear on one hand, and of ecstacy on the other provide the mainspring of the opera, and are unpredictable states to which contemporary man in particular is precariously vulnerable. Both states are constantly confronted in music of the new Romanticism.

Tippett's output in the decade from *The Knot Garden* to *The Ice Break* fashioned a newly expressive language whose underlying aesthetic can be seen to resonate sympathetically with the work of other major contemporary composers. In 1985 one can stand back from the decade sufficiently to recognise common factors that can, with some confidence, be recognised as Romantic, and these are symptomatic of deeper impulses which were re-shaping the basis of our society itself. Tippett's neo-Romanticism has never implied a mere resuscitation of nineteenth-century Romanticism. Writing in the early 1970s he affirmed that for him Schiller's romanticism, which could believe that joy was universal and inevitable, was out of date.[24] This he went on to prove with the most powerful means at his disposal in the Third Symphony, but in that he proposed an alternative, he confirmed his belief in the capacity of his art to make statements that touch the sensibilities of contemporary man. From his earliest days as a composer, Tippett believed that 'there was a necessity for art of our time . . . to be concerned with what was happening to [the] "apocalyptic" side of our present time'.[25] In his last phase Tippett has been demonstrably anxious to reach out to an even wider public, but such a public has been made up of perceptive individuals, and diametrically different from the universal humanity addressed by Beethoven and Schiller. Tippett has sought no more and no less than a cathartic response from the individual who is attuned to the insights communicated by the composer. He would go no further, and together with other artists of his day, he would deny that art is able to affect political events. He specifically implied that Shelley's claim that 'Poets are the unacknowledged legislators of the world' was a delusion.[26] On the other hand he would probably have been reluctant to endorse the reckless cynicism of W. H. Auden who wrote in 1939 that 'if not a poem had been written, not a picture painted, not a bar of music composed, the history of man would be materially unchanged'.[27] Tippett's view is probably closer in spirit to that

189

expressed by Wilfred Owen and quoted by Benjamin Britten at the head of the score of the *War Requiem*: 'All the poet can do today is warn.'

Tippett's self concept as an artist comes closest perhaps to that of Owen and Britten, and recognises the capacity of art to touch individual sensibilities with an ethical statement while being powerless to alter the corporate affairs of men. This capacity has given him a positive and responsible role, but he would strongly reject the romantic notion of the artist as hero, or the decadent notion of the artist as anti-hero. There is a passing representation of the artist with intuitive insights in the psychedelic messenger Astron in *The Ice Break* III sc. 5. Surer of his own insights than needing the adulation of the fickle crowd, he ironically rejects their praises with 'Saviour?! Hero?! Me!! You must be joking.'

Tippett's own journey towards self-knowledge and wholeness has been a life time's odyssey, but it was given significant impetus in the mid-1960s by factors both internal and external to the composer. That journey would have remained the private experience of one man had it not been for the incomparable power of his music that was able to transform his vision into a means of intimately touching the experience of many. That potential was always present in Tippett's music, but since the mid-60s, it has flowered, propelled by new Romantic impulses of spirit and style to produce a body of music that powerfully and eloquently articulates some of the major concerns of our time.

NOTES
1. J. Warrack, 'Romantic', *The New Grove*
2. M. Tippett, *Moving into Aquarius* (St. Albans: Paladin, 1974), p35
3 *Ibid*, p35
4 *Ibid*, p167
5 *Ibid*, p167
6 *Ibid*, p42
7 *Ibid*, p42
8 *Ibid*, p156
9 *Ibid*, p156 which refines a passage first appearing on p100.
10 M. Bowen, ed, *Music of the Angels* (London: Eulenburg, 1980), p234
11 I. Kemp, 'Tippett', *The New Grove*.
12 M. Bowen, *Music of the Angels*, p235
13 *Ibid, p237*
14 *Ibid, p236*
15 *Ibid, p238*. Tippett borrowed this particular usage of 'rhetoric' and 'poetry' from W. B. Yeats.
16 See *Moving into Aquarius*, p18
17 M. Tippett, *Moving into Aquarius*, p156
18 *Ibid*, p167
19 M. Bowen, *Music of the Angels*, pp235–8
20 M. Bowen, *Michael Tippett* (London: Robson, 1982), pp119–20
21 BL Add. MS
22 Tippett, *Moving into Aquarius*, p40
23 This chord was settled in collaboration with Paul Crossley (information conveyed in conversation with the author). It seems that there was no conscious attempt to find a chord that made anything other than an arresting conclusion to the work. That this particular chord was chosen is indicative of the concentration of the harmonic language of the Sonata, and the necessity of arresting the movement with an element that in itself grew so inevitably out of that movement.
24 M. Tippett, *Moving into Aquarius*, p159
25 *Ibid*, p152
26 *Ibid*, p150
27 Humphrey Carpenter, *W. H. Auden: a Biography* (London: Allen and Unwin, 1981), p256. Auden could nevertheless salute music as being demonstrative of a freedom of spirit if not of body: 'Every high C [in opera] accurately struck demolishes the theory that we are the irresponsible puppets of fate or chance.' *The Dyer's Hand* (London: Faber, 1975), p.474

TWO FANFARES *for the 80th birthday of Sir Michael Tippett*

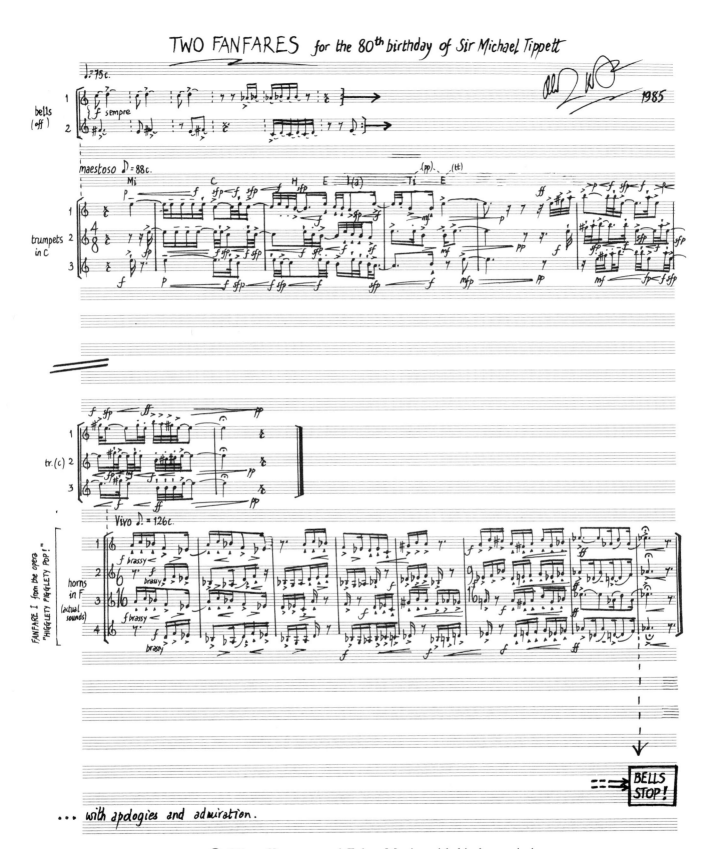

191

Tippett at an Opera Factory/London Sinfonietta Press Conference at The Royal Court Theatre, June 1984. (Photo: Malcolm Crowthers)

SIR GEORG SOLTI
Tribute

MY FIRST association with Michael's work came long before I had the pleasure of meeting him. It was in my early years in Germany in the mid-1950s, when I performed the Concerto for Double String Orchestra in Frankfurt. I thought it was a wonderful work and the public acclaim was very great.

It was during my first year as Music Director at Covent Garden that I met Michael in person. We performed *King Priam,* a magnificent opera which is enormously imaginative, as indeed are all his works which I have come to know since that time.

In 1972, on the occasion of its own 80th birthday, the Chicago Symphony Orchestra commissioned five European and five American composers to write a work each. It was a very obvious choice to commission Michael Tippett and to our great delight he accepted the commission. This was to be his 4th Symphony, which we had the pleasure to première in Chicago and to take with us shortly thereafter on our European Tour, with performances at the Salzburg Festival and the Promenade Concerts in London. Clearly the work was written with the Chicago Symphony's virtuosity and sonority in mind. It is very typical of Michael Tippett's music – most imaginative and with a remarkable feeling for orchestral sound-elements and brilliance. I worked on it with the greatest joy and love and when I first met with Michael in London in the course of the work I was amazed to find how well he knew the piece. So often composers write quickly and once one piece is completed it is forgotten in favour of the next on which they start work. He, however, came here and not only knew every single tone and articulation but described with the clearest imagination how things should sound. It was the most enormous help to me in its preparation and I think that as a result we were able to achieve very much what he wanted. I realised how much one could absolutely trust his sound-imagination. My orchestra and I very much enjoyed the work; it was a challenge, difficult technically for both players and conductor alike. Following the performances we had the great chance to record the Symphony (together with his earlier work, the *Suite for the Birthday of Prince Charles*) and I hope that everybody will hear from this what a marvellous piece of music it is and how wonderfully the orchestra plays it.

193

It is extraordinary to think that Michael will be 80; his body and spirit are that of a man one-half, if not one-third, of his age. I send him my warmest love and deepest personal admiration and wish him at least another 80 years of composing.

Georg Solti

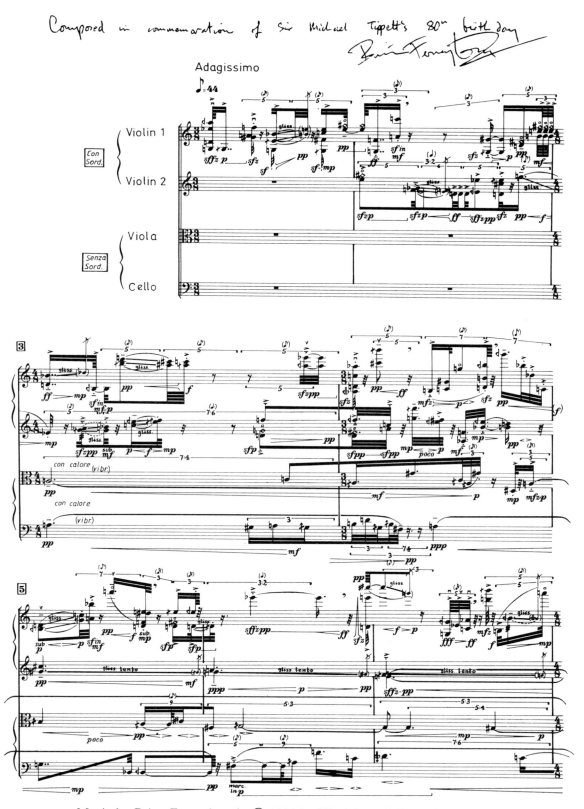

Music by Brian Ferneyhough, © 1984 by Hinrichsen Edition, Peters Edition Limited, London. Reproduced by permission of the copyright owners, Peters Edition Limited. All rights reserved.

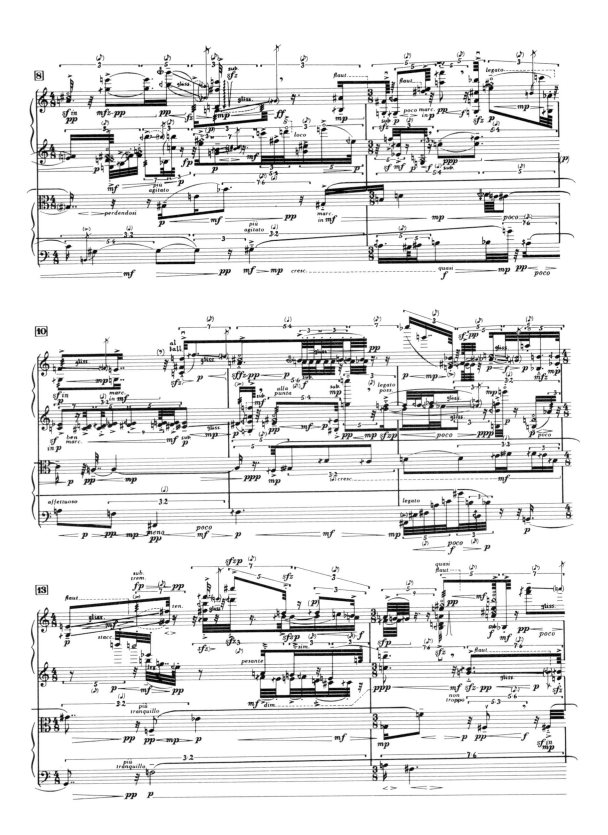

196

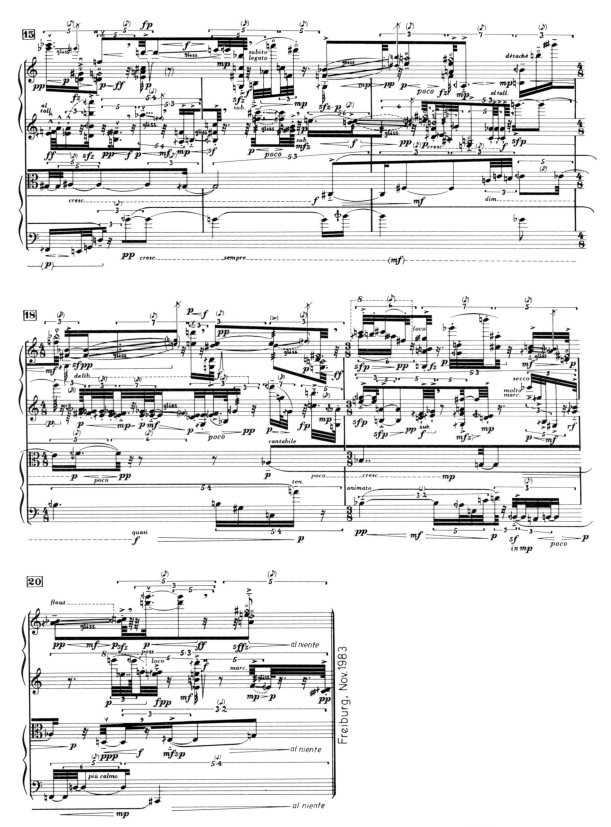

Freiburg, Nov. 1983

197

GERAINT LEWIS

'Spring come to you at the farthest
In the very end of harvest'

THERE IS a scene in *The Ice Break* where music is reduced to barbaric onomatopoeia and words to agonized screams. The stage-action at this point is a graphic presentation of a mob-fight – volleys of gunfire echo around the theatre and bodies are stamped to death. It is a horrific moment.

In an opera where realism is frequently tempered by mild surrealism the stark immediacy of this scene is so strong that it is not surprising to recall rumours that the chorus at Covent Garden initially refused to perform it. That in itself is, paradoxically, a tribute to the power of Tippett's achievement. The eruption of violence in the opera is both sudden and shattering, but this very impact is the result of careful dramatic preparation.

Many critics have noted that *The Ice Break* is often cinematic in subject-matter and technique. It is important to realize that the subject-matter at times ideally suggests the technique and that the technique is at the same time a natural extension of Tippett's dramatic development. It is also worth noting that an awareness of the technical possibilities of the cinema was no recent phenomenon – a result perhaps of the composer's American interests. In the essay *The Birth of an Opera* (written just after work on *The Midsummer Marriage* was completed) Tippett wrote of the film *Citizen Kane:* '. . . the cutting and the shots themselves (that is scene-changing *in excelsis*) become part of the artistic experience and put the old-fashioned scene-changing of the operatic stage to shame.' In its context in the essay this passage relates to Wagner's belief that 'dramatic material which needed a lot of scene-changing should be left as romance or novel.' Tippett suggested that Verdi would not have agreed with this, but that he might have done had he seen a film like *Citizen Kane*!

The implication here therefore is that dramatic material requiring a lot of scene-changing is today best left to the cinema. In *The Midsummer Marriage* Tippett's stage-mechanism is at least partly Wagnerian – scene-changing is effected mainly by constant manoeuvring of characters and chorus on and off a largely static unchanging set. Even so, his mind was open to the possibility of reversing this position. In the postscript to the essay (presumably written at an early stage in the conception of *King Priam*) he writes that there 'is no guarantee that for the purposes of a new opera I shall not turn it upside down.'

The Brechtian tradition which he utilised as a background to *King Priam* gave Tippett the framework for greater fragmentation of stage-presentation and by the time he composed *The Knot Garden* he developed the notion of vivid scene-cutting to the point where a musical 'dissolve' can act as a signal for a psychological scene-change – a re-grouping of characters and attitudes rather than of location. Here – to some extent – is a technique proper to the novel transformed into operatic terms, and so a general affinity with the world of Iris Murdoch is underlined yet more firmly, though on a different level. What is remarkable about *The Ice Break* is its striking synthesis of Tippett's previous attitudes to the stage, which is at the same time (as is surely true of any truly enriching synthesis) a new departure.

The compression of *The Knot Garden* is taken a stage further in *The Ice Break*: in three short acts there are nearly thirty scenes. This might suggest that the stage-action is very bitty, but in practice this problem is skirted by a partial return to the fluidity of *The Midsummer Marriage*. The opening scenes in an airport lounge develop sudden juxtapositions of dramatic-time in which the manipulation of characters and chorus produces interlocking patterns of stasis and speed which very broadly recall the multiplication of contrasted cells in the first movement of Symphony No 3. It would be perverse to push the parallel too far, but there is no denying that this general scheme gives to the first two acts a sense of ebb and flow which enables Tippett to control the dramatic pace effectively over a large span. As the two acts unfold, longer, sustained sections fall naturally into place and are much less sudden in their impact than the corresponding arias and ensembles of *The Knot Garden*. So while *The Ice Break* is shorter than *The Knot Garden* it actually has greater breadth of perspective.

The elaborate musical scene-changing of *King Priam* is abandoned in *The Ice Break*, even though scene-changing as such is reintroduced. Tippett's confidence in the growing sophistication of stage-production encouraged him to shift locations instantaneously. This can partly be achieved by musical means – sudden cross-cutting for instance – and lighting techniques obviously play an important role. The action can therefore move from one part of an airport to another, and from the airport to a private apartment without any disruptive pauses. A cinematic effect is dramatically effected very vividly, but is also truly operatic because it becomes a thoroughly musical expression as well. Some hitches in the technical presentation of the first production do not actually blur the brilliance of Tippett's conception, but merely underline that the challenges presented to both producer and designer are very steep. The one bad miscalculation of the Covent Garden production – the psychedelic trip in the Paradise Garden – could be remedied by being projected entirely in terms of lighting, so that the long awkward pause before the scene started would disappear. The dramatic timing is indeed balanced on a knife-edge here, even though the desired musical effect – of an immediate shift away from

Nadia's death-scene – is very clear. The surrealistic highlight of the opera should in fact be allowed to emerge very vividly.

Surrealism plays a part in heightening the realism of the opera's climax. Having split into black and white factions in the aftermath of greeting the black athletics champion Olympion in Act I, the masked chorus is summoned to action by the spine-chilling keening of siren-like trumpets and pulsating drums and it proceeds to self-righteous identification – the whites for instance sing a barbershop-like parody of a hymn favoured by the Klu Klux Klan. When however the two sides confront each other with provocative tribalizing (each stage of the de-humanizing chorus-action is punctuated by opposing scenes of increasing intimacy and depth of individual characterization) the dancing and chanting is projected with an almost ridiculous and comic air. The dancers hold instruments with which they mime *while* dancing – and the audience actually laughed! This scene could even set up a resonance as a bizzare parody of the identically placed *Ritual Dances* in *The Midsummer Marriage*. In that scene, as the hawk is about to swoop and kill the bird, Bella screams, and the threat of violence recedes. In *The Ice Break*, the tribal dancing swirls ahead in an increasingly meaningless fashion, and is then very abruptly cut-off. Violence does not seem to recede, for it has been kept at bay here by the surrealistic stylisation and so remains an ominous backdrop to the scene of impotent cat's-cradling between Lev and Nadia which follows. Without warning their agonizing is engulfed and the mob-stamping is upon us.

Any recollection of laughter at the previous chorus-scene is now brutally stifled. Even though some eventual violent dénouement was clearly on the cards about two-thirds of the way through Act I, the barbaric riot itself breaks out so suddenly that it is overwhelming in its impact and so seemingly unexpected. As spectators in the opera-house we virtually become part of the action – silent, stunned witnesses. This is partly why the effect of this violence is greater and far more disturbing than that of a similar scene actually shot for the cinema, and as if to emphasize this the scene which follows is presented as a set of crude cinematic clichés in which bodies are examined by policeman and doctor with almost callous indifference. This however is the turning-point of the opera. As Lev learns that his son Yuri is gravely injured he seeks comfort from the sympathetic black nurse Hannah. Very gradually a solo violin and a 'cello weave long lyrical lines of warm compassion around which a supportive texture on electric and bass guitars and horns seems further to echo the scene on stage. At this moment in the opera such music of tender, but brave hope is hard-won. It is more sustained in profile than a similar gesture in the slow movement of the Third Symphony and is different in kind to the rapturous dream which is the slow movement of the Third Piano Sonata. Given indeed the generally dark and violent character of Tippett's music since *The Vision of Saint Augustine* (an impression highlighted by the outer movements of the Sonata) which had now come to a head in the preceding scenes in *The Ice Break* it was perhaps not fanciful to feel at the first performance that the composer had just turned a crucial corner not only in the opera but also in his career. Lines from a Rilke sonnet adapted in the libretto of *The Mask of Time* seem very appropriate here:

> 'Who alone already lifted the lyre among the dead
> dare divining, sound the infinite praise.'

Act III of the opera emerges – bruised – from the violence. Everything in it is tempered by the preceding action and consequently its qualified note of optimism is all the more moving. Tippett portrays – as far as is possible – a reconciliation and a rebirth, and it becomes clear that the theme of the opera is but a further stage in his continuing obsession with the central message of *A Child of Our Time*: 'I would know my shadow and my light, so shall I at last be whole.' In his article in the new Grove Dictionary Ian Kemp quotes the composer in saying that this is likely to be the one truth that he will ever utter, and in one preface in *Moving into Aquarius* Tippett writes that 'the deep relationship between all dualities is a problem of abiding fascination for me. I return to it again and again.' It has driven Tippett here to the absolute extreme of his concern for mankind and the world in which he lives. The opera does at one point stand at the abyss, and the harrowing effect on the composer himself of pursuing his dark vision to the end should never be underestimated.

This particular pursuit is not however undertaken in any directly didactic sense – there is no condemnation, for, as Tippett has written, one of the opera's messages is that any form of self-righteousness is a grave danger. Nevertheless it cannot but be a powerful warning, and though another of its messages is given to the androgynous two-voiced visitor from outer-space called Astron (who is obviously a send-up of Madame Sosostris), its content is surely meant to be taken passionately to heart:–

> 'Take care for the earth
> God will take care for himself'

These lines from a letter by Jung were clearly in the forefront of his mind when he quoted them towards the end of the Postscript to the 1974 paperback enlargement of *Moving into Aquarius*. They were then preceded by Caliban's soul-melting song ('Be not afeard;) from *The Tempest*. In the opera they are followed by a 'blessing' from Juno's masque in the same play:–

> 'Spring come to you, at the farthest
> In the very end of harvest.'

The *Tempest* of course played a prominent part as an allusive layer to *The Knot Garden* and so together with a Jungian reference we are unmistakably in Tippett's most precious area of visionary thought. Given the overall context however, the sobering experience of the opera is very crucially connected to the spirit of forgiveness and renewal at the heart of Shakespeare's late plays, and it is very aptly summed up in its heading which is quoted from Francois Villon:

> 'Brother humans who may live after us,
> Do not harden your hearts against us.'

The metaphor of polarity and reconciliation which *The Ice Break* portrays so vividly can be pursued through Tippett's whole output. An early work like the Concerto for Double String Orchestra for instance could be interpreted as an abstract portrayal of such an image. Indeed it may even emerge that such a pattern can be seen to underlie the whole progression of his musical development. In this view a work like *The Midsummer Marriage* (and its surrounding satellites) very clearly occupies the 'light' while *King Priam* stands as the sharpest and 'darkest' split – a split which the works following the opera (with the striking exception of *The Vision of Saint Augustine*) carry still further. However, the synthesis promising reconciliation in the works written since *The Ice Break* can clearly be seen as the natural culmination of the whole development. The generalisation is obviously dramatic and an over-simplification, but it does help to elucidate the sometimes seemingly disconcerting stylistic changes in Tippett's development without denying the unity of purpose at its very heart. (Such movements as the central slow cantilena of the Concerto for Orchestra and Part I of Symphony No. 3 – among others – are microcosmic metaphors for the concept.)

An awareness of intense contrasts, dualities and polarity has indeed been present in Tippett's art from the start. A scheme of this kind lay behind the original first two movements of String Quartet No. 1 (1934–5) and at the head of the *tour de force* of a fugal finale stands a quotation from Blake's *The Marriage of Heaven and Hell*: 'Damn braces: Bless relaxes.' (This could also now be aptly applied to the initial polarity of Symphony No. 3). It is clear that if a synoptic view of Tippett's compositional career from the metaphorical position outlined above *is* taken, *The Ice Break* represents a crucial step. The war-cries of Achilles in *King Priam* and the distanced hieratical violence of that Homeric epic become uncomfortably real in the later opera. Even if the great risks taken are so enormous that it is inevitably open-ended and to many minds obviously and disastrously flawed (it is manifestly the riskiest work of a composer who relishes risk) it should never be wished that *The Ice Break* could ever have been a comfortable expression. That would be to deny its very nature and to suppress its true significance in Tippett's compositional and operatic journey.

The extreme violence of *The Ice Break* also provoked a different kind of polarity. Before the opera's first performance in 1977 when asked to describe the already-completed Fourth Symphony, Tippett said that it 'is the first of the works in which I'm turning my back, with some pleasure on the cruel world. It may even appear to be polarized against *The Ice Break*.' This statement is perhaps most interesting for its insight into Tippett's perception of the direction his music was taking at the time. He was for instance then just started on the Fourth Quartet and contemplating the Triple Concerto which was to be 'radiant' and free from 'dramatics'. On the horizon too was *The Masque* (sic) *of Time* for which the composer was then still 'looking for metaphors'. The Symphony No. 4 has indeed been interpreted as the start of a new phase in Tippett's work, but it has also been taken as a work of tension and struggle. By and large, the arena for its struggle is obviously far removed from *The Ice Break*, but even so the Symphony's distance from the opera is not absolutely clear-cut. For example it pursues the stylistic synthesis already emerging in *The Ice Break* (and which is even evident momentarily in the Third Symphony and Third Sonata) to a much deeper level, and it establishes certain traits that will resound through most of the works written subsequently – even to the point of powerful quotation in *The Mask of Time* and the Fourth Piano Sonata. Its new radiance however is surely a continuation in general terms of the hard-won lyricism of the opera's later stages, and the context provided in the Symphony for the emergence of this radiance has not entirely obliterated the shadow of *The Ice Break*.

The relationship between Tippett's symphonies and his operas is especially fascinating. Both Symphonies 1 and 2 are certainly transitional works. No. 1 retains some of the brooding intensity and angularity of *A Child of Our Time* as well as the idiosyncratically neo-classical madrigalian and contrapuntal impulse of String Quartet No. 2. Symphony No. 2 meanwhile is at times bathed in the beneficent light of the Piano Concerto and is often roused to the rhythmic exuberance of *The Midsummer Marriage*. They both also pose interesting paradoxes. The first two movements of Symphony No. 1 both end with understated lack of finality and the scherzo similarly evaporates airily. The confident fugue subjects and their associated textures in the finale might therefore be expected to issue in a triumphant resolution in A, and for a while the music almost seems about to gratify this expectation. With hindsight it might even be on course for a conclusion like that of *The Midsummer Marriage*, which is in A too! However, Tippett in fact disperses his fugal material over an insistent, rather menacing pounding bass on the dominant, and this is eventually all that's left. The work's apparent goal is therefore not reached and the inconclusiveness of the earlier movements is retrospectively heightened.

In Symphony No. 2 the first three movements end with schematic neatness quite in keeping with their sense of logical continuity. The finale however is a discrete movement. Its deliberately unrelated sections (together with a few passages in the previous movements) foreshadow the disjunctiveness of *King Priam* in the same way that the First Symphony's texture and continuity prefigure the visionary warmth of *The Midsummer Marriage*. Where the refusal of that symphony's finale to follow its logical course seems simultaneously at odds with the emergent stylistic development that is carried forward into the following opera (though structurally true to the other movements), so the very end of Symphony No. 2 builds out of its disparate progression an obstinately affirmative and logical conclusion which links cyclically to the first movement's opening – Tippett again seems reluctant to follow the path on which the movement seems set.

These endings can be read merely as manifestations of the 'finale problem' but they also underline the transitional nature of the works in relation to their individual dramatic unity and their general operatic surroundings. As a totally dramatic entity Symphony No. 3 has no such obvious problem. The text of its second half seems concerned to extend the sense of compassion and frustration opened-up in *The Knot Garden*. The blues and *Scena* seem almost an externalised projection of the opera's tortured freedom-fighter Denise – her

Songs as it were (the jazz-like idiom is sometimes akin to the *Songs for Dov*). The widening of Tippett's humanistic message in the Third Symphony is also a natural upbeat to *The Ice Break*. Polarities are the essence of the Symphony and its concluding series of tough chords momentarily transmuted into tender counterparts is one of Tippett's most powerful archetypal statements. No further reconciliation is possible. The subsequent breaking of the ice in the opera however is both the promise of some gestural rebirth and a fragile hope for musical reconciliation, and it is indeed as the first fruit of this gradual move that the Fourth Symphony is perhaps most clearly interpreted.

Considered purely as a structure Symphony No. 4 is one of Tippett's most ambitious large-scale abstract designs. In common with Quartet No. 4 and the Triple Concerto (and indeed Piano Sonata No. 3) it is cast as a single movement. Unlike the earlier one-movement Piano Sonata No. 2 though, these later works are essentially contractions of multi-movement designs rather than expansions of a single movement. Of the late examples however, Symphony No. 4 comes closest to brooking some degree of compromise. It is only as the argument unfolds – in Tippett's own terms – that we become aware of its references to traditional symphonic archetypes. The journey is one of continuous development and accretion leading eventually to a modified recapitulation. It is instructive to recall here a remark Tippett made in a radio interview to the effect that it took him a long time to develop the necessary confidence in his ability to write a one-movement work of this kind. Sonata No. 3 is much more obviously concerned with stark polarities: the vigorous athletic profile of the first movement cut abruptly in mid-flow to give dramatic emphasis to the still meditative rapture of the slow movement before this atmosphere in turn is rudely shattered by the violent concluding toccata. This kind of scheme is not abandoned in the later pieces, for, in modified form it figures prominently in both Quartet No. 4 and the Triple Concerto.

In Symphony No. 4 there is a much tauter network of interlocking ideas. Although sonata-terminology can be easily applied to the component parts of the first span of music – slow introduction, first subject, bridge, second subject and codetta – it is not done out of any sense of academic duty. Tippett's music proceeds so lucidly that the traditional sections are immediately perceived as an archetypal, even metaphorical extension of the music's life-blood. The means of articulating this expository span is largely rhythmic – Tippett's argument is unfurled in three main rhythmic stages so that the whole represents an organic acceleration. When a burst of violently hammered chords (reminiscent of the equally insistent chords in the Third Sonata's finale), some battering on percussion and a rasp in the brass (a momentary slip back to *The Ice Break*'s roughness) halt the acceleration in being followed by a slow chordal build-up on six horns (its immediate relaxation makes it virtually a musical metaphor for the inhalation/exhalation of breath so prevalent in the wind-machine writing in the Symphony), it is clear that the argument must proceed on expansive lines.

The symphonic mechanism is of course crucial, for this is what ultimately gives the work its coherence – it is a symphonic argument and not some set of ritual dances. The process of development is most obviously one of variation and the accumulation of music related to that already heard in each section of the exposition. In this way the articulation of the structure is easily comprehended, for the initial sequence of tempi is repeated (more or less) a further four times to cover the whole work. The first of these 'replays' – in establishing the pattern – emerges naturally as the 'development' section, but the schematically linear plan being set up does not seem to promise an immediate recapitulation – the scale is too large for that. In allowing the third replay to start with the same punctuation on horns as opened the second, Tippett conjures up broader vistas. Each tempo section is now elongated – they are thus sections in themselves, and the acceleration is drawn out over the whole central section of the Symphony. This is how the slow movement and scherzo grow naturally into the design, and in having a fugal development placed climactically between them the three sections can be seen to belong to both multi-movement and single-movement patterns. In other words while a degree of independent profile is established, these middle sections are simultaneously an enormous extension of the preceding 'development' proper and become an adjunct to it. They also kindle an expectation for some form of the recapitulation previously frustrated. After the scherzo (and its trios) the punctuation which had always followed the fast sections returns and the two concluding spans are beautifully symmetrical. Another development section suggests a mirror or arch-like return and it clinches, in synoptic fashion, the relationship of the three central panels to the initial development procedure in being an enormously compressed review of both stretches. It seems to squeeze the central expansiveness into the earlier straitjacket and it leads, via a cunning juxtaposition of the so-far unrepeated codetta fanfares to the actual recapitulation of the exposition. In this guise it is the only point of 'arrival' in the Symphony and so acts very naturally as the 'finale' – the 'finale problem' therefore being dealt a convincing blow here. It is however a point of arrival and not the climax of the whole work – that came at the height of the second panel in the central developmental span. The Symphony's dramatic curve is always kept in focus, for the recapitulation *is* a finale and not just a re-run and it incorporates music from the scherzo's trio towards the end, as it dissolves in tensely dramatic polarities.

The sonata-mechanism is also the clearest way of approaching (albeit tentatively) the nature of the Fourth Symphony's synthesis. Having abandoned diatonic tonality and a traditional sense of developmental continuity in favour of a freely chromatic virtual atonality (without entirely giving up points of tonal locality) and a disjunctive juxtaposition of thematic blocks in *King Priam* it was natural that an initial return to 'symphonic' sonata-form should be achieved by reinterpreting the classical sense of duality (or indeed polarity!) in terms of the newly-established idiom. Symphony No. 3 therefore grows from two dramatically-opposed cells – the one basically chordal (*Arrest*) and the other essentially linear (*Movement*). These interact, until they are eventually superimposed. Some six years later the Fourth Symphony's exposition – in that it proceeds in clear stages – presents a realignment of the classical prototype (expressed most succinctly and masterfully by Tippett in the first movement of Symphony No. 2) with the cellular expansion of Symphony No. 3. It is as if the ground-plan of the Third Symphony's first section is here stretched out to accommodate the discursiveness which it could not itself contemplate. In this opening of the Third Symphony perhaps can be seen the germ of the kind of single-movement organization that Tippett was to favour, and it must not be forgotten that the two parts of the Symphony each contains two movements dramatically linked. It is interesting too to note that the structure of the first 'movement' is foreshadowed in a tonal context in the *Fantasia Concertante on a theme of Corelli* – two sharply contrasted ideas expanding on repetition into extended variants which develop an individual profile before returning to their original form for a pithy conclusion. If this is compressed (atonally) in the Third it is enlarged over the whole structure of the Fourth Symphony. That the Fourth also reconciles the elements of sonata and fantasy (as many commentators have pointed out) is therefore given further weight by this particular structural analogy.

As to its surface, the Symphony No. 4 presents just as dazzling a synthesis. Its introduction immediately opens a sound-world which has a breadth and spaciousness new to Tippett, even though the transfiguring glow of *The Midsummer Marriage* resonates distantly in the clear tonal anchor on A with which the Symphony opens, as also in the radiantly lucid textures. In the subsequent expansions of the Symphony's slow music the world of the opera becomes increasingly tangible both harmonically and texturally. Much in the music is metaphorical – the implied progression from 'birth-to-death' is obviously one instance, and the labelling of ideas in the exposition (and elsewhere) as being characteristic of 'power', 'lyric grace' and more is further evidence of an attitude not only manifest in Symphony No. 3, but also in No. 2. As another ingredient in the synthesis fairly rigorous fugal writing is reintroduced in the central development and the scherzo's second trio. In the latter a tune from Gibbons's 3-part viol Fantasy No. 8 is treated in this way (suitably on strings only), and it also provides another echo for it was also quoted in the *Divertimento on Sellinger's Round*. The very end of the Symphony too is an echo. The surging fast music, with everything caught up in its wake vanishes without warning to reveal a procession of slow and intensely moving brass chords. Hectic bursts of the fast struggling semiquavers return (only a few bars each time, getting gradually shorter) but fail to stop the inexorable growth of the chorale with which the Symphony eventually expires. This is in fact a dramatic intensification of the concluding stages of the Piano Concerto's slow movement (and by way of that work the slow movement of the Second Symphony too) and harks back therefore to the slow movement dialogue of Beethoven's Piano Concerto No. 4. As described above its significance as the metaphorical climax of the Symphony is abundantly clear.

With hindsight, much of the Fourth Symphony's music will now be inextricably coloured by its quotation in *The Mask of Time*. This has in fact enriched the strong affective power of the Symphony in rather the same way (though in a less specific context) that fragments of the Third Symphony's first part are given associative weight and significance when quoted in conjunction with verbal ideas in the work's final *Scena*. The pounding ostinato of Symphony No. 4's first subject comes vividly to life as a metaphor for Shelley's voyage to death on the Ligurian coast, and the slight rhythmic changes it undergoes give it greater strength and inevitability. The tense breath-like horn chord (and the lyrical interlude which follows it) acquires great poignancy when it is recalled in the final stages of *Hiroshima mon amour* – with the inhalation transferred to voices. Such inter-quotation is part of the rich synthetic fabric of Tippett's late music (though quotation itself can be traced back further even than the *Suite for the Birthday of Prince Charles*) and goes simply to reaffirm the metaphorical implications of the music. In this way the magical opening of the Fourth Symphony is confirmed in *The Mask of Time* as a symbol of *Time* unfolding into *Space*.

String Quartet No. 4 contains many elements which betray its close relationship to Symphony No. 4, and the same is true of the Triple Concerto. In the Quartet for instance the extended slow introduction appears as an elaboration of the Symphony's birth-image, even to the point of a similar gesture of rhythmic multiplication which ushers in the assertive first subject of the ensuing sonata movement. Some moments of linear angularity here recall passages in the first movement of the Third Sonata, and its three very similar panels suggest a parallel with the scherzo of String Quartet No. 2. Although the three sections of the Fourth Quartet's second movement do imply a very symmetrical sonata-allegro there are scherzo-like touches which contribute to a nicely calculated sense of structural ambiguity. While the rest of the quartet expands naturally as a slow movement, finale and coda there emerges gradually a greater concentration on the work's central issue – polarities of speed and stasis – which is pursued in a structurally less schematic way than the binding of rhythmic patterns in Symphony No. 4. The unity of the one-movement structure, though just as convincing, is achieved not in terms of recapitulation over and beyond the boundaries of the inner movement divisions – rather, this is eschewed in favour of an intense web of motivic interconnections, which centre around densely organized networks of tones and semitones.

In the Triple Concerto the tranquility which eventually settles at the end of Quartet No. 4 finds its fulfilment. There are once again, however, certain polarities in the work. The outer 'movements' have great forward momentum of the kind associated with classical sonata-music. The opening movement is essentially a remodelling of the first two sections of Symphony No. 4 – a slow introduction, quick first subject (here texturally episodic), lyrical second subject and an ostinato-like codetta. Even the gestures are in places remarkably similar. The overall tone is however rather more benign and relaxed. The second section of the Concerto's first movement is another interesting instance of structural illusion. Everything heard in the first section is re-presented and often elaborated, but there are also significant additions to the flow, which are very cunningly placed to flesh-out the design already heard – to the point indeed that much of the material is structurally reorganized (the slow introduction for instance is cut up to unify the whole section and the first subject is split down the middle) but in such a way that the original prevailing symmetry is maintained. It therefore relates to the Mozartian structural concept of a 'soloist's' exposition in a concerto first movement, or, that is, to the analytically erroneous 'double-exposition' where the expository skeleton (tutti) is maintained as a background while a new foreground is fleshed out. When the music rushes to a headlong and breathless halt, it is immediately clear that the scale of the music so far (as in Symphony No. 4) could not admit now to an immediate recapitulation. That will be the goal of the extended finale, which gradually picks up the sense of forward movement which the central slow section of the Concerto manages to suspend for over fifteen minutes.

The polarity presented is once again between movement and stasis, and the gentle presence of Javanese colouring in the scoring and structure in places encourages a feeling that we have here (even if not deliberately) an encapsulation of a Western notion of dynamic music giving way to a contemplative oasis of Eastern stasis and tranquility. It is wonderfully enhanced by the static interludes surrounding the lyrical outpouring of the slow movement proper – the one gentle and trance-inducing and the other (equally static in effect) serving to crack the dream. I am grateful to Ian Kemp for disclosing that this second interlude is connected to the dawn-image in Yeats's poem *High Talk*. It is interesting therefore to note that a setting of part of the poem appears at the start of *The Mask of Time*, even though the Triple Concerto's interlude is not quoted at the relevant point. In the concerto it is followed by a rich string cantilena which galvanizes the music to life by recalling the 'second-dawn' music from *The Midsummer Marriage*.

As a structure the Concerto combines the clear-cut design of Sonata No. 3 with the sense of sub-structure present in Symphony No. 4. This surfaces in the double-exposition, interludes and finale. Everything in the finale is ingeniously devised, from a structural point of view, to lead to the reprise of the Concerto's opening section, which having been expanded on its second appearance is now suitably compressed. This compression provides the key to an understanding of the finale. Its exuberant opening tune is structurally crucial as an archetypal landmark and so it is strategically placed; its continuation however tells us that it is only a notional rondo. All we get is a mini-rondo complete with tiny sequential episodes, and just as the return of the rondo is instantly upon us it immediately peters out. All the sections from (and including) the second interlude onwards are stages in a journey, and its most exciting part is the sequence of tonally-rooted ostinato pedals which gradually build up momentum in order to arrive at the very opening of the work – the proportions of this final stage are therefore totally different to those in the Fourth Symphony. The journey now virtually over the music's sense of arrival is such that the coda (actually a codettetta!) just peters out again – having come full circle a further cycle is whimsically dismissed. As with Symphony No. 4 (but much less so) parts of the Triple Concerto will now connect with *The Mask of Time*. The gentle shimmering of bells and whirring pizzicato strings (the codetta figure) which ends the Concerto opens the first of the *Three*

Songs in *The Mask of Time – The Severed Head* in which sections of the Orpheus legend are described. The inclusion at its heart of the lines from Rilke already quoted earlier in this essay provides a clear indication of how far removed the Triple Concerto is from the shadow of *The Ice Break*, and it is interesting to note that when Tippett quoted the same lines in the preface to *Too Many Choices* in *Moving into Aquarius* he used a slightly different English translation, in which one word is perhaps significantly different:

> 'Only he who raised his lyre also under *shadows*,
> may with divining tongue sound the infinite praise.' (Schatten)

The path towards a realignment and rejuvenation of the spirit is now fully realised – a renewed spring indeed towards the end of the rich harvest of a life's work. But it is also a metamorphosis of idioms in which the varied and chastening experience of a grim century is manifestly transcended but never discarded. Coincidentally the setting of Shakespeare's blessing 'Spring come to you' in *The Ice Break* and the unison melody of the Triple Concerto's slow movement not only share a similar melodic profile, but they both also set out from F without returning to it. F being an archetypally autumnal key it is perhaps no coincidence that the Triple Concerto ends in the equally archetypal vernal E. There is a profound wisdom in Tippett's late music alongside the continued questing. Although there is no direct quotation from the Triple Concerto in *The Dream of the Paradise Garden* in *The Mask of Time*, the use of solo strings makes the connection crystal clear. The Triple Concerto is pre-eminently the work of reconciliation in Tippett's output and this progression reaches its fulminant fulfilment in *The Mask of Time* – that much is evident in the heading to the work:

> in the beginning and now
> creation, falling away and the marriage of opposites

The Mask of Time is in no way the end of the road, even though it may now momentarily seem to stand as the climax and crown of Tippett's output. The three works which have been composed after it continue to explore, in different directions. Paul Crossley has expressed his eager anticipation that the Fourth Piano Sonata will be Tippett's 'definitive' work for solo piano. The Sonata for Guitar – *The Blue Guitar* – is a delightfully transparent and nimble work, in which lines from Wallace Stevens' poem of the same title give rise to three contrasted movements:

Transforming: Being the lion in the lute/Before the lion locked in stone.
Dreaming:　　Morning is not sun,/It is this posture of the nerves,
　　　　　　　As if a blunted player clutched/The nuances of the blue guitar
Juggling:　　the old fantoche/Hanging his shawl upon the wind

It has been suggested that at the start the guitarist appears to be improvising gently to himself before capturing the essence of his discourse. The slow movement is a vivid dialogue between lyrical musing and declamatory passion, while the finale entertainingly touches on some jazz-like inflections in its exhilarating flow.

　　Blues figure prominently of course in *Festal Brass with Blues* – Tippett's first work for brass band. With the notional sound of the flugelhorn in mind what could be more appropriate than to actually realize the original intention behind the finale of the Third Symphony – an 'instrumental' blues. After a vital reinterpretation of fanfare-like ideas (related to the glowing brass writing of Symphony No. 3's first movement) the sudden quotation of the fanfare of chaos from Beethoven's Ninth Symphony unmistakably ushers in the world of Tippett's own Symphony. The work's axis thus dramatically tilted the composer beautifully and movingly instrumentalises the vocal lines of the first and second blues songs from the Symphony before a brief coda disperses the emotion. This abstraction of the Symphony's polemic is proof that *The Mask of Time* did not exhaust Tippett's engagement with either metaphor or abstract theatricality or even the blues! *Festal Brass with Blues* is also yet another work which – like Quartet No. 4 and its rhythmic allusions to Beethoven's *Grosse Fuge* – has strong Beethovenian affinities, and there is evidence already that the Fourth Sonata will maintain this tradition.

In 1980, just after completing the Triple Concerto and before embarking on *The Mask of Time* Tippett declared in the Preface to *Music of the Angels*: 'I feel further that all, but all I have to dream with now is metaphor and theatre.' *The Mask of Time* indeed proved to be his most metaphorical work. It is heartening now to learn that even though *The Ice Break* was described at the time of its premiere as the 'fourth and final opera', there is a new theatrical work in progress. Early rumours of the presence in the scenario of a giant panda and a flying saucer were a tantalising glimpse of another Tippettian world in the making, even if it is unlikely that they will survive into the final draft of this new stage work. After the references to Shakespearean masque in *The Ice Break* and the stated link between *The Mask of Time* and the Renaissance masque it would be highly appropriate if the new work revitalised the masque tradition in some way. As *The Ice Break* demonstrated so emphatically Tippett's dramatic development has from the start been a process of constant evolution.

As to *The Mask of Time* itself, there is a sense in which it transmutes much that is central to *The Ice Break* and projects the central concerns of Tippett's artistic vision on a universal platform. To have presented such a broad world-view with such a sweep of single-minded vision and musical richness perhaps stands as one of the four most extraordinary feats of Tippett's compositional career, alongside the creation of *A Child of Our Time*, *The Midsummer Marriage* and *The Vision of Saint Augustine*. Even though the tenor soloist is frequently given lines which seem to echo some of Tippett's most personal artistic expressions, so falling into the tradition traceable through *Boyhood's End*, *The Heart's Assurance*, *Songs for Achilles* and *Songs for Dov* there is also a sense of pure detachment. I find a passage from Iris Murdoch's *The Sovereignty of Good* peculiarly apt to Tippett's achievement in this respect:

'The talent of the artist can be readily, and is naturally, employed to produce a picture whose purpose is the consolation and aggrandizement of its author and the projection of his personal obsession and wishes. To silence and expel self, to contemplate and delineate nature with a clear eye, is not easy, and demands a moral discipline.'

The Mask of Time does not avoid polarities in its striving for a union of opposites, and it contains one such polarity that may well stand eventually as the most dramatic in Tippett's whole output. It is certainly one of the quintessential moments in his music. As the course of work moves inexorably through images of Creation, Man, the Fall from Paradise, artistic striving and human mortality to the discovery of science and technics, the music is propelled with a seemingly inexorable and demoniac force through the third chorale-prelude prefiguring the statement of Mankind's potentially destructive misuse of technology (a message which repeatedly resounds in Tippett's writings from 1945 onwards) to the emergence of an unspecified but explicit moment of cataclysmic destruction – 'Shiva dancing our destruction', a reversal of his *creative* dancing. It could well be surmised that the horrific violence of the scene from *The Ice Break* which I took as the starting point of this essay is here transformed. The music is blindingly insistent and has an awesome mesmeric grip. Where the opera's violence was all too human in its inhumanity the image presented here has a totally numbing and complete inhumanity – in a sense it is non-human. Then in a flash there is no noise and we are aware only of a deep, initially almost inaudible low humming for male chorus over which a soprano slowly pours out a heartrending lament. There is no moral, polemic, message or propaganda at this overwhelming moment – here is just threnody and remembrance of *all* victims of Man's inhumanity to Man. Even though the purely musical effect rivals the moment of transcendent vision in the finale of Stravinsky's *Symphony of Psalms* (another Boston commission) as one of the great moments in our musical heritage, there is more to it than that. In acknowledging that few composers of the present century have achieved such a perfect equilibrium of the heart and mind as has Tippett, the greater significance of this climactic gesture in *The Mask of Time* is that it is the most important and fundamental single expression that is open to Man today. In one overpowering collective moment Tippett sings for the whole world – and the art and the message are indivisible. From a moment of total polarity immediately flows the deepest reconciliation. This moment is merely the musical manifestation for stating (though it be of no significance to the composer himself) that Michael Tippett is not only a supreme musician, but one of the great men of our time. At a point in his setting of Anna Akhmatova's words under the heading *Hiroshima mon amour* the words are totally consumed by music of compassion from the Fourth Symphony which wells up underneath the singer's declamation:

'I have woven a great shroud for you out of those poor words I overheard you speak. I shall remember always and everywhere shall not forget come fresh evil days. And if they shut my tortured mouth through which a thousand million shout then, shall you remember me on the eve of my remembrance day. Slowly it floods my mind like a melody in music . . .'

But our eyes are already flooded with tears, and we are speechless, humbled and grateful.

Opposite
© Schott and Co. Ltd. The opening of *Hiroshima, mon Amour* from *The Mask of Time* in Tippett's autograph.

A rehearsal in Boston (April 1984) for the world première of The Mask of Time. *Tippett listens with Meirion Bowen, dedicatee of the work. (Photo: Ted Dully)*

MEIRION BOWEN

'Dare, Divining, Sound'

The Mask of Time

TIPPETT'S compositional development during the 1960s and 70s could credibly be depicted as an Orphic descent and return. For, in a succession of works during this period, such as *The Knot Garden, Songs for Dov*, Symphony No. 3 and *The Ice Break*, he was impelled to tackle themes explicitly concerned with the turbulence of the modern epoch and the sufferings endured by both individuals and whole societies. The ultimate messages of these works are invariably bleak:

> If, *for a timid moment*
> we submit to love,
> Exit from the inner cage,
> turn each to each to all . . .
>
> (*The Knot Garden*, Act 3)

> My sibling was the torturer.
> He takes his place . . .
>
> It is our agony
> We fractured men
> Surmise a deeper mercy;
> That no god has shown.
>
> (Symphony No. 3)

> Chastened, together,
> We try once more . . .
>
> Yet you will always be brought forth again,
> glorious image of God,
> and likewise be maimed, wounded afresh,
> from within or without.
>
> (*The Ice Break*, Act 3)

Nevertheless, Tippett has always possessed an instinct that allows him to detach his creative endeavours from the tensions and upheavals of the outside world and suggest possibilities for hope and regeneration. Earlier in his career, for instance, just when the concentration camps were being opened and atomic bombs had been dropped on Hiroshima and Nagasaki, Tippett had conceived and brought to fruition the most radiantly lyrical opera of the twentieth century, *The Midsummer Marriage*. This gift of being able to envisage an entirely separate realm of experience constantly obtrudes in his work, producing odd, almost un-analysable music, like the fourth movement of his String Quartet No. 3, or unexpected suspensions of the stage-action in his operas while mysterious Messenger-figures – Madame Sosostris (in *The Midsummer Marriage)*, Hermes (in *King Priam*) and Astron (in *The Ice Break*) hold forth: and it became virtually the subject-matter of *The Vision of Saint Augustine*. If it was necessary in the last twenty years or so for him to travel down into the abyss of contemporary turmoil, it was equallly incumbent upon him to journey back towards the daylight of a sustaining vision. That return journey is steadily manifest in the Symphony No. 4, String Quartet No. 4 and Triple Concerto. *The Mask of Time* encompasses both the descent and return and additionally provides a cosmic context for it all.

To think of *The Mask of Time* only as a summatory work, as Tippett in old age making one great last effort to deal with the transcendental, is to limit its essential scope. Certainly, in part, such a view is accurate: and as such, the work can be compared with the late poetry of William Blake, Yeats' *Last Poems*, Gauguin's *Where do we come from? What are we? Where are we going?* – etc. A more apposite analogy would be Rilke's *Duino Elegies*, the product of ten years' hard effort (as was the case with Tippett's composition). For here, too, is an allegory of lament culminating in an affirmation. Rilke's lowest note is sounded in his 'wintry' fourth Elegy. By the time he reaches his ninth and tenth Elegies, he is in a position to affirm and praise. Likewise, Tippett in his sixth, seventh and eighth movements plumbs tragic depths: the triumphal chariot of life in Shelley's poem throws bodies off in all directions, and later Shelley himself drowns at sea; knowledge and science are perverted to produce ultimate weapons of destruction; a threnody for the victims of a brutal world is unavoidable. But then in two linked final movements, Tippett brings a succession of individuals into focus, offering images of creative vitality, hope and reconciliation, and at the last, an intense visionary moment which can be shared by everyone. It is not far-fetched to discern in all this an expression of creative self-confidence on the composer's part. Having reached this point, he can assuredly contemplate further works.

Significantly, in the ninth movement, the first individual to stand up and sing is Orpheus: the Orpheus of mythology returning from Hades without his beloved Euridice; after his death and dismemberment by the Furies, his head floats down the river, still singing. The mythological Orpheus is fused, however, with Rilke's who – in the course of two cycles of sonnets (55 in all, written, unlike the *Elegies*, at great speed) – is not there so much in person, but is used to underpin an exposition of the poet's own world-view. Tippett, for the purposes of his ninth-movement song, seizes upon a specific aspect of Rilke's theme: 'only a person who has known and suffered the dark side of the world can truly praise; Orpheus visited Hades and therefore experienced this darkness.' Hence his quotation from the ninth of the first cycle of Orpheus sonnets (sung, in fact, by the solo baritone):

> Who alone already lifted
> the lyre among the dead
> dare, divining, sound
> the infinite praise.

At the end of the song, the severed head of Orpheus sings further lines from Rilke, this time sonnet 26 of the first cycle:

Woe! where are we; Ever yet freer,
like torn-loose kites,
We flitter half-high, with edges of laughter,
bounced by the wind.
Order the screamers, O singing God!
That they may wake flowing,
bearing on the river-race the head and the lyre.

As with Rilke, it is not merely the myth of Orpheus that matters in Tippett's song, but the Orphic *vision*, and the problems that arise out of it. *The Mask of Time*, like the Orpheus sonnet-sequence, is diverse in its ingredients and in some ways illustrative of the Orphic vision: some of it is celebratory, some of it tragic, and some of it is polemical, setting the modern world and its technology in sharp contrast with the Orphic world-view. But we reach the crux of the work quite clearly in this song.

More generally, the composer of *The Mask of Time* and the poet of the Orpheus sonnets have traits in common. At the start of Tippett's work, the tenor intervenes in the choral rhetoric to sing:

All metaphor, Malachi, stilts and all
Malachi, Malachi, all metaphor.

And indeed, *The Mask of Time* is *all metaphor*. The point is reinforced when Tippett allots the final song of the ninth movement to a *young actor*, a choice which echoes Shakespeare's famous lines:

All the world's a stage
. . and one man in his time plays many parts.

The work is all metaphor because everything within it moves towards fusion and metamorphosis. The threshold between the visible and the invisible is the locus of redefinition and transformation as, again, the tenor continues:

A barnacle goose
far up in the stretches of night;
night splits and the dawn breaks loose.

It is the same with Rilke: the emphasis always is on *Bezug* (relationship), *Umkehr* (reversal) and *Wandlung* (transmutation). These are the pervasive processes that enable the Orphic metamorphosis of the earth in Rilke's sonnet-sequence to become a reality here and now. In the concert-hall, when *The Mask of Time* is performed, exactly these processes underly its eventual change from intense, violent fulgurations resulting in catastrophe, to soaring aspirations and an affirmative outpouring.

To cap this comparison, one could say that with composer and poet, not only are all the images inward-bound, but even their context has to be drawn into the metaphorical realm. Each, in a word, is a poet of *Weltinnenraum* (world-space interiorised). Thus, in the opening movement of *The Mask of Time*, the chorus and tenor soloist *both* offer metaphor: the former ululate upon a single word, *Sound*, expressive of the infinity of time and space; the latter sings 'from within the poignant and immediate here and now', identifying with the whiffler of Yeats' poem, *High Talk*, who stalks about on stilts in front of a circus-parade – an apt analogy for the efforts of an individual to survive amidst the mêlée of human experience, as well as for the artist attempting to sustain the integrity of his message. This polarity is maintained throughout the work: e.g. against Orpheus 'stalking on into the daylight' (in the ninth movement), the chorus once again vocalise upon the word *Sound*.

How and why *The Mask of Time* came to be written can only be fully understood when one bears in mind these co-existing processes: to discover relationships, reversals and transmutations that could be applied not only to the heterogeneous ingredients offering themselves for inclusion, but also to their contexts, was the basis of Tippett's entire creative effort. It was always evident that the work would be compounded from Tippett's earliest memories, lifelong obsessions and various recent experiences. How he sifted, selected and shaped them all into a coherent composition was an elaborate affair.

As is probably now evident, the seeds for many of his major compositions were sown early on in life. Seeing Toller's *Masse und Mensch* in his youth, for example, provoked resonances which were to make an impact later in *The Ice Break*. Visiting the Pitt-Rivers Museum of Anthropology in Dorset and seeing a film of foetal development left an indelible mark: the opening birth-motif of Symphony No. 4 (which recurs in *The Mask of Time*) related directly to that memory. As a child of five, Tippett was held up by his father to see Halley's Comet. His memory was reactivated in the 1970s when he read Loren Eiseley's *The Invisible Pyramid*,[2] where the comet (which Eiseley, too, had seen as a child) is the presiding metaphor, and it assumes that role in *The Mask of Time*.

What fascinated the composer about the comet was that it would *reverse its course*: not only would he himself be around to see it again when it returned in 1986, but the idea of reversal tied in with other such concepts as Jung's *enantrochromia*, the mechanics of the pendulum, reversal psychology, and ancient theorising about reversal in Heraclitus and the *I-Ching*. Halley's comet reversing its course could be polarised against the inexorable forward motion of the cosmos in general. It could suggest not merely a set of linked images and ideas, but a vital method of articulating them within the structure of the piece:

Eternal
Reversal

as the chorus sings in the first movement, might even be regarded as a way of understanding how the entire universe came into being. Hence also the presence of both Orpheus who, through music, brings order to a disordered world, and Shiva who, here, dances the world into existence and, later (in the seventh movement), 'dances our destruction'. There are other reversals. In the fourth movement, Man the nomadic wanderer finds a home and ritual

218

within the depths of a cave; with the genetic accident that makes available breadgrain-bearing plants which can be cultivated, Man moves up overground, forms settled societies and enacts rituals at the *top* of pyramids and temples. The two halves of the fifth movement, similarly, show at first a blissful communion of Man, Woman, the animal world (represented by a Dragon) and the supernatural (represented by the Ancestor), which then goes into reverse: the change is signalled by an allusion to the *I-Ching*:

> In the moment of perfection
> of the six-fold graph,
> a line is about to . . .
>
>   . . . too late, ah, too late, a nine-line has reversed.

Notions of time have figured prominently amongst Tippett's lifelong obsessions. Already, as a student, he was aware that new concepts were coming into existence through the exercise of the scientific imagination. He read, currently, H. G. Wells' *Men Like Gods* (1921) and was much enamoured of its presentation of a future socialist utopia. One of his earliest efforts at composition, was a piece for chorus and orchestra based on a didactic passage on time in the book. And the ruminations of Wells' Mr Barnstaple, a sub-editor on *The Liberal* who finds himself in utopia, almost anticipate the kind of thinking that eventually became central to *The Mask of Time*:

'Time was when men could talk of everlasting hills. Today a schoolboy knows that they dissolve under the frost and wind and rain and pour seaward, day by day and hour by hour. Time was when men could speak of Terra Firma and feel the earth fixed, adamantine beneath their feet. Now they know that it whirls through space eddying about a spinning, blindly driven sun amidst a sheeplike drift of stars.'[3]

Years later, reading Henri Bergson and Jung alerted Tippett to other ideas on time which had a bearing upon musical experience:

'At the other pole to painting, music offers images of the inner world of feelings perceived as a flow. As our concept of external time is itself an equivocal one, it is perhaps less easy even than with space in painting, to realise that the time we apprehend in the work of musical art has only a virtual existence in contrast with the time marked by the clock hands when the work is performed.'[4]

The Vision of Saint Augustine (1963-5) crystallised out of Tippett's perception of the psychological nuance which Augustine had given to concepts of time. The present is nothing if not an experience in the soul; the past is a memory image in the soul; and the future exists only as our psychic expectations. Ordinary time is transient and meaningless. It disappears when the soul unites with God. 'Divine time' – or 'Eternity' – is thus separable from measured worldly time. The soul is forever distended in all directions without a centre. To achieve a centre, concentration is necessary. Augustine's two visions, the prime concern of Tippett's composition, gave him an intimation of such a centre. And this landmark in Tippett's music in the 1960s became a beacon for the future. Only at the end of *The Mask of Time*, having completed the Orphic descent and return of the past fifteen years, could Tippett once more justify an outpouring of ecstatic, visionary music.

Travel and television figured prominently amongst the more recent experiences fuelling Tippett's inspiration in *The Mask of Time*. In the late 1960s and 70s, Tippett visited America many times and fell in love with the canyons and mesas of the Far West. Monument Valley, an Indian reservation in Arizona (and home of many a John Wayne movie) haunted him especially. With its red rocks eroded into pillars and castles over millions of years, it seemed to him the living embodiment of timelessness. Watching television – which he does, not only for diversion but for stimulus – he once heard an astronomer say that with the possibility of putting one of the newest telescopes on a satellite outside the earth's atmosphere: 'We can see beyond the edge of the universe and the beginning of time.' 'What happens,' Tippett asked himself, 'when we reach the "edge" of the universe? Do we fall over it; do we meet God; or what?' Such notions opened up for him new dream territory: and at one stage Tippett used as his motto for *The Mask of Time* a quotation from Eiseley's book, encapsulating both the scientist's and artist's situation, given the potency of such dreams:

'But I dream, and because I dream, I severally condemn, fear and salute the future. It is the salute of a gladiator ringed by the indifference of the watching stars.'[5]

Referring to Cocteau's image of the theatre as a 'trick factory where truth has no currency, where anything natural has no value, where the only things that convince us are card tricks and sleights of hand of a difficulty unsuspected by the audience', Eiseley comments:

'The cosmos itself gives evidence, on an infinitely greater scale, of being just such a trick factory, a set of lights forever changing, and the actors themselves shape shifters, elongated shadows of something above or without. Perhaps in the sense men use the word natural, there is really nothing at all natural in the universe, or, at best, that the world is natural only in being unnatural, like some variegated, color-shifting chameleon.'[6]

In formulating a composition of transcendental compass, Tippett could not thus ignore the scientific advances which, in this century, have pushed back the frontiers of knowledge and perception, vastly expanding our conceptions of time and space. He had to put on one side 'standard' Biblical accounts of Genesis and other religious orthodoxies: and he even had to discard 'alternative' though composite philosophies exemplified in such works as Delius' *A Mass of Life* and Mahler's Eighth Symphony. If Messiaen could respond to the canyons of Utah and Arizona with an expression (in *Des Canyons aux étoiles*) of total faith, confidence and wonder, Tippett had to show an opposite world of doubt, scepticism and uncertainty.

The chief model for *The Mask of Time* – or, more accurately, what exemplified for Tippett the kind of project he would most like to emulate – was Jacob Bronowski's *The Ascent of Man*, which he saw first on television and then read in its subsequent book form.[7] Bronowski's unitary conception, its blend of scientific and artistic insights – these he knew he could not rival. But he

220

thought he might match its humane vision and even something of its imaginative breadth. In writing and compiling his text, Tippett often paraphrased Bronowski. For example, in the seventh movement, where he is depicting the alchemists' research into the possible mutation of elements –

> O rose-red cinnabar, you sombre metal
> hell-heated
> hotter, hotter!
> radiant
> look, look!
> a silver and liquid pearl of mercury,
> For fire is alchemy.

Tippett is drawing directly on the opening of Bronowski's Chapter 4, 'The Hidden Structure':

'They [the alchemists] took the red pigment, cinnabar, which is a sulphide of mercury, and heated it. The heat drives off the sulphur and leaves behind an exquisite pearl of the mysterious silvery liquid metal mercury, to astonish and strike awe into the patron.'[8]

Later in the chapter, Bronowski writes of the 'dizzy hope that we can march from the primitive processes of the first coppersmiths and the magical speculations of the alchemists to the most powerful idea in modern science: the idea of the atoms'.[9] In the same movement of *The Mask of Time*, Tippett walks that route:

> unbind the structured atom.

Earlier in the work, in 'The Ice-Cap moves South-North', Tippett's text is indebted to Bronowski's account of nomadic life at the mercy of the elements and the emergence of settled societies as a result of a 'genetic accident' amongst wild grasses producing 'the first breadgrain-bearing plants cultivated by, and indeed dependent upon, the post-Ice-Age man'.[10] The threat to the Paradise Garden in the succeeding movement is signalled by the Centaur that jumps the wall: 'In a sense, warfare was created by the horse,' writes Bronowski.[11]

Tippett and Bronowski are not, however, identical in their viewpoints. For Bronowski, the scientific achievements of the century, and their imaginative and intellectual background, justify confidence in the future ascent of man, notwithstanding the upheavals and catastrophes, and evidence of a loss of nerve, a retreat into Zen Buddhism, 'falsely profound questions' etc.[12] Tippett is more reserved, more sceptical. His stance is that as an artist he has to defend values that are in danger of being ignored or obliterated by societies which have put their economic resources primarily at the disposal of technology. It is a theme to which he returns repeatedly in his talks and essays, e.g:

'The barrenness of the age lies in the deprivation of man's imaginative life once he has put value into machines. As man becomes more and more capable scientifically, the debasement of the world of imagination produces human beings who find it harder to use decently the material abundance thus provided.'[13]

So, in *The Mask of Time*, there is no celebration of science, of the new world of metaphor opened up by quantum theory or whatever. Instead, it is the perversion of scientific discovery which is brought sharply into the foreground. Tippett recognises that a younger composer might take a different line. He himself – as someone almost as old as the century, who had lived through two world wars, Hiroshima, some major revolutions, and any number of small conflagrations – could not, by temperament, shut out of his mind those many inhuman consequences of technological advance. For him recent human history has often come close to the natural world in which there are 'fixed' and often horrific and pointless cruelties, an everlasting struggle of prey and predator. The Jungle movement in Part 1 of *The Mask of Time* (drawing considerably upon Annie Dillard's *Pilgrim at Tinker Creek*[14] and the experience of watching television programmes by David Attenborough and others) has its human counterpart in Part 2: not just the historically distanced Shelley movement, but the searingly immediate Hiroshima Mon Amour. The polarity between intellectual knowledge and that derived from deep inner sensibilities – something ever-present in Tippett's work as a whole (*cf.* the alto solo, 'Man has measured the heavens with a telescope' in Part 1 of *A Child of Our Time*) is a constant ingredient of *The Mask of Time*. Yet his decision to centre the second song in the ninth movement upon a scene in which the *I-Ching* is consulted came as a result of discovering, by chance, that 64 was a magic number for both the ancient Book of Changes *and* molecular biology. Here was a resolution of apparent opposites which seemed entirely relevant to his theme.

The layout of *The Mask of Time* – 'fragments or scenes from a possible "epiphany" for today' – is consciously indebted to T. S. Eliot's *The Waste Land*. Eliot's method of quoting and juxtaposing sharply contrasted images is reflected in Tippett's text. The music itself is similarly presented, enhancing dramatically the verbal ideas and structuring them into a coherent whole. In this respect, the music is closer in conception to Monteverdi's *Vespers* of 1610 than to the symphonically organised large-scale compositions of a later period. For a start it is dominated by *singing*: in its entire 93 minutes' duration and ten movements there are only a few purely orchestral episodes. There is also a Monteverdian variety in its scoring. Although it entails a large choir, four soloists and an orchestra with a sizeable contingent of percussion, six horns and a saxophone amongst the brass and woodwind, there are relatively few big perorations in the piece involving absolutely everybody. Tippett describes the work as being 'for voices and instruments' since he tends to use the singers and instrumentalists in many different ensembles and textures, making up an elaborate mosaic scheme altogether.

Quite unconsciously, Tippett came curiously close to Monteverdi in certain features of *The Mask of Time*. For instance, just as Monteverdi began his *Vespers* with a chorus centred upon repetitions of a single D major chord, so Tippett, at the start of *The Mask of Time*, makes one chord the fulcrum of his invocation of an immense, eternally present universe (ex. 1):

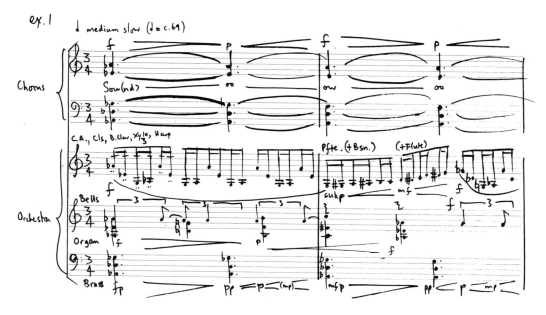

And again, inadvertently, Tippett followed Monteverdi in ending the work with a great surge of multi-layered polyphonic writing, the initial sound-metaphor now transformed into something visionary and transcendent. Whereas Monteverdi's ending is, however, thematically unconnected with his opening, Tippett's final movement is a kind of metamorphosis: the decorations and sequences of fourths surrounding the original chord in the first movement are lifted into the foreground (ex. 2).

The Mask of Time has fallen foul of those who consider the development sections and goal-orientated designs of the Viennese masters to be intrinsically (indeed, to judge from the tone of their advocates, morally) superior to the block-building, mosaic methods favoured as much by Monteverdi as Tippett. In the case of this work, few doubt its actual coherence. For there are many transmutations of its thematic material (such as the one cited above), counteracting any piecemeal effect arising out of the composer's section-by-section treatment of the text and wide diversity of idiom.

The opening gesture on 'Sound' recurs memorably as a significant symbolic 'presence' near the end of the Jungle movement and at the climax of the cry of Orpheus (in the ninth movement) – 'Dare, Divining, *Sound*'. The stuttering rhythm of 'Exploring, Exploding' and the winding lyrical phrases of 'Turning, Returning' are also aptly inserted at the start of the Shelley setting and of Orpheus' song, respectively. 'Resounding' also offers an important motif to which Tippett can refer in 'The Ice Cap Moves South-North' (*cf.* fig. 147) and at the close of the Shelley movement (fig. 289), in each case a *contextual* image, enabling individual deaths to be interpreted in a milieu of unavoidable human mortality. In this way, linked verbal and intellectual ideas are translated into musical metaphors.

There are, additionally, in *The Mask of Time*, a number of straightforward devices of a purely musical nature which Tippett uses to ensure continuity

and logic. For instance, in the third movement, there are recurrent 'calls to attention' on the drums; the four-bar introductory orchestral motif returns to introduce the final section; also, the tiny interlude for woodwind and organ preceding the section, 'Clamber downwards to the dark' comes back in an inverted form before 'We clamber *up* the staircase stone by stone' – a simple, though obviously effective mode of musical 'reversal'. The dawn music of the opening movement returns at the start of Part 2 and is developed in the second section of the movement (centred on Shelley himself). Depicting the tragic, triumphal chariot of life, Tippett uses a ground-bass – one of his favourite tools for keeping order in music whose fantastic inventiveness would otherwise get out of control. Yet here it also has a semi-pictorial, semi-symbolic function. Scored for tuba, bassoons and contra-bassoon, it has two triplet components, separated by a thump on the bass-drum, conveying vividly the lurching forward of the chariot (maybe it has a broken axle!). This 'naive' pictorial/symbolic aspect of the music is very much in the tradition of Monteverdi, Bach, Handel and others. Hence the struggles of predator and prey depicted in the choral writing of the 'Jungle' movement; the percussion stampede at 'Images of bison running' in the next movement; the violent rhythmic roulades on brake drums ('Shiva dancing our destruction') introducing the brass chords symbolising atomic explosions in the seventh movement; and so on: these elements in the music supply an essential richness of meaning in much the same way as when Renaissance or Baroque composers setting the Mass respond musically to specific words (*Crucifixus*, *Ascendit*, *etc.*).

The musical idiom of *The Mask of Time* exemplifies further the composer's habit of synthesising influences from disparate sources. A typical instance is the gentle interlude in the manner of a sarabande in the fifth movement, scored for three flutes, harp, three double-basses and percussion: this emulates an interlude late on in Berlioz's *L'Enfance du Christ*, but takes its rhythmic gait from the middle movement of Ravel's Sonatine for piano. The final amalgam is unmistakably Tippett's own. When he wanted a purple passage for the soprano and mezzo-soprano duetting exaltedly together at the end of the third movement, as 'the mocking-bird falls and time unfurls across space like an oriflame', he turned again to Monteverdi (especially *Nigra Sum* from the Vespers). The choral textures and madrigalian writing in particular in the Paradise Garden movement, memorably setting Milton's lines, are already part and parcel of Tippett's compositional style. The orchestra is often an extension of this kind of baroque vocal writing: so, again, when he wanted a blissful nature-evocation at the start of the fifth movement, he was irresistibly tempted to use as his starting-point the rhythm of Monteverdi's madrigal, *Ecco mormorar l'onde*.

It has been widely observed that *The Mask of Time* contains Tippett's most torrential flood of musical invention since *The Midsummer Marriage*. This invention, of course, does not at any stage in the work seem merely experimental, since the composer was inventing within a well-matured and individual style. In retrospect, that style may be regarded as the accumulation of all that he has written in the last two decades or so: its breadth can encompass an Orphic descent and return. The violence and *angst* of the Third Symphony and *The Knot Garden* are there; the speculative, incandescent exultation of *The Vision of Saint Augustine* are also there. These are the extremes of the work. They are synthesised in the concluding bars, where the florid vocalisations of soloists and chorus are set above orchestral chords that are tense, tough and stoic.

Two idiosyncratic features of Tippett's musical language are evident in the work as a whole. One is its rhythmic exuberance, never more brilliantly deployed than when the plainsong *Veni creator spiritus* is incorporated into the three preludes of the seventh movement. Another is the empirical treatment of harmony to achieve contrasting connotations for the thematic ideas: for instance, the richly sensuous string chords flowing through successive

225

interrupted cadences to bring balm and solace in the Hiroshima Mon Amour
movement (ex. 3):

and which have antecedents (for instance) in the Beethoven-inspired piano
writing of the final song of *The Heart's Assurance* (ex. 4):

are present as a dissonant, expressively distorted mirror-image in the opening
movement (ex. 5):

They reappear in that form (though rhythmically modified and embellished)
in the fourth movement (*cf.* fig. 143) and in the final section of the Shelley
movement (*cf.* fig. 289 onwards). Tippett's mature music of the last few
decades has such integrity amidst its diversity, that in *The Mask of Time* he can
quote from past works without any disturbing staleness or over-familiarity.
The opening of the Fourth Symphony, for instance, has a bluesy clash of
minor and major thirds which is a trait in Tippett's music as a whole, and
when he quotes the same motif near the start of *The Mask of Time*, the tenor line
superimposed upon it can continue in the same vein – the last B flat of the
tenor's phrase is very much a blues-note, in fact (ex. 6).
When this recurs near the close of the 'Jungle' movement the soprano and
mezzo-soprano lines (especially the latter) intensify this bluesiness (ex. 7).
And of course it is entirely appropriate that he should use this motif against
the word 'space', for it belongs originally in a work which was opening up a

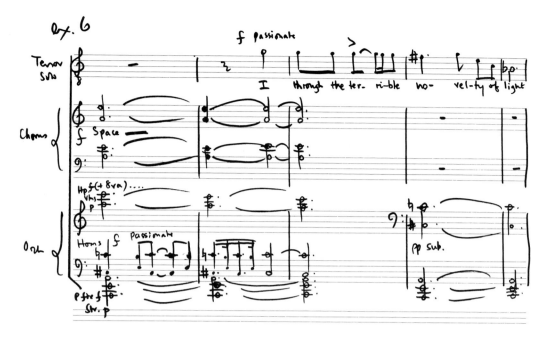

ex. 6

cosmic context of exploration in Tippett's *oeuvre*. Those well-acquainted with *King Priam, The Ice Break* and the Triple Concerto might at first not catch the significance of quotations from these works in *The Mask of Time*. Greater familiarity with the latter encourages one to accept them as *belonging* there, both because of the specific images they contribute and because of their relevance to the stylistic amplitude of the work.

Writing of the creative processes that led to *The Midsummer Marriage*, Tippett declared:

'I hold for myself that the composition of oratorio and opera is a collective as well as a personal experience.'[15]

The Mask of Time is certainly that kind of collective work; indeed, if Stravinsky could say of *Le Sacre du Printemps*, 'I am the vessel through which *Le Sacre* passed', so, Tippett, within his entire output during the 1960s and 1970s,

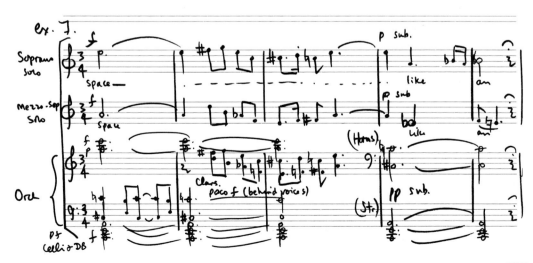

ex. 7.

suffered the composition of many such collective compositions. *The Mask of Time* is the most comprehensive of them all.

*   *   *

To conclude on a personal note, watching Tippett gradually bring *The Mask of Time* through successive stages in its conception and realisation caused me many surprises. For he is both responsive to the widest range of influences and suggestions, and yet so self-aware, that nothing tends to get through his defences which is not consistent with or relevant to the acts of creation that he endures and enjoys. In the seven-year period that preceded actual formulation of the text and music for the work, I myself was involved in bringing him books, accompanying him on travels, helping him test out a plethora of possibilities for the words, the structure, the sounds in the piece. The work became more than just a vague desire to return to the concert-hall and to choral composition when, around 1973, I talked to him about the notions of paradise I had found fascinating in my own recent reading. I lent him Joan Evans' *Paradise Lost and the Genesis Tradition*,[16] and for months afterwards he tantalised people with questions about the origin of the Zodiac, and entertained them with accounts of pre-lapsarian and post-lapsarian sexual intercourse. I also brought him Walter A. Strauss' *Descent and Return: the Orphic Theme in Modern Literature*,[17] which reawakened his love for Rilke (and my own essay, here, is much indebted to Strauss). Sometimes I was over-eager. I saw listed in a journal a new book entitled *Milton's Paradise Mislaid*[18] and immediately ordered it for him. This turned out to be the autobiography of Billy Milton, a well-known cabaret pianist and singer. Tippett quickly read it and revelled in its pervasive scurrility,[19] but ultimately, he decided the contents of this book were not germane to *The Mask of Time*! Quite crucially, though, I suggested that instead of using Wilfred Owen's poetry for the threnody of the eighth movement, he should consider Anna Akhmatova, who seemed to offer something less centred upon one particular war, a single continent and tradition.

I shared, too, his fascination with the Mexican pyramids. We went to see them twice and Tippett climbed and explored with unremitting zeal and excitement. Both trips were adventures. In retrospect, I don't know how we entertained such risks. Nevertheless, the sites in the Yucatan – particularly those at Chichen Itza, Uxmal and Palenque – left an indelible impression. They are not actually named in *The Mask of Time* but there are references to them: the resounding trumpets of the third movement and final scenes of sacrifice refer specifically to the famous echoing courtyard at Uxmal and the rituals enacted at the top of its pyramids.

I also accompanied him on a few occasions to Monument Valley and all around the canyons and mesas of Arizona, Utah and New Mexico. I was however, often tempted to puncture his transcendental *afflatus* and mock his musings upon what might equally well be treated literally as piles of stones and earth. Fortunately, we have in common a streak of irony and a delight in deflation.

228

When it came to the music, I found myself playing brake-drums down the telephone to him, bringing to his home tapes of animal noises, bird-calls and a Welsh male-voice choir singing *Myfanwy* (he had heard the latter on the soundtrack of a television presentation of *Off to Philadelphia in the morning* and thought it the ideal sonority for the chorus in Hiroshima Mon Amour). Likewise, other friends and colleagues were inveigled into providing ideas and materials for possible inclusion in the text and music. A friend who stayed once at my London flat dreamt he was in the situation described in Wallace Stevens' poem, *Metaphor as Degeneration*. He related the dream to the Nocketts Oracle[20] (as we know the composer) the following morning. It so intrigued him that I was immediately deputed to send him a copy of the poem. In an initial draft of the text of *The Mask of Time*, a substantial portion of this poem was included. All that now remains, however, is:

> My ear rehearses 'river noises'.

Early on in the conception of the work, I felt that it might become a twentieth-century equivalent to the Renaissance masque, and suit the theatre rather than the concert-hall. However, the dramatic ingredients of the first versions of the text were either so thinly spread, or so eccentric (e.g. the fifth movement was at first a bizarre Mad Hatter's Tea Party in the Garden of Eden) that this form of presentation had definitely to be discouraged. Even so, the Jungle movement and Paradise Garden *scena* almost fall between two stools. The coming and going of the animal noises in the former movement could probably have been better accomplished with discreet electronic amplification of the voices: and their intermingling with narration (whose words are not always apposite) is somewhat uncomfortable. As theatre, the Paradise Garden episode is too compressed: the characters are not established and it is tempting to want the Man and Woman, at first, to sing a love-duet to depict their paradisal state more fully,[21] but Tippett does not even allow them some pre-lapsarian canoodling. Accepting the movement for what it is, however, as part of a spectrum of ideas about the world expressed in a variety of different formats, one does get used to it. The music sees to that.

The projected ending of *The Mask of Time* worried me for some time. I tackled the composer about it not long after he had commenced writing the work. In fact, while on a brief holiday on Maui Island, Hawaii, we had a protracted argument one morning over breakfast. Originally, Tippett intended to finish with the ninth movement and the lines from Mary Renault's novel, *The Mask of Apollo*:

> O man, make peace with your mortality
> For this too is God.

In my view this would arouse expectations of a Mahlerian rhetoric which Tippett was unlikely to deliver: indeed, he would shrink from it. In that case the work might peter out. Given my knowledge of the trouble he had encountered with the final pages of previous works (including, most recently, the Triple Concerto), it seemed reasonable to prevail upon him to deal with this matter now.

229

I proffered one solution for an extra movement which might be based on lines from 'Ode to Joy' by the Czech poet-cum-biochemist Miroslav Holub:

> You ask the secret:
> It has one name: again.[22]

Tippett liked this a lot and turned it over in his mind for some time. In the event, he opted for a wordless extension of the ninth movement, which caused me even further doubts. I am still not too happy with the setting of the Renault lines, where the choral and brass writing are both too constricted and static. But the tenth movement is incredible! I am glad I harangued him over the papaya that morning.

Generally speaking, our disputations over details and occasional eruptions over major aspects of *The Mask of Time* have proved fruitful. Such irreverence on my part might well seem outrageous and arrogant to those who don't know the composer well or who are inclined to put him on a pedestal. But the Nocketts Oracle likes to have his pronouncements challenged. Such impiety would never affect our dealings with each other: he would still love me and I would still love him; and with anyone else it would be exactly the same.

The greatest surprise was receiving the score of *The Mask of Time* a few months before the world premiere, and realising just how extraordinary it was – something instantly evident, also, at the first rehearsals in Boston. It disposed of any claims that I or anyone else might make about having a hand in its creation. He had done it all himself.

NOTES
1. My italics
2. New York, 1970; see also Ruth S. Freitag: *Elliptical Designs: Halley's Comet as a Medium for Advertising Messages* in *The Quarterly Journal of the Library of Congress* Vol. 40, No. 3, Summer 1983, pp267-77, for a general account of the impact of the Comet in 1910.
3. Book Three: *A Neophyte in Utopia*, Ch. 1
4. See 'Towards the Condition of Music' in *Music of the Angels: Essays and Sketchbooks of Michael Tippett* (Ed. M. Bowen) (London: Eulenberg Books 1980) p21
5. *op. cit.*, p2
6. *op. cit.*, p119
7. London, 1973
8. *ibid.* p123
9. *ibid.* p150
10. *ibid. cf.* chapter 1 and chapter 2, esp. pp64-8
11. *ibid*, p80
12. *ibid*, pp436-8
13. 'Poets in a Barren Age' M. Tippett: *Moving into Aquarius* (2nd edn. London: Paladin Books 1974) p154
14. New York, 1974
15. *Morning into Aquarius*, p50
16. Oxford, 1968
17. Harvard, 1971
18. London, 1976
19. see esp. pp13, 70, 103, 110, 112
20. The composer usually signs himself in visiting books as 'Michael Tippett, Nocketts, U.K.'
21. *cf.* Paul Driver, *The Mask of Time*, Tempo. No. 149 (June 1984), pp39-44: 'But I have one especial criticism of the work: in its scheme of things no place is assigned to erotic love. While *agape* is enshrined in the Akhmatova setting, *eros* does not particularly figure in the 'Dream of the Paradise Garden nor anywhere else, and is in fact kept under the floor. A movement on erotic love could be conceived of; if it were to be added, a twelfth movement too would probably have to be found, in respect to epic patterns. Such an increase from 10 to 12 parts would, oddly enough, make another parallel with *Paradise Lost*, which Milton reorganised in like fashion between its first and second printings.' (p43)
22. M. Holub, *Ode to Joy* (in Selected Poems, transl. Ian Milner and George Theiner, London, 1967), p38

PAUL CROSSLEY

The Fourth Piano Sonata

AS I PUT pen to paper I have just finished learning the third movement of Michael Tippett's Piano Sonata No. 4; there are two more movements to come and, of course, by the time this is read the whole work will have been played and recorded: inevitably this is not the time for any categorical statements. In any case, I become wary of such statements – as I look over what I wrote about Sonata No. 3 (can that really be 12 years ago?) I see that it is allegedly 'the work of an artist at the height of his powers'. In the wake of Symphony No. 3, which remains one of the peaks of Tippett's output, that did, and does not, seem an exaggerated estimate and yet I would not make it now in that it implied an earlier lesser stature, and perhaps presupposed a future descent, planned or unplanned. Now that we have Symphony No. 4, the Triple Concerto and *The Mask of Time* it seems rash indeed.

Not only has the invention gone on unabated since Sonata No. 3, but for those of us privileged to know the composer, there has been a noticeable change in the creative process – the 'strain and effort' to which he referred in the sleeve-note of my 1973 recording of the Sonatas seems to have lifted.

I should say that Sonata No. 4 is very much a product of this almost mystical (if that is not too strong a word) process. As opposed to a work like *The Mask of Time*, which is the result of many years of deliberation and is, in some measure, drawn, to use Tippett's own words, from some 'collective as well as personal experience', the Piano Sonatas perhaps inhabit a world of more private fantasy. Despite the composer's acknowledged ponderings over the title 'Sonata' for his piano solo works, it seems to me particularly suited to pieces of such pure, abstract, unpremeditated invention.

As I discover the work step by step, apply my technique and insight to it until it begins to be defined as an entity, the opening at once presents me with the basic guidelines for my exploration. The first thing you hear is a single, loud note in the bass whose resonance is then prolonged and expanded through a series of gestures. (At a public performance you would, moreover, *see* this being done, dramatically – the right hand crossing over the left to produce the required sound.) The exploitation of resonance is very much what Sonata No. 4 is about. The first movement begins with five of these 'expansions of resonance', the bass notes being B flat, C, A, C sharp, D – these are fundamental to the piece (and totally justify the use, later, of material from Symphony No. 5 – if such justification were needed!), as is the number 5, but expect no serialist rigour: the B flat is sometimes B natural for example. The middle of the movement presents transpositions of this set underpinning a delicate, shining figuration; and the last part of the movement recapitulates the first with even more added resonance – resonance on resonance.

The second movement is a fugue which prolongs, in its unitary form, the drama and the contrast (so central as gestures in the first movement), its subject being, in essence, two notes (or a set of two-note phrases), the first short, loud and sharply attacked; the second long, quiet and tender. As the fugue proceeds entirely in two-part writing, the short notes are embellished with ever-varied strong, tough gestures, the long ones with crisp, delicate, dancing gestures; the centre of the movement is a lyrical interlude of the most moving simplicity.

Movement three sets out, in ABCBA form, three types of passionate rhetoric which might, simplistically, be described as 'harmonic', 'melodic', and 'rhythmic' and which, in turn, derive from Symphony No. 4, the Triple Concerto and *The Mask of Time*. The A section uses the opening gestures of Symphony No. 4; this is *not* a 'quote' but, rather, a new version of pre-existing material. First and foremost, there is a completely new *sound* – the piano 'attack' is quite different from that of the orchestral instruments, one is much more aware of the sustained lower resonances than the higher; and there is a much more 'pianistic' discharge of energy. Moreover, there are five gestures rather than three (that is, two entirely newly-invented ones) and their context, function, and emotion are not only different from Symphony No. 4, but also from their use in *The Mask of Time* where, at least, their sound is the same. Similarly, the B section, though it recalls a passage in the Triple Concerto (not the same notes this time, however), 'sings' differently. The C section uses the same rhythmic figure that opens the 'Dream of the Paradise Garden' movement of *The Mask of Time*, though, in point of fact, both ultimately derive from Monteverdi.

One should not be misled by these references to orchestral works. Sonata No. 4 is very much a piece 'about' the piano, its material much more conditioned than usual both by the inherent properties of the modern concert-grand (including, incidentally, its *three* pedals), and by the necessarily augmented technical resources of the modern pianist, notably his ability to create the impression of not only the two hands, but three, or even four, at one keyboard.

The composer has given me tantalising glimpses of what is to come. Movement four will be about 'speed' and will be very virtuosic – after a day spent struggling manfully with an incredibly difficult passage in an earlier movement, he rang me up and said, 'I hope your thirds are good – you'll really need some fingers for the fourth movement!!' The final movement is to be a set of Variations (five, of course), almost entirely lyrical and poetic, the end being a restatement of the opening – like the last movement of Beethoven Op.109.

I was asked recently whether I had any ambitions left now that I have had not just one, but *two* Piano Sonatas written for me by my favourite, and our greatest living composer. It *is* an extraordinary honour: though I commissioned Sonata No. 3, it was a real act of faith to place it in the hands of a young man at the outset of his career; the new sonata was a gift, a surprise, and I must confess to feeling rather like a little boy for whom it is Christmas every day!

Sonata No. 4 is dedicated to my friend Michael Vyner and is, I think, a magnificent tribute to all he has achieved for music, to that blend of 'right knowing and right doing' – that *culture* – which singles him out. As such, the title page will bracket together the names of the two people who have had the profoundest influence on my musical life. I am reminded that as Michael Tippett enters his 80s, we enter our 40s and that we have known him for our entire adult lives. Happy birthday, Michael, and thank you for being alive.

Tippett at a ceremony to receive the Gramophone Record Award, 1981, for the London Sinfonietta's performance of King Priam.
(Photo: Mike Evans)

ALAN BROADBENT & GERAINT LEWIS
Tippett on Record

It is now a well-established fact that appreciation of Tippett's music was dramatically enhanced in the mid 1960s and early 70s by means of gramophone recordings. Although some of his earlier works were recorded in the 1940s and 50s, the major pieces grouped on either side of *The Midsummer Marriage* were not as fortunate in being committed to disc so quickly, and their generally poor first performances contributed to the widespread misunderstanding of Tippett's output at the time. When, however the Concerto for Orchestra (1963) was issued in a splendid recording in 1965, awareness of his developing style was immediately increased and most of the subsequent major works were released in good accounts fairly swiftly – often by those giving the first performances. Simultaneously, previous works were either recorded for the first time, or re-recorded, and so the earlier part of Tippett's output was readily available for critical rehabilitation. This discography is a brief guide to these recordings – grouped in their respective categories.

ORCHESTRAL MUSIC

Symphonies

To mark Tippett's 80th birthday, the four Symphonies have been sensibly and conveniently re-issued in a boxed-set (Decca 414 091/1 – tape 091/4). Nos. 1, 2 and 3 are performed by the London Symphony Orchestra conducted by Colin Davis (who gave the first performance of No. 3 with soprano soloist Heather Harper) while No. 4 is played by the Chicago Symphony Orchestra (who commissioned it) under Georg Solti. The oldest recording is of No. 2 (1968) but the original *Argo* tape has a warm immediacy which has worn well, while the performance is notable for its zestful elan – sweeping the music forward exultantly. The sensitivity of the playing captures the intimate ritualism of the slow movement just as effectively. In their account of No. 1 for Philips in 1976 the orchestra is captured with greater clarity which at the same time reproduces a rich radiance. At times the string playing sounds a little strained in the upper register and the performance is a tiny bit disappointing when compared with the definitive version of the Third Symphony released by the same company and performers a year earlier. This vivid recording is often searingly immediate and Heather Harper's committed and moving singing of the Symphony's 'blues' and concluding dramatic scena is stunningly caught. The 1981 (really 1979!) digital sound Decca provided for the Chicago Symphony's recording of the Fourth Symphony is quite spectacular, and most aspects of the performance are virtually ideal – this is the revised performance, which is greatly superior to the actual premiere in its handling of tempi. Furthermore the amplified human breathing is convincingly handled.

Concertos

Of the four concertos only that for double string orchestra has been recorded more than once. In 1952 Walter Goehr (who conducted the first performance of *A Child of Our Time* in 1944) made a sterling recording with the Philharmonia Orchestra, and just over ten years later the Bath Festival Orchestra and the Moscow Chamber Orchestra joined forces under Rudolf Barshai. This can now be heard in another compendium box re-issed for Tippett's 80th birthday (EMI Ex 2902283/5 – tape) and co-incidentally Maestro Barshai has just recorded a new version with the Bournemouth Symphony Orchestra also in time for the continuing birthday celebrations later in the year. In 1972 the most celebrated recorded performance of the Double Concerto was made by the Academy of St. Martin-in-the-Fields and Neville Marriner [ZRG 680], and hard on its heels in 1974 came Vernon Handley's account with the London Philharmonic Orchestra [CFP 40068]. The Piano Concerto had to wait nine years for its first recording – by John Ogdon and the Philharmonia Orchestra under Colin Davis in 1965, (now in the box mentioned above – Ex 2902283). Considering that Philips produced a magnificent recording for the Concerto for Orchestra in the very same year (just a couple of years after its première by the same performers – the L.S.O. and Colin Davis) it is a great pity that E.M.I.'s sound quality for the Piano Concerto is so opaque and badly focused, for it is a good performance. The Concerto for Orchestra emerges with dazzling clarity and is now deservedly re-issued, (Sequenza 412 378/1 – tape 378/4). Even better is the superbly authoritative account of the Triple Concerto which Philips recorded with digital splendour in 1981. Featuring the original performers – Pauk, Imai, Kirshbaum, the L.S.O. and Colin Davis – it went on to win the *Gramophone's* Record Award in 1982. The only pity is that the continuity of this 34 minute work is interrupted by an irritating turn-over, which is even retained – perversely – in the taped version (6514 209).

Miscellaneous works

The early *Fantasia on a theme of Handel* is a little ponderous and not quite stylistically assured, and its performance by Margaret Kitchin with the L.S.O. under the composer's direction [*RCA SER 5620*] is a bit clangorous.

236

The *Little Music* for strings is rather more idiomatic and is radiantly realised by the Academy of St. Martin's [ZRG 680] who – in direct competition with the Orchestra of St. John's Smith Square [*Pye TPLS 13069*] – also give the *Fantasia Concertante on a theme of Corelli*. The Academy's first performance is a little more indulgent than their re-make in 1983 [(ZC) DCA 518] and it has an unfortunate and audible tape-join around fig. 19, but both accounts are superbly assured and sound ecstatic when compared to most inadequate performances by large orchestras. Best of all perhaps is Tippett's own performance with the Bath Festival Orchestra in EMI's 80th birthday reissue.

The two lighter works are especially delightful. *The Suite for the Birthday of Prince Charles* (1948) was recorded by the Leicestershire Schools' Symphony Orchestra under the composer's baton in 1968 and has subsequently been featured as a filler on records by the L.S.O. and Colin Davis (currently 412 378/1) in 1976 and the Chicago Symphony and Solti in 1981. Davis' performance is the more relaxed and genial whereas Solti is a little unrelenting. The *Divertimento on Sellinger's Round* (1954) takes the Suite's ingenious use of quotations a step further though its chamber-orchestra texture is rather more acerbic. The English Chamber Orchestra and Norman Del Mar give a dextrous performance – (Lyrita SCS 111).

Rather surprisingly, Tippett's most frequently performed and popular work for full orchestra, the *Ritual Dances* from *The Midsummer Marriage* as arranged in his concert version is not over-represented on disc. Philips has in the past spliced together the relevant sections from their complete recording of the opera, but this is not a satisfactory solution – Dance 3 is for example faded out so that we avoid the voices of Jack and Bella! The original performers at Covent Garden under John Pritchard did record the suite in 1958 (currently DPA-Argo-571/2)) and this is surprisingly adequate considering its age, but it is good that Barshai and his Bournemouth forces have just recorded the only other version – (No. not available yet).

Record numbers in italics are currently unavailable – numbers refer to the previous incarnation, which can always be heard via record libraries.

INSTRUMENTAL MUSIC

Quartets

The recording of Tippett's Quartet No. 2 by its original performers the Zorian Quartet in 1948 is now unavailable, as – sadly – is the celebrated 1956 performance by the Amadeus Quartet. The rather scrawny recordings of the first three quartets by the Fidelio Quartet on Pye (1967 and 1970) are adequate but no match for the deeply intense accounts by the Lindsay Quartet issued in 1975 (OSLO 10). Even though the recording quality can seem a little constricted and close at times these authoritative interpretations reveal Tippett's three early masterpieces as a central contribution to the 20th century quartet repertoire – and they did after all provide one source of inspiration for Quartet No. 4 (1977–8).

Paul Crossley's stunning first performance of the 3rd Piano Sonata was a good opportunity for a retrospective grouping with the first two sonatas in 1974 (*6500 534*) and now that the Sonata No. 4 has just been written for him it is a magnificent gesture on the part of the C.R.D. to allow Tippett's prime instrumental interpreter to repeat the exploration after a gap of ten years.

Especially fascinating (in view of revisions to the score in 1942 and 1954) would be Phyllis Sellick's 1941 recording of Sonata No. 1 (on 78s) of which she gave the first performance in 1938. The work was then recorded in 1960 by Margaret Kitchin, who in 1962 gave the first performance of Sonata No. 2 – which she surprisingly did not subsequently record. Later in the 1960s John Ogdon recorded both sonatas, and these powerful interpretations are now fortunately available again (Ex 2902283). As a definitive document however Crossley's new recording of the complete canon will probably be the most significant addition to the catalogue in the composer's 80th birthday year.

Another Sonata – for four horns (1955) – has been recorded with remarkable virtuosity by the Tuckwell Horn Quartet (it was written for Denis Brain's Quartet) as a coupling to the original issue of the 2nd Symphony in 1968 (Argo ZRG 535).

Tippett's shortest solo instrumental piece the *Preludio al Vespro di Monteverdi* (written to precede one of the earliest British performances of the Vespers in 1946 and incorporating quotations of plainsong used in the Vespers) has been recorded by a number of organists – most effectively perhaps by Simon Preston in 1967 (ZRG 528).

CHORAL MUSIC

Tippett's most popular single work – *A Child of Our Time* – has been recorded twice. John Pritchard's 1958 RLPO account (Argo 571/2) has a warm compassion which Colin Davis' BBC recording in 1975 (Philips 6500 985) seems to eschew in favour of greater distance and objectivity. This later account is hampered by the rather dry recording but the performance is immediately enhanced by the presence of Janet Baker and Jessye Norman as soloists. *The Vision of Saint Augustine* was given an intense performance under Sir Michael's direction in 1972, but the RCA recording (*SER 5620*) is not really rich or clear enough to project the work's complex yet incandescent textures. It is however an enormously valuable document which should be re-furbished and re-issued – John Shirley-Quirk's performance should on no account be missed.

Of the smaller choral/orchestral works the most important is *The Shires Suite*. The stylistic exuberance of the piece is infectious – it ranges from an elaboration of *The Knot Garden's* jazz-breaks (Interlude 2) to the unique layered lyricism of Interlude 1. Taking its cue from the *Prince Charles Suite* and the *Sellinger's Round Divertimento* and its predecessor *The Crown of the Year, The*

Shires Suite takes the mature 'allusive' technique of *The Knot Garden* and the Symphony No. 3 to remarkable heights. Each movement quotes a canon – from *soomer is i coomen in*, through John Smith, Byrd and Purcell to the setting of a proverb by Blake which Alexander Goehr composed as a tribute for inclusion in Ian Kemp's 1965 Symposium. (One wonders what might be suggested by the present collection of offerings!) The choral writing is fresh and direct and the virtuostic orchestral writing makes frequent use of amusing effects – literal hunting horns, and what Tippett describes as 'visual sounds' . . . 'the pop-pop can be done with the finger in the cheek (or actual corks and bottles) and the clinks with real drinking glasses. The ff crash can be metal trays of cutlery dropped.' As a work in progress for the Leicestershire Schools Symphony Orchestra Tippett recorded the final movements (of which the setting of Byrd's *Non nobis Domine* as the *Epilogue* is perhaps his most noble re-creation) with these forces in 1970. In 1980 the complete *Suite* was brilliantly performed by a new Leicestershire generation under Peter Fletcher for Unicorn (UNS 267).

Tippett's most important short choral work (and one of the landmarks of liturgical music) is the *Magnificat and Nunc Dimittis* for St. John's College, Cambridge. The College Choir under George Guest with the late Brian Runnett (organ) recorded a remarkable, authentic performance in the year of its première – 1963 (*Argo ZRG 5340*) – which remains stunningly vivid. Most of the smaller choral works (including the Magnificat) were conveniently recorded together in 1978 by the Schola Cantorum of Oxford under Nicholas Cleobury. The collection includes the *Two Madrigals; Plebs Angelica; The Weeping Babe; Dance, Clarion Air; Bonny at Morn;* the *Four British Songs;* the Spirituals from *A Child of Our Time* (a capella); *Music* and *Lullaby.* These are spirited, refreshing performances, even though the organ sonority in the *Magnificat* is a pale reflection of that in St. John's College Chapel!

VOCAL MUSIC

The recordings by Peter Pears of *Boyhood's End* and *The Heart's Assurance* with Noel Mewton-Wood (1953) – (*Argo DA 34*) – and the *Songs for Ariel* with Benjamin Britten (1965) – (*ZRG 5439*) – are sadly not generally available, and neither is the 1968 performance of the first *Song for Achilles* by Richard Lewis and John Williams (the original performers). However, all these works were recorded with mellifluous insight in 1976 (*OSLO 14*) by Philip Langridge and John Constable, with Timothy Walker (guitar). Those wonderful performances of crucial works should be immediately re-issued, as should the 1973 recording by Robert Tear and the London Sinfonietta under David Atherton of *Songs for Dov* (*ZRG 703*). Even if the jazz-influenced opening is tentative when compared to the later recording of *The Knot Garden* (where the first song originally appeared) the allusive textures of the second and third songs are brilliantly conveyed.

OPERA

Perhaps the crucial step in the awakening of interest in Tippett's music both here and abroad was the issue in 1971 of a recording of *The Midsummer Marriage*. This is a faithful representation of the contemporary production of the opera (its second) at Covent Garden – soloists, chorus and orchestra are conducted by Colin Davis. Even though certain cuts which the stage-version made are observed (it would be fascinating now to see and hear the full version) the sense of continuity and 'staginess' in this recording is impressive. All levels cohere beautifully and a sense of corporate identity is powerfully conveyed (Philips 6703 027).

King Priam on the other hand was recorded in the wake of a superb 1981 concert performance, in which David Atherton (who had then plentiful experience of conducting the work in the opera house) conducted the London Sinfonietta. Heather Harper and Norman Bailey sound a little elderly at times (maybe appropriately so) and their intonation is not always ideal. It is also a pity that Hecuba's accompanying violin figuration is played by one violin only (presumably on grounds of corporate difficulty – which Kent Opera's recent performance brilliantly repudiated). These are however small blemishes in an otherwise stunning performance (Decca D246D 3).

Most definitive of all undoubtedly is *The Knot Garden* which was recorded by Philips after a revival at Covent Garden of the original production (1974 – *6700 063*, now re-issued – 412 707/1). Colin Davis' direction is incisive and vibrant and the dramatic immediacy of the performance seems virtually to leap out of the grooves. Especially great is the interpretation of Josephine Barstow as Denise – a searingly intense performance. Robert Tear's Dov too is masterly.

Much, therefore, of Tippett's output is satisfyingly represented on disc. There are of course certain works which are in need of new recordings – the Piano Concerto (with Paul Crossley) and *The Vision of Saint Augustine* spring straight to mind. Others need to be re-issued, but more urgently a number of major works need to be recorded for the first time. *The Ice Break* and *The Mask of Time* are the most glaring gaps at present (and sadly there seem not to be any plans in prospect now) and the Quartet No. 4 is quite *inexplicably* unrecorded. There can be no sensible reason either for the fact that the cantata *The Crown of the Year* and the *Praeludium* for brass, bells and percussion are also languishing – they are after all quite often played now.

While acknowledging the blessings bestowed by many recording companies and supportive bodies it remains a sobering fact that the world of commercial recording is often haphazard and hazardous!

ALEXANDER GOEHR
Tribute

In times when it is only too easy to despair, to be
shocked and frightened, to look for certainties which
have never and can never exist, and for gratification
and comfort in art, when we would like to shelter
behind the achievement of older and wiser men, but
when only the old questions occupy our minds, and
when the hope of progress in the self, or in the world
appears as a chimera, we turn to Michael with
gratitude, not because he has solved these problems,
or has suggested a right road for us, but because he
tells us that no such roads exist, but that we can
rejoice in expressivity, can create out of conflicting
prolixities, and can sing of things together so that the
sounds leap over each other, the rhythms lift off from
mundane reality, so that there is colour and light.

Printed by kind permission of The London Sinfonietta and Michael Vyner.

To Michael Tippett

The Fields of Praise

Song-Cycle for Tenor and Piano

1. In the beginning

Dylan Thomas

William Mathias,
Op. 74

Lento con moto

In the be-gin-ning was the three-point-ed star, — One smile of light a-cross the

em-pty face; One bough of bone a-cross the root-ing air, The sub-stance forked—that mar-rowed the

first sun; And, burn-ing cy-phers— on the round of space, Heaven—and hell— mixed— as they spun.

242

WILLIAM MATHIAS
'And all is always now'

I T IS EASY to forget that Michael Tippett is partly of Cornish stock. His Celtic inheritance, indeed, goes a considerable way towards an understanding of why his music has always sounded significantly different from that of his English contemporaries. It also casts a revealing light on three aspects of Tippett's vision: (a) his consistent role as a celebrant of life, (b) his instinctive pluralism, and (c) his involvement with the nature of Time.

Anthony Conran has said of the Welsh bardic tradition that 'the poet was one who, at the coronation of the king and at his funeral, and at sundry important events in between, chanted the praises of the king, invoked ancestral strength and piety, and unified (in a kind of communion-rite of song) the whole tribe around its leader. This *magical* content of Welsh poetry waxed and waned in importance; but it was always there, and it was always acknowledged.' Disposing of tribal connotations and in relation to the twentieth century 'there arises in us some kind of need for eulogy, even for formal eulogy, on a number of occasions where, in our culture, such a need is likely to go unsatisfied. For praise is a difficult art; it is normally done badly, or not done at all.'[1]

Precisely. There was certainly little time for the concept of praise in the European music of the mid-1950s when apparently leading minds were more concerned with technical matters such as total serialism or the aleatoric. The musical 'images of abounding, generous, exuberant beauty' with which Tippett filled *The Midsummer Marriage* left many operagoers and critics behind, unused as they were to such a generosity of spirit in a reductionist age – let alone to a Jungian, mythological background of ideas. There were those, however, who instinctively understood that this was one of the glowing masterpieces of twentieth-century music, and one which (irrespective of the touch-line games of the avant-garde) would create its own time, as masterpieces have a habit of doing. It had to wait. Norman Del Mar conducted a crucially revealing broadcast performance in 1963, and Colin Davis a successful Royal Opera House revival in 1968 followed by a disc recording. All the same, when in 1976 the Welsh National Opera under Richard Armstrong mounted a superbly passionate production in Cardiff, it was in order to feel that the work had reached at least one major spiritual home.

Even though we have here perhaps the clearest example of Tippett as 'yea-sayer', the Celtic, celebratory nature of his vision is to be heard in one form or another throughout his output to date, always allowing for the distance encompassed between the Concerto for Double String Orchestra of 1939 and the Triple Concerto of 1979. And in that forty-year journey he has proved to be the ultimate pluralist in what is (above all else) an age of multiplicity. In terms of musical language his precise opposite is Boulez, for whom 'every musician who has not felt the necessity of the serial language is useless', and who wrote at the time of the establishment of *Ircam*: 'Despite the skilful ruses we have cultivated in our desperate effort to make the world of the past serve our present needs, we can no longer elude the essential: that of becoming an absolute part of the present, of forsaking all memory to forge a perception without precedent, of renouncing the legacies of the past, to discover yet undreamed-of territories.' Such views may be helpful in psychological terms to Boulez as a background to his compositional processes, but they go no further than that in terms of truthfulness. The Celtic mind, indeed, finds them illusory in its knowledge that the discovery of undreamed-of territories requires of necessity a profound psychic integration between the present and the relevant past – something concerning which Tippett's music has much to say for those who have ears to hear.

The first unambiguous example of Tippett's pluralism lies in the use of spirituals in *A Child of Our Time*; but even this had been preceded by the influence of jazz and blues rhythms in the First Piano Sonata and the Double Concerto for strings. Amongst English contemporaries of genius Britten was largely untouched by jazz, while Walton overtly acknowledged its influence in some of his finest music; but Tippett is unique in creating an amalgam in the 1939 String Concerto between the rhythms of jazz and madrigalian technique, and it is the extraordinary propulsion thus produced which gives the work its ecstatic and luminous grace – a grace equally pervasive in the Second String Quartet and *Boyhood's End*. English music of the Renaissance hovers in the air around these early mature works, but the sense of Celtic ecstasy they also embody is without an equivalent in this century's music. It is certainly possible to use the term 'ecstatic' in relation to much of Messiaen's output, but in a special affinity to Christian mysticism; Tippett's very pluralism precludes his taking the stance of an orthodox believer, even when enhancing his deep sense of the numinous.

His prolonged engagement with the *anima* gave birth to the works which surround *The Midsummer Marriage*, but it is in the latter that we find it at the highest sustained point of lyrical intensity. It would hardly be possible to go significantly (or immediately) further in this direction, and as such it should have come as no surprise to the intelligent observer that *King Priam* (and its surrounding constellation of works) would need to be fired by other aspects of the composer's psyche. The *anima* principle conquered, it was now safe (and necessary) to set out in new formal directions relating to the integration of opposites. The collages and juxtapositions of the Concerto for Orchestra point the way to *The Knot Garden* and *The Ice Break* in which widely dissimilar

244

Michael Tippett with William Mathias at a Proms Press Conference in June 1984. (Photo: Malcolm Crowthers)

musics are fused in ever more challenging combinations. It is fascinating in this process to see Tippett expand his terms of reference, and in particular to watch his eyes and ears turn to a more personal engagement with the new world of America (with Blakean overtones?). What was in 1941 an inspired, deeply moving, but necessarily distanced use of blues and spirituals becomes in *The Ice Break* a wild engagement of personal (slavery and freedom) and ethnic (black and white) opposites, even permitting the not too distant influence of the rock musical. Here is still 'light and shadow', the 'grave passage' is still being dared, but at greater risk in a seemingly more dangerous world. Whether or not the later operas will be accorded the status of Tippett's first, remains an open question; what is not in doubt is the consistent act of bravery which constitutes this kind of composer's ever-widening psychic journey – and above all, his truthfulness to his time in seeking a kaleidoscopic multiplictiy in terms of musical exploration. It is, however, also fascinating that in the process the concept of tonality has been strained, pulled out of focus, juxtaposed – but never *lost*; one reason, of course, why the music has remained archetypal and communicative even when complex. A lesser man could easily have sought the air of other planets (pace Schoenberg, who was right to do so in that he derived from a great but different tradition): Tippett has chosen to remain in contact with this one. Here one understands the abiding reverence for Beethoven, even though Tippett's music is for the most

245

part more oriented towards the sensual, and the Third Symphony's use of the *Schrekensfanfare* does not achieve its purpose for all listeners. Ives (a seminal pluralist) can be invoked, but not overstressed – the path is Tippett's own, and one which can be viewed as opening new vistas to a new generation.

Closely tied to the question of pluralism is Tippett's constant, almost obsessive concern with the nature of Time. This is, of course, the ultimate problem which musicians are only just beginning to explore. As such, let us remove Stravinsky from the argument in the light of his unique position as the first great composer to have deliberately and purposefully used musical history to enhance his creative gifts; a profound Russian who needed the example of Western music in order to proceed – to lapse into cliché, Bach for *Dumbarton Oaks*, Tchaikovsky for *Le baiser de le fée*, Mozart for *The Rake's Progress*; less into cliché in suggesting that such models were at least partly necessary to overcome Stravinsky's lack of a pronounced melodic gift – a flaw for which Beethoven was undeservedly berated in *The Poetics of Music* (which strengthens the argument). Given Stravinsky's genius, we don't notice the lack, even when revelling in what Lambert quite reasonably called his time-travelling. There are, however, different kinds of traveller, and it is useful to examine Tippett's stance more closely in respect of four particularly apt works.

In the 1953 *Fantasia Concertante on a theme of Corelli*, Tippett's relation to the past is singularly different from that of Stravinsky. We begin three hundred years ago unequivocally in Corelli's world, and move almost imperceptibly into Tippett's; there is a magical (Celtic) moment towards the end of the first variation where a scale in thirds (which Corelli could have written) suddenly becomes a scale in fourths – we have fully entered the 'now' of Tippett's world. Later, there are two short quotations from Bach embedded in this twentieth-century work; we end with Corelli, but the work is Tippett's throughout. It is a sleight not of hand, but of Time. The technique employed bears no relation to the Romantic era as in, say, Brahms' *Variations on a theme of Handel* (curiously, Tippett's own fantastic relationship with Handel via Butler in 1939–41 hardly seems successfully integrated – perhaps it was too early). Also, it bears little or no relationship to treatments of the past as evinced in the music of Kagel, Maxwell Davies, Stockhausen, Cage, Zimmermann or Rochberg. Maxwell Davies' parodistic use of Handel in *Eight Songs for a mad King* is enormously effective as music theatre, but quite different in kind. Vaughan Williams' great *Tallis Fantasia* comes a little nearer, but is complicated by the fact that the modal language used by that master is throughout very closely allied to that of the work's progenitor. The finale of Berg's Violin Concerto provides a closer comparison, though it seems unlikely that it would have proved a direct influence. None of these parallels will really do. The *Corelli Fantasia* is unique in the very particular manner in which it presents a convincing synchronicity between the eighteenth and twentieth centuries; Tippett creates an ethos of reciprocity and transmutation between Corelli, Bach and himself in the sense that the music moves freely backwards and forwards over a space of three hundred years. The work is one

246

of his greatest achievements because it exhibits an aspect of newness upon which we have only begun to touch in depth – a fully integrated synchronicity between two different Time-worlds. Perhaps the active influence of Jung's thinking remains here most potent of all.

The superb, proud Symphony No. 2 was generated, we are told, as a result of hearing a pounding Vivaldi bass-line. There is here no similar affinity in terms of Time; Vivaldi is merely the start for take-off, and he is soon lost in a celebratory work which succeeds in expanding in purely musical terms (like the Piano Concerto) on *The Midsummer Marriage*. Rhythms abound, but the labyrinthine slow movement (as also in the Concerto for Orchestra) is clearly the opposite aspect of a deeply Celtic imagination.

The String Quartet No. 4 is the work in which Tippett so far finally comes to terms with Beethoven. Here again, the Time-world between the *Grosse Fuge* and ourselves is broken down. The Quartet does not *depend* on Beethoven to make its case; it engages the earlier composer on its own different terms of intellectual sensuality (no contradiction here – merely paradox), so that one-hundred-and-fifty years become as nothing. Tippett engages in a grappling of minds in a common cause, and the manner in which it is done is highly personal. He does not parody, refract or distort; he once again synchronises, and in doing so subtly changes our understanding of the nature of Time. Such a thing is so much in the nature of music that it is barely possible to do it in words; the only writer to have attempted to do so in English at a profound level in this century is that other great pluralist John Cowper Powys in *A Glastonbury Romance* and *Porius* – novels of peculiar genius arising out of a Celtic, mystical fusion of Time-elements, and written by (in his own words) an 'obstinate Cymric'.

Tippett relentlessly pursues the question yet further in *The Vision of Saint Augustine*. As explained in the opening composer's note, Augustine's great second vision 'concerns the dispersal of his mind upon the evanescence of things, and came to him through his prolonged inner struggles as to the meaning of Time . . . We cannot in this temporal existence experience a true present. In fact we only know Time through the mind, which is constantly shifting from the immediacy of sight (*contuitus*) towards the future (*expectatio*) or the past (*memoria*) with such rapidity that the soul is for ever distended (*distentus*) in all directions without centre. To have any inkling of such a centre the contrary is necessary, *viz.* concentration (*intentio*).'

The earlier quotations from Boulez are one way of looking at the question; rationalistic, reductionist, Cartesian – and out-dated in that this linear, clock-bound view is already well behind the post-quantum physics understanding of Time and reality.[2] Tippett in *The Vision of Saint Augustine* shows a way forward on a quite different spiritual level through an astonishingly courageous attempt to capture in music the 'now' of Eternity – to use Music, in the terms of Lévi-Strauss, as a 'machine for the suppression of Time'. Despite the composer's codiac 'I count not myself to have apprehended', the leaping act of imagination involved is clearly that of (at least in Jungian terms) a religious and mystical soul – 'In you, O my mind, I measure my three kinds of Time!'

247

Bach composed against a consistent background of belief in Eternity, and needed therefore only (but in what manner!) to reflect this in the musical near-certainties of his time. In a different age, lacking certainties, Tippett must first synchronise and then fuse different Time-elements in order that he can attempt a musical reflection of Augustine's vision. In doing so he makes use in Hebrew and Greek of an ancient musical tradition drawn upon when 'ecstasy forces from us a jubilation beyond words, beyond sense, expressed by melismata of vowel sounds only' – for which the technical name is glossolalia. We should not be surprised to find that (though it has little meaning in English) such a state of ecstasy is also deeply enshrined in the Celtic/Christian tradition; in modern Welsh it is in the proper sense known as 'hwyl'.

> Sailing to Samos over the wine-dark sea
> memorialise the seer
> who named the nodes of music and of time . . .[3]

In Masking Time Michael Tippett points to a liberated concept of 'newness' in Music. Do we remain intellectually trapped amongst the litter of reductionist ideas which surround us, or can we summon the imagination and understanding to see through the window (fenestram!) which he has opened?

Time, of course, will tell.

NOTES
1. The Penguin Book of Welsh Verse
2. 'For us believing physicists, this separation between past, present and future has the value of mere illusion, however tenacious' (Albert Einstein)
3. From The Mask of Time (Part 7: 'Mirror of Whitening Light')

© Schott and Co. Ltd. Part of 'Mirror of Whitening Light' from the composer's autograph of *The Mask of Time*

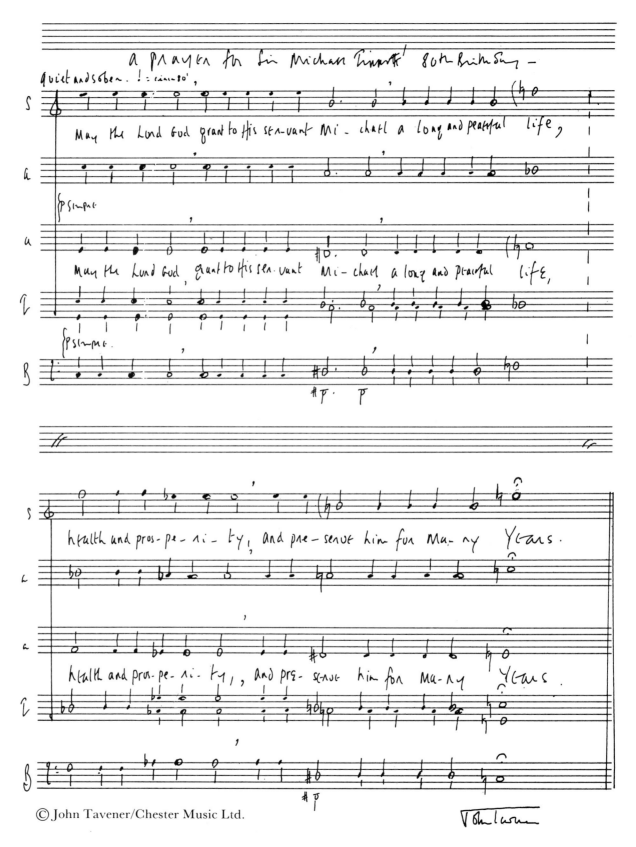

250

ENDPIECE

'Dream of the Paradise Garden'

A FEW MILES from where I live is Avebury – one of the most fascinating and extraordinary relics of our distant past. It is a strange place, full of magic, where certainly art and religion were practised together. It is four thousand years old, coming right out of our ancient past, and it's so enormous that it must have required a colossal feat of social organisation to have raised those great stones into those circles. And it wasn't for things like defence or for living in, it was for practising ritual . . . Once we are inside this sort of sanctuary, we feel that the necessity, the drive, the instinct, to make such a place where this kind of ritualistic art could occur, and where all the functions that we think art has are comprehended, is something so fundamental and deep-seated in human beings that there is no doubt that it must have existed always. Whenever I come back to the places where the great seas meet the primeval granite, I am curiously refreshed. Because as I look I get the sense that it's been there long before human beings, and that it has been made under the fantastic pressures of the cooling earth and the sea which is totally destructive of anything that comes in its way. And even further, if we look around at all that has happened to us as human beings, we feel that we too are susceptible to just the same choas, the same violence, the same unpredictability, the same kind of impersonal passion of the irrational forces, that it makes a mockery of all our idealistic and rationalistic intentions. But, however much we may be aware of the chaotic forces we also have the opposite within us, the complementary need for harmony and goodness. Deep within me, I know that part of the artist's job is to renew our sense of the comely and the beautiful. To create a dream. Every human being has this need to dream.

The quotation from Michael Tippett above comes from his BBC Television documentary Poets in A Barren Age *in the series* One Pair of Eyes *recorded in 1972.*

251

INDEX

The Major Published Works of Michael Tippett

One Pair of Eyes

(Photo: Malcolm Crowthers)

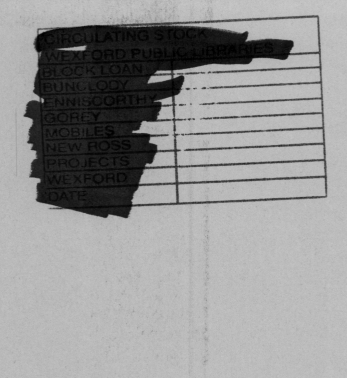